Every Woman's Guide to Retirement

T0359385

Alice Mantel BA, LLM

First published by Busybird Publishing 2019
Copyright © 2019 Alice Mantel

ISBN
Print: 978-1-925949-27-8
Ebook: 978-1-925949-28-5

Cover design: Busybird Publishing
Layout and typesetting: Busybird Publishing
Editor: Jessica Waters

Front cover:
Dorrit Black
Wings, 1927 – 1928
Linocut on paper
Purchased, 1976
Collection: Art Gallery of Ballarat

Busybird Publishing
2/118 Para Road
Montmorency, Victoria
Australia 3094
www.busybird.com.au

Contents

Preface

"Old age was growing inside me. It kept catching my eye from the depths of the mirror. I was paralysed sometimes as I saw it making its way toward me so steadily when nothing inside me was ready for it."

Simone de Beauvoir, author, Force of Circumstance

The kernel of this book grew out of my reluctance to accept retirement as a real possibility in my own life. Despite my dissatisfaction with the demands of professional life and a growing desire for more personal freedom, I resisted making a declaration of retirement until I realised that unconsciously I had taken steps towards a post-work life.

As a lawyer working in many facets of legal practice for over 30 years, the personal and intellectual demands of the profession have always engaged and challenged me.

However, eventually I realised that I wanted to disengage from the constant stress of working in family law to set up a new legal practice focused on the needs of older clients.

I was reading voraciously to understand the financial side of aged care to better advise clients, but I was also clear that I did not want full-time work. I wanted to share my knowledge in a more creative context, so I slowly retired from the daily practice of the law and took the jump into the retirement pond.

In the course of my practice, I had visited many aged care facilities and recently been to more funerals than weddings. From both my clients' experience and my own, I was finding this stage of life both confusing and draining with few guidebooks to assist. Looking for advice, I found most retirement books either too blokey, too financial or too optimistic and nothing quite right. Writing an accessible, practical book to assist women to have a fulfilling retirement seemed a logical goal for my post-work life. From my perspective, women experience retirement differently to men. Women are the unrecognised carers and the charitable volunteers of later life. But books about retirement often do not meet or reflect their interests and needs. My focus is to remedy that situation.

Researching and writing this book combines both my professional and personal experience. Retirement gave me the opportunity to withdraw from legal practice in order to reflect and develop this project. Most surprisingly, I discovered that there were many stories out there waiting to be told. I hope that readers' input will improve the reliability and usefulness of this book in the future.

My heartfelt thanks to my patient and knowledgeable reviewers, Dr Sally Denshire and Charles Jago for their comments and ideas throughout this work, and to Geoff Harper for his comments in respect of the finance chapter.

1

What does retirement mean to you?

"Ageing is not lost youth but a new stage of opportunity and strength."
Betty Friedan, author *The Feminist Mystique*

Mention "retirement" to some people and immediately they think of freedom. Freedom from work, freedom from the drudgery of dealing with clients, and freedom to travel to all those places on their bucket list. For others, however, the idea of "retirement" strikes fear into their heart. They wonder how they will manage if they are not employed, receiving a regular income and having a daily routine.

Whether you cannot wait to leave your job or cannot bear the thought of leaving it, retirement will bring a profound change to the way you are now living your life. It can be a period of great activity and productivity – if that's what you want. Or, it can be a v-e-r-y long series of afternoons reading a book.

Retirement represents approximately a third of your lifespan, with no instruction booklet handed out on how to spend that time. At the end of the day, your last decades literally represent your own work. Have you done a good job of making a meaningful life? What will your legacy be?

Why would you need a book to assist you in the perfectly natural process of getting older? Well, you probably don't need a book, any more than a mum-to-be needs a book to explain the process of giving birth. Theoretically you understand the process of retirement, however this book can alert you to how to better manage some of the issues likely to arise in this long and unpredictable period.

In my experience, many women are not well-equipped for the practicalities of retirement. I admit that this very generalised statement may not apply to you specifically. But I am constantly surprised how many women are not interested in the financial and legal decisions being made in their household. Not because they are not capable of being well-informed, but because many women think that it's boring, or it's not important for them. This is not a question of age, education or income: it's an attitude of leaving it to the spouse to decide how joint money will be spent or how the paperwork will be done. Any lawyer who has worked in family law, as I have, will likely have encountered this attitude amongst many of their female clients.

Despite our participation in the workforce and our major role in the upbringing of our children, many women still avoid involvement in the details of their finances. Sometimes it's because the partner uses his control over the family finances as a means of asserting his position and it's easier to let him decide. But what happens when unexpectedly, for any number of reasons, a spouse may no longer be around? Suddenly without their decision-maker, women realise they don't know who is their insurer, what their super provides or where their title deeds are located.

This book is intended to assist you to be informed and understand the implications of your very important decisions before a crisis occurs and you rely on someone else's opinion. Let me be clear – getting a second well-informed opinion is always a good idea, but you are the best person to know your own needs for your situation.

Here are my supporting credentials: professionally I have been a lawyer for 30 years advising others to make good decisions; I have personally experienced many of the issues about which I write; and I have researched as much as I think you, as a reader, will want to absorb in a practical handbook. For further information you can refer to the online resources in the final Resources chapter.

Defining retirement

Traditionally, retirement has many negative connotations associated with a retreat from relevance into dependence and ill-health. Retirement used to be primarily a male experience.

As the main breadwinner, once the man stopped working the family lost its main source of income. The family moved into a "grand parenting" role before the man died a few years later. Being retired was a relatively short period of decline before death for men, while women carried on their domestic duties as widows.

Acknowledging the increasing life expectancy of humans, modern sociologists often divide our life span into four ages:

- The first age: childhood, education and dependency;
- The second age: adulthood – younger and middle-aged;
- The third age: no longer working, children have left home;
- The fourth age: frail and dependent.

In this third age, retirement generally represents a significant period of over 20 years in everyone's life. Although women spend a significant part of their life in the working environment, it is more likely that their domestic role continues very much unchanged into the retirement period. This factor probably enables women to make the transition into unpaid work with far greater ease than their male breadwinners.

Over the past 50 years, the scope of retirement has grown immeasurably. Retirement has become a marketer's playground, as retirees can expect to contribute to the economy as consumers, spenders and the targets of new opportunities over several decades. Retirees can now participate in a huge range of "seniors" events – festivals, cruises, tours – which attract the active, healthy group of older people who have both the time and money to create a new sector in the economy.

Those retirees in the "third age" also known as the "young-old" between 60 and 80 years, are more likely to experience at least a decade of good health and active involvement. Those in the "old-old" group are loosely described as being over 80 years and in their "fourth age". This is the age of increasing disability, frailty and interdependence. Thanks to medical and lifestyle improvements, women can expect to spend many more years in this latter stage.

It is a sobering perspective that most of us will move from the one group into the other before we shuffle off our mortal coil. It is likely we will experience most of the medical and social aspects traversed in this book, so an informed attitude better prepares us and our families for the uncertainties of older age.

Why write a book intended mainly for women?

I have titled this book "*Every woman's guide…*" because I believe that with some planning and a basic level of financial and physical health, every woman can expect to look forward to a further 20 years of productive living after retirement to reveal her real talents and character to the world. As a reader, your circumstances may not be identical to those that I propose. You might not yet be old enough to see retirement on the horizon personally, or you may be a carer for ageing relatives. In any case, I have tried to forecast the issues that you may encounter, guiding you to make more confident, better informed decisions for those you care for.

This book therefore intends to be a realistic but positive guide to venturing into the retirement stage of your life. It attempts to cover the broad range of predictable life issues faced by women in their mature years. While owning your home and holding substantial superannuation should put you in a comfortable position, financial security only contributes to part of the picture. An open attitude and participating in meaningful activities will promote your well-being over time as much as a good income. Continuing to learn and being involved with others will bring personal satisfaction beyond mere dollars.

Modern Australian women can expect to have an active retirement and not a retreat to the stereotype of carpet slippers and cups of tea as it might have been 50 years ago. This period can be an opportunity to make a significant contribution to your community, to learn a new language, skill or follow an interest unrestricted by having to earn an income. Exploring and embracing retirement can lead to a whole new lifestyle that gives depth and colour to an otherwise ordinary life.

While male readers may also find this book useful, I recognise that women have different experiences and needs to men. I encourage women to use their life experience to rediscover and rejuvenate themselves in their later years, freed from the restrictions and obligations to either their birth family or their own family. After a lifetime of caring for others, this book advocates that women balance their caring obligations with their personal interests, skills and friendships to meet their own needs into the future.

As workers, carers and creative individuals, women take responsibility for many decisions, for themselves and their children, but also for parents and partners in their later years. Prior to retirement, examples of questions you might ask:

- Can I continue working after 65? I really need the money.
- When can I access my superannuation?
- What options do I have to care for my elderly parents?

In your later retirement, you might be thinking about different issues, such as:

- Can I get some extra help at home?
- Should I move in with my son's family?
- Have I organised everything for when I am gone?

In writing this book, I aim to answer questions about topics that I think you should understand as you approach retirement. Having basic information will assist you to be better prepared and steer you in the right direction to get more help. In researching each topic, I am writing from both a professional and a personal perspective. As a lawyer, I have shared in the lives of many clients and tried to advise them as best I could. While in my own life, I have learned about the experience of others in their early retirement phase, as well as my own.

Of course, this book cannot promise you with certainty is how to make the last third of your life a time of happiness and satisfaction. Your attitude is the main driver of that experience, mostly unrelated to your financial position. Realistically, we all need a basic level of financial security, but humans are complex creatures and more money does not automatically bring more happiness. Our health and our relationships with family and friends contribute at least as much as, if not more to our happiness quota as abundant financial resources.

2

Preparing for retirement

"Yes, you can have it all, but not all at the same time. Set your own priorities, trust your gut and follow your heart."
Quentin Bryce, former Australian Governor-General

If you are reading this book, chances are that you are planning for the future, perhaps your own, or perhaps for a family member. Retirement is a confronting issue, not only for us personally but also because we are likely to play a role in someone else's life – whether a parent, a child or our partner. Once we reach the age of 50 or thereabouts, ageing becomes a reality we can comprehend. We experience our bodies changing, we become aware of our parents' growing frailty or we notice that our career expectations are shrinking.

Our sixth decade can be a time of consolidation. We have become experts in our work; if we are lucky our income reflects our experience. Our expenses and child caring responsibilities have reduced while our financial situation will often have stabilised. Provided we remain healthy, it can be a very fulfilling time in our lives. But the decade of "middle age" also brings a subtle but growing realisation that things will not stay the same as we progress towards the latter end of our allotted span.

Without wanting to stereotype whole generations of the population, I find it convenient to use a framework that tags each generation with a characteristic. "Baby boomers" refers to people born between 1946 and 1965 who were born into an extended period of peace and economic growth after World War II. Being born into economic stability, gave the baby boomer generation the confidence to explore and innovate, developing concepts such as a youth culture, and equality for women and other groups in society which still continue today.

This generation also witnessed change across Australian society. The previously largely Christian, homogenous population, experienced waves of immigrants (from Europe after WWII and from Asia after the Vietnam War) bringing new foods and cultures to Australia.

Over time, innovations such as accessible contraception, home computers and mobile phones have created an "activist" generation that welcomes technology and change and brings a perspective that will permeate the aged sector now and into the future. That ongoing determination to challenge the status quo can be seen even as the life expectancy of baby boomers increases and they insist on changing the previous paradigm of rigid medically-based nursing homes.

Women of the "baby boomer" generation have seen their lives grow with greater opportunity in employment, education and awareness of personal capacity. However they still suffer great financial disadvantage – on average coming to retirement with less than half of the superannuation benefits of men. At the same time, they are likely to live longer and are more likely to care for ageing parents, their older partner and their grandchildren.

Working baby boomers have had some of the benefits of the compulsory superannuation scheme, but, coupled with a gendered pay difference, their financial situation is still more precarious than the subsequent X and Y generation workers. Women in their 50s now have more financial security since the introduction of compulsory superannuation contributions in the 1990s.

However, they still carry the burden of lower pay and an interrupted working life in order to take up caring responsibilities, for children and often for other family members. Women also comprise the largest group of casualised and part-time workers, which again reduces their ability to accumulate superannuation benefits needed to protect them from a life of poverty.

The take-home lesson from these economic realities? It is never too early to start planning for your retirement. It isn't easy to simply contribute more to your super, as many writers suggest, when it's all you can do to pay the mortgage and your electricity bill. But it is a goal that you can include in your weekly budget.

This book does not assume that all readers have the benefit of being in a two-income family. If you are – great! You should be consciously reducing your personal debts and putting more into your super towards your retirement. However if you are just managing on one income, whatever even small amount you can save represents a step in the right direction.

I am not suggesting a life of grim austerity as you head towards retirement, but small changes in your daily expenditure can reap long-term benefits. Living in a prosperous first-world country, many Australians see subscription TV, a weekly manicure or a cleaner to keep the house under control as a necessity. These are nice-to-haves, but certainly not essential if they prevent you putting $100 per week towards paying off your credit card or into your super.

But retirement is not only about super. It is also about what you want to do for the next third of your life. It's about having interests and activities beyond paid work and developing new friendships that reflect your independent and mature self. There is more about managing financial matters in Chapter 4, and developing your interests and activities in Chapter 9.

More than a worker or a homemaker

With work being so central to our identity and role within society, many have said that modern Western society classifies us all as workers first and as individuals second. For women this can be a real dilemma as they try to juggle the roles of worker, homemaker and one's own creative life.

Until 1966 the Commonwealth Public Service barred the employment of married women. Married women were employed only as temporary employees who could not be supervisors, and were restricted in their ability to accumulate superannuation. This reflected a societal view that homemaking was the ideal female occupation, even though to an extent this reflected an upper/middle class world view.

Women who lost their male provider – whether through death or separation – were normally relegated to work in the most menial and low-paid jobs, such as cleaning, cooking or waiting in order to support their families.

While working-class women always needed to earn an income, middle-class women usually only entered the paid workforce for a short time prior to marriage. Female workforce participation has therefore been marginalised both in terms of contribution and financial need. This historical attitude persists today.

With the rise of the feminist movement, women aimed for equal choices in education and representation in professions such as law, accountancy or the sciences. Increased participation of women in the whole employment spectrum has continued in the last 30 years, although a large and increasing part of these roles remain part-time or casual. This directly reduces female accumulation of superannuation and job seniority.

In 1975, 46% of women aged between 15 and 64 years held a job. In 2015, the Treasury reported that 66% of women in that age group worked, with an increase to 70% expected by 2054-55. By 2019, the Workplace Gender Equality Agency reported that there were 73.3% women in the workforce, reflecting how changes in welfare benefits can affect employment attitudes[1]. Few women now see being solely a homemaker as a desirable goal (except perhaps for some of the very wealthy), not only because of a perceived lower social status, but also because it lacks economic benefits such as superannuation and a separate income.

Since the 1970s, generations of women have grown up with the expectation of having it all – a well-paid job, a fulfilling relationship, as well as 2.2 children. In Australia, particularly in the capital cities, this identity has come at a cost. In recent decades, for most families buying a house, having holidays and a comfortable lifestyle has required two full-time workers, often with a sacrifice of personal fulfilment and a compromise of family relationships. Most single women, single parents or women who have become single find it almost impossible to enjoy the same living standard as their partnered friends.

Working longer

Australian government policy reflects international policies in encouraging people to work to a later age. This policy aims to both reduce individual reliance on public funds and also improve a person's health and their income-earning ability. For some, poor health or family needs can initiate the move to retirement. However, for many successful women, leaving a hard-fought career without a future direction can lead to much personal anxiety.

There are alternatives for women who are not ready to slow down. The retirement phase offers women many opportunities to use the experience and skills of previous employment in a new and more satisfying personal context, once they venture beyond the traditional work environment.

Where once women were unlikely to work beyond 60, economic pressure will now likely force many to continue until they reach age pension eligibility, which has been steadily increased. With insufficient superannuation benefits or an existing mortgage, many women cannot afford to retire until they are assured of a pension income. Currently around 12.9% of persons aged over 65 are in the workforce, with this figure expected to increase to 17.3% by 2054-55.[2]

Of course, even if we remain willing to take on a new employment role, our future employer might not be. While discriminating against potential employees on the basis of their age is officially reprehensible, anecdotally any job applicant 50 years or older would have had suspicions that they had been discriminated against because of their age. I look at the issue of ageism in the workforce in more detail in Chapter 3.

However even involuntary retirement can bring fresh choices to enable you to redefine, rediscover and reinvent yourself. You can explore a range of options – ceasing work, working part-time, changing work and starting another business, or finally accepting a non-employed life and making that a worthwhile project in itself. Finding the right path requires a certain amount of exploration before you can enjoy this time in your life.

When is the right time to retire?

Ending one's formal work career is a significant step in any worker's life. Once marked by gold watches and congratulatory dinners, these days the event tends to be more subdued, with retirees experiencing mixed emotions of relief or regret.

Whether we retire voluntarily or due to changed circumstances such as personal or family health issues, it represents the loss of our work identity, the income and the recognition that accompanies a successful working life. These issues affect single people just as much as couples. In fact, singles are more likely to depend on their work for their regular income and more subtly, they rely on work colleagues as a source of social interaction.

Difficulties in the transition to retirement period extend beyond stereotypes. Any well-prepared individual can experience emotional challenges at retirement, even with significant preparation. You may have defined yourself as a professional for many years, with confidence in your knowledge and your ability.

Respected in your position, you have achieved the status of a senior role model. Then suddenly, everything that has defined you disappears. Your income falls, while your job description becomes "retired", with all the inherent associations of old age and incompetence. In your own mind, just another week has passed and you are the same person, but now you have lost your daily compass.

Of course, we don't just work for the money. We want structure, purpose and recognition in the public arena – and these aspects rank as highly as our income – especially in our later career. The first year of retirement can be personally challenging for many subtle reasons.

We may experience regret for the career achievements we did not have; there can be guilt because we are receiving an income without apparently doing anything to receive it. We may feel a real loss of identity – I used to be a senior manager, now I am a has-been. What's more, I no longer have the work colleagues and contacts that I used to have because they are busy working. So now I am bored as well. It can be a questioning time with no immediate answers.

Finishing up at work is also likely to accompany other transitions – children starting work and leaving home, and ageing parents requiring more assistance. Despite our best attempts, our bodies also start to show signs of ageing in our skin, our joints and our muscle tone. We may no longer feel able – or want - to manage the demands of a busy workplace and may want to have more spare time to improve our fitness.

None of these factors may be a reason to leave fulfilling work, but eventually we face a decision about whether to continue full-time work. Of course, a few people will say that you never have to retire, that you can still go into the office at 81 years and make a worthwhile contribution.

No doubt some exceptional individuals will continue to not only be productive but enjoy the work process beyond the usual retirement age. That's fine if you happen to be the well-known Ita Buttrose and you're invited to the board.

However, the vast majority of workers who have been employed for the last 40 years and have reached their 60s with fewer financial responsibilities will be ready for a less demanding role.

For many, retirement generates a profound sense of relief from the daily grind of early rising, managing workplace relationships and rushed weekends. Often at this stage, being able to assist other family members becomes a very welcome objective, with retirement being a way to be available to support the wider family. Continuing and sustaining relationships is an important aspect of having a meaningful retirement that enables you to contribute to others, receiving support and recognition in return.

Not just a long holiday

This book intends to assist women transitioning to this new stage in their life to make it fulfilling and worthwhile. You are not going on a very long holiday. If you were, your life would be boring and empty in a very short time. By creating your own goals and schedule of meaningful activities, you will have a renewed sense of purpose and accomplishment in the early years of transitioning to this new lifestyle.

This next statement is deliberately harsh – *none of us get out of here alive*. No matter how carefully we eat, exercise and meditate, eventually we will experience illness, pain and disability. If we are lucky, this period will be relatively short and we will not be a burden either to ourselves or to our friends and families. More likely, we will experience some years of declining health, loss of memory and increased dependency before we pass away.

Death marks the end point of retirement. We fear retirement with good reason, because we know we are entering a tunnel without a light up ahead. In this century, retirement represents nearly a third of our lifespan. The preparation for our end stage can be as fulfilling as any other stage in our life.

After all, when we decide to marry, we are well aware that we may end up being divorced, but we marry anyway because we expect there will be some benefits from the experience. Whether those benefits are children, personal fulfilment or financial growth, they will also require effort, persistence and possibly some pain.

Transition to retirement can be a worrying time

Many unknown factors can exacerbate the initial transition from worker to retiree. To name just a few – sources of income, health, housing, cost of living, excess spare time – all of these require changes to the routine of a lifetime. Hopefully, you will have started to prepare many years earlier for this time.

However, many people don't consider what their own needs and goals beyond finishing work might be. Typically, having a long overseas holiday figures high on most wish lists, but returning to reality can lead to periods of a depression before we come to terms with our options.

Research has shown that planning for a retirement future will provide a better outcome, not only financially but qualitatively in the range of choices that we make. Later, I will propose some alternative options to assist you in achieving a fulfilling retirement that relies on more than an income stream.

With a few statutory exceptions, Australia has no compulsory retirement age. Federal legislation is gradually increasing the age for eligibility for receiving the age pension (67.5 years by 2023) but there has been steady resistance to a 70 year pension age.

People can choose to retire earlier and have conditional access to their superannuation after the minimum 'preservation age' of 55 years (you can't normally make use of your super when younger than that age). But many people actually retire earlier than pension age if they can afford it. Since compulsory superannuation was introduced in 1992, most employees will likely have some savings in their funds. Yet significantly, women are likely to retire with an average of $138,500 in benefits while men are likely to have $292,500.[3]

Given this disparity, women unsurprisingly prefer to keep working until they can receive a pension. Women remain very vulnerable to financial pressures throughout their longer lifespan and are more reliant on age pension income. Consequently, I have provided a brief, comprehensive introduction to our social security system for individuals and carers in Chapter 10.

Our long-lived population

To put the retirement period into perspective, let us begin with a few facts and figures. According to Australian Treasury figures, in the early 1900s Australian men could expect to live to 54.3 years and women to live to 57.4 years. Since then, our life expectancy has steadily increased and a male born today can expect to live to 80.4 years and a female to 84.5 years.[4] As of 2018, there were over 5.5 million people aged between 53 and 72 years. By 2055, statisticians expect that Australia's population over 65 years will double in proportion to the general population, with those aged over 85 years then representing 4.9% of the population, or nearly two million people.

At the same time, it is likely that proportionally there will be fewer younger working people to support a growing cohort of older people[5]. Younger workers are required to provide labour and taxes to support the older generation who need and use health and aged care services and need aged pensions.

Is there an aged care crisis?

From my perspective, the statistics showing a growing number of 'old-old' people in care appear to be beyond doubt. However, I would not support any conclusion which sees aged people as a burden on society, or that interprets this trend as a crisis.

Using the term 'crisis' suggests that older people are an increasing burden, with a substantial drain on government funds and insufficient working age people to support them. Some also suggest that Australia will not be able to afford paying the aged pension to retirees and government rhetoric certainly suggests that older people should be self-supporting.

In my view, such arguments do not indicate that a crisis exists but rather suggests that, as a society, we do not value the lifelong (and still continuing) contribution of a whole preceding generation.

From my perspective, the increasing number of older people certainly raises a number of complex issues requiring attention. However, solutions will require working with older people, not kneejerk reactions.

One key issue remains – employment for older people. Of course, many older people (and I include anyone over 50 years in this category) are quite willing to work, but figures show that once they lose employment, they find it harder than any other age group to get another job. Positive changes to employer attitudes will support older people who wish to work and benefit society as a whole.

Supporting a large non–working population over a long period is a new challenge for our society. It requires development of new social paradigms to provide appropriate activity, services and housing for people over 65 years of age. Fortunately to some extent, Australia has largely escaped this global first-world experience because our immigration policy has favoured younger workers who make an active and longer-term contribution to the economy. Pre-conceptions about the burden of older people can be balanced by recognising the contribution of seniors to the unpaid workforce that supports both families and non-profit organisations.

Government policies encourage self-sufficiency in the older population. For example, recent changes to the superannuation legislation encourage older people to downsize to smaller houses, allowing the excess funds to be contributed directly to their own super funds. Such innovative policy makes more appropriate housing available to a younger generation while giving the retiree financial independence.

Housing providers have recognised the need to cater for an older population by providing alternative housing options such as retirement villages, retirement 'resorts' and group housing to meet the growing demand. Choosing the most suitable long-term housing in the maze of options can have both financial and psychological consequences. I discuss this in more detail in Chapter 5.

While we can plan to eliminate as much uncertainty from our lives as possible, reality will nevertheless intrude whether through events of the individual or another family member. Arranging your legal and financial affairs to reduce problems and disputes in the family should begin in your 50s. It should include planning for your own care over the coming decades, in case of unexpected events leading to physical or mental incapacity.

What is successful ageing?

A widely used 'successful ageing' model[6] from the 1980s describes successful retirees as having long lives; generally avoiding disease and disability; retaining their mental and physical functions and remaining engaged with life.

One of the most fascinating studies that I have encountered suggests that having a long and successful retirement depends more on our innate personal make-up and an absence of trauma in our early life, rather than wealth, intelligence or luck.

Entitled 'The Longevity Project',[7] this study was conducted by Stanford University (USA) over eight decades beginning in 1921 when Dr Lewis Terman selected 1,500 11 year-old children and followed them throughout their lives. He collected extensive information about them that included family histories and relationships, teacher and parent ratings of personality, hobbies, jobs, education levels, marriages, and finally, their age and cause of death.

While Dr Terman died in 1956, his colleagues continued the study and concluded that a number of key character traits offered better predictions of longevity than any other factor. Those characteristics are prudence and persistence, which the study amalgamates into the trait of 'conscientiousness'. Conscientious people are prudent, persistent and well-organised and even if these traits are not obvious in childhood, a person can become more conscientious as they age.

Because of their very nature, conscientious people are more likely to live healthy lifestyles, to not smoke or drink to excess, to wear seat belts and follow doctors' orders when taking medication. Second, conscientious people tend to choose happier marriages, better friendships and healthier work situations. The third factor appears to be a biological predisposition to avoid risky behaviour which might result in violent deaths and to avoid diseases caused by risky habits.

According to the study, early influences such as family wealth, parental divorce, education and intelligence do not generally determine how long an individual may live. Even experiencing stress through having a stressful job to which a person is strongly committed caused less unwanted health effects than might be expected. In later life, the study found that having social support networks, religiosity, life satisfaction and marital happiness were positive factors, while neuroticism and catastrophic thinking had negative effects.

The take-away from this research? Whatever our biology or our birth situation, we can change our attitude and behaviour to reduce our risk of experiencing traumatic events and to increase our support networks when we become less capable. We cannot completely prevent illness or disability, but we can retain an optimistic attitude to obstacles that arise. In fact, this optimistic thinking appears to become easier to achieve as we age.

Stages of retirement

Obviously not everyone approaches life transitions in the same way, but a US study by Merrill Lynch[8] categorised retirement into four stages following an extensive survey of American retirees. You might want to compare your own experience with their findings.

Stage 1: Winding down & gearing-up: from five years prior to retirement

In the five years prior to retirement, many pre-retirees felt overwhelmed with work and looked forward to more time for the non-work activities they love. Not surprisingly, 74% said they were stressed and burned-out, with work acting as a barrier to more fulfilling leisure. Leisure travel in this stage was about escape (43%) and recharging one's batteries (46%). Optimism and financial preparedness rose compared to earlier pre-retirement.

Stage 2: Liberation & self-discovery: retired for two years or less

Early retirees experienced an enormous sense of liberation and relief as most (78%) felt they finally had enough free time. However they continued to deal with the challenge of adjusting from a work-centered identity to one defined by leisure and other interests. During this transitional period, some still felt unsettled, anxious, or bored but many sought opportunities to expand their personal growth, to travel, to volunteer and a significant percentage continued to work on a part-time basis.

Stage 3: Greater freedom and new choices: 3-15 years into retirement

During the first 15 years of retirement, retirees continued to enjoy their leisure and embrace their new identity. Their spontaneity peaked while anxiety waned. As retirees were better able to structure their time, they further separated from full time work and became comfortable with their post-work selves. Fewer had feelings of guilt when not using leisure productively, increasingly replacing 'do-ing' with 'be-ing'. Everyday activities included: exercising, shopping, reading for pleasure, volunteering, taking classes/learning, and socialising with friends. Spending on leisure travel rose, with interest in immersive experiences such as 'voluntourism', cruises, adventure travel, international sightseeing and camping travel. Some (9%) still worked, often in different ways to their core careers.

Stage 4: Contentment and accommodation: over 15 years retired

After 15 years of retirement, retirees were most likely to strive to maintain health and independence as well as enjoying familiar activities rather than new ones. They spent much of their leisure time connecting with family and friends.

Compared to other stages, people were most likely to prioritise simplifying their lives and continuing with familiar leisure activities, rather than trying new things. Retirees in this stage were less energetic, more physically limited, and more worn out than earlier in retirement. They preferred travel with family, including multigenerational travel with grandchildren. At this stage, health conditions (72%) were more pervasive and limited leisure experiences. Increased doctor visits and medical care were also barriers to leisure activities for 61%, as well as caregiving for a partner for some.

Designing your own retirement

Unless you have been a politician, received a substantial inheritance or been incredibly successful, most people will have a reduced income in retirement. That means you will need to reduce your discretionary spending to some extent. On the plus side, your expenses will also reduce – you don't need the smart work clothes, the city commute or the city lunches. You will probably spend more on holiday travel though – but that figure might depend on how much you want to keep for any children to inherit.

The largest financial decision ahead for many retirees will be paying for a transition to residential care. While many retirees can remain in their own homes, others will of necessity have to enter supported accommodation, such as a residential village or nursing home. When this decision arises, the deposit on your accommodation will require a large commitment of resources. It will also substantially complicate your spending decisions. Many people (reluctantly) sell their home to make the deposit for residential aged care but equally, few of us would want to delay enjoyment of our retirement for such a prospect.

Your mental health and attitude will be the most important factors in managing the inevitable difficulties that arise in retirement long-term. Explore your own feelings and be honest with yourself, rather than believing overly optimistic self-help books (you can do it all!) and soft-focus adverts. Leaving work naturally brings welcome relief for many people. However others (myself included) know that we are not ready or able to abandon paid work overnight.

Personally, I enjoy the intellectual challenge of work, the contact with new clients and resolving their issues. But I also enjoy not having to work to a deadline every day. I deliberately include a variety of activities in my regular weekly schedule such as going to the gym, meeting up with friends and taking on volunteer roles.

If you cannot afford to cease paid work because you have not yet have reached age pension eligibility, take the opportunity to plan for your eventual retirement while you continue to repay debts and accumulate super. Pre-retirement planning in the form of re-aligning your personal relationships, leisure and lifestyle decisions can have a positive effect on your personal satisfaction in retirement.

Women on average hold less financial resources than men, but have more personal relationships outside their families, and wider intellectual interests that they can follow in their leisure time. Their social connections provide a key factor in retirement well-being.

Prepare your own retirement narrative by ensuring that you don't idealise your previous work situation. Remembering only the good parts (including the salary) will make you more disenchanted with your new stage of life. Recall the more boring aspects and conflicted moments of your work as well. Taking a balanced view of your past work life will assist you to realistically assess how much work you take on through the transition into retirement.

Eventually I expect to cease all paid work and to settle into the routine of a retiree. For me, having a routine in early retirement is essential to successfully transition from the structure of work to the independent satisfied life of a successful retiree. Your social and emotional resources will bring opportunities for growth and development, both personally and to the community.

Creating your retirement routine

In retirement, your routine centres around you rather than an employer. However, developing some basic routines to structure your week is still advisable, for example:

Give every day its own routine. Get up at the same time and walk the dog, feed the cat or water the garden. Break your fast and share the domestic chores such as doing the washing, tidying the house or doing the shopping.

Find a reason to leave the house every day whether for a social event, to participate in a class or to read in a café.

Take up some physical activity – whether the gym or more organised sports like golf, tennis or croquet. Make sure you participate every week to keep up your fitness levels.

Do a course. It could be something you have always wanted to know about, or it can be more practical, such as doing Asian cooking or woodwork. Short-term or long-term, it will stretch your grey matter and keep you healthier longer.

Give yourself regular time out. It could be in the form of attending your local religious group or participating in meditation or mindfulness groups.

Do your family a big favour and start de-cluttering your clothes, books and furniture. Remember to only keep those things that give you joy.

Structure in at least one key unique activity for each week. This will add variety and spontaneity to your week and perhaps introduce you to a different future interest. It could be:

- **Catching up** with a long-lost friend, or going to a musical show or the art gallery.
- **Take a day trip** by car or by public transport and visit a place you haven't been lately.
- **Join an organised bus tour for the day** arranged by your local community centre or other club that you have joined. It's a good way to meet other local residents and visit an unfamiliar area.
- **Spend time in nature** without your phone, iPad or any other electronic device. Just be. Unplugging yourself will provide exercise, reduce stress and revive you.

Take care of your relationships with family and friends:

- **Make time for your family,** with both close and extended family members. You don't need to interfere but they might appreciate your help.
- **Invite people to your** home and enjoy some joint social events with your partner.
- **Have some separate social time from your partner.** Join a club on your own and meet other people whose interests align with your interests, rather than your partner's.
- **Stay connected via social media.** Being able to use Facebook, Snapchat, Instagram and emails keeps you in contact with distant friends and brings you international news without leaving home.

Even if you took up only half of these suggestions, every week would be busy and before long you would have a multitude of new friends and interests.

Defining your own meaning and purpose

Giving structure, purpose and involvement to your day-to-day activities makes the transition to the post-work world easy and satisfying. When you define your own purpose you will be motivated to work towards meaningful activities in this fruitful time of your life.

The equation for purpose is G+P+V=P
Gifts + Passion + Values = Purpose
Richard Leider,
author, *A Year of Living Purposefully*

Just as I have suggested that you create an everyday routine that will accommodate your transition into post-work life, I also believe everyone should find a purpose that reflects their values and gives their life meaning. That purpose might be something that has always been present but undefined in your earlier life, or it may be something that you have only come to recognise as being significant to you once you have disengaged from your former working life.

For me, a meaningful purpose implies being part of something greater than myself, where I can contribute my talents to a bigger idea that benefits and involves others who are not my direct family. Finding your own purpose might take time.

There are many examples in the media where people have been touched by tragedy, such as losing a child to cancer, and become ambassadors for advancing that research. But it is by no means limited to good causes. I know of someone who discovered his passion for playing the trumpet, joined the local brass band and has since toured all around Australia playing in competitions and festivals with other bands. Others have taken up permaculture and volunteered their time at local community gardens or used their professional skills to assist refugees with their legal cases. 'Making a difference' is an oft-used trite phrase, but the meaning behind this phrase can become a reality for you in a world where time is a luxury.

In this 'Third Age' of your life, being happy means more than just being financially secure. Being happy means also being aware of others in the 'big picture' of life and living according to your own principles and values.

3

Leaving work

"I find endlessly fascinating people's notions of scarcity and abundance. Somebody can have a lot and feel that they don't have anything. Somebody can have nothing and feel they have a lot."

Karen Mahlab AM, Australian business woman

Although retirement means a withdrawal from employment, there is also an implication that it is a withdrawal from the relevant world – that is, the world of work. Most people find the fear of becoming irrelevant more overwhelming than just leaving a job. We have spent most of our adult life striving for recognition as being competent and valuable in our role.

Many of us have sacrificed time with our family or our personal interests to attain our respectable position. Yet, here at the epitome of our productive life, we give it all away for the promise of freedom.

No wonder that amidst those fond workplace farewells, many of us resent and resist the new phase of our life opening up. We all need to remember that our job does not solely define our identity. We also have innate interests and abilities beyond the obligations of work and family responsibilities. Whether or not we actually believe in the

Protestant ethic of hard work, discipline and frugality as being the true measure of our worth in society, we effectively adopt that view throughout our working life.

While retirement may mean stepping back from the employer/employee roundabout, we can continue to offer a relevant contribution. We can take the opportunity to make a life of our own choosing.

We can continue to work, paid or unpaid, to participate in activities that really interest us, and to give practical assistance to our family and friends that otherwise would not be available. We can contribute real value to others and to ourselves in being there for them.

This chapter examines two options that face mature-age workers – leaving paid full-time employment at a time of your own choice, or leaving paid employment involuntarily as a result of some major intervening event.

The process and the consequences are different, initially at least, but can also have long-term impacts on how we live the last third of our life. I also suggest some alternative income-generating options.

Retirement is complicated in that it is not just a personal decision. Besides leaving your work friends and colleagues and the daily routine, your decision also impacts your relationship with your partner and your children, with whom you are likely to become much more involved. The initial retirement year can be a bewildering time, but thoughtful planning can reduce anxiety and encourage ongoing exploration.

If you have built your life around your work identity and your work status is central to your life, it is only to be expected that leaving work means leaving the most relevant and important part of yourself behind.

Unless you consciously adapt your skills to a different focus you are likely to experience a great sense of grief. Having a less flexible personality can make such a transition quite damaging as demonstrated in this case study:

CASE STUDY

Dr P was an extremely successful law academic. During the course of her career she had been on many boards and represented the legal profession in international events. With no significant personal relationships, she resisted retirement until close to 70 years when she finally bowed to colleagues' pressure that it was time for younger staff to step up.

Despite a healthy superannuation pension, Dr P felt that she was no longer "well-off" and curtailed her spending on food to a bare minimum. When her former colleagues visited, they reported being offered supermarket packet biscuits in a cold and barely lit apartment. Their visits and invitations continued for several years, but eventually ceased as she became more cantankerous, leaving her to the care of her neighbours.

After Dr P was diagnosed with early stage Alzheimer's disease, one of her former colleagues agreed to act as her Attorney and Enduring Guardian to assist in her transition to an aged care facility that could better manage her day-to-day personal care.

This case study demonstrates the difficulty of leaving a work role which has been central to a person's identity. In contrast, another person who is just leaving their more mundane job, gladly anticipates their forthcoming leisure activities. The second person will feel freed from onerous conflicts and management duties and can now exit from their position in a socially acceptable path. They are more likely to look forward to this new phase and to adapt existing skills to new challenges. Our heavily-invested colleague is more likely to feel the loss of position and purpose once retired.

If you are enjoying your present position and feel appreciated, by all means continue in your work. But also recognise that choosing to leave is a far better experience than being forced to leave when you have not planned for it.

Managing change in our lives

You need to think about retirement and make changes to your lifestyle at least 6 months before your proposed retirement date. Why? So you can initiate an ongoing new routine that will take you into that first year as smoothly as possible. While most planned retirees do experience a brief honeymoon period as they enjoy a long holiday and morning sleep-ins, that is likely to be followed by periods of aimlessness or depression if they have not made longer term plans.

Involuntary retirees who are thrown into retirement because of redundancy or illness are far more likely to experience anger and depression for extended periods as they try to readjust to an unwanted lifestyle. Besides difficulties arising from health issues, involuntary retirees are often not mentally open to accepting new opportunities because they have not been able to prepare for the change that being forced out of employment brings. They may also struggle with their perception of retirement as a bleak financial wasteland without any positive characteristics.

Each person has a different way of coping with change, whether welcome or not. Whether you are starting a new job, expecting a baby or being down-sized, we all have individual coping mechanisms, some of which may make the transition actually more difficult than it might be for others.

Some types of change only happens if we proactively encourage it. Other types of change can be thrust upon us, unexpected and unwanted. Here are some suggestions to make the adjustment to changed circumstances easier, regardless of how it has come about.

1. **Acknowledge that change is occurring.** Denial blocks positive steps to managing change.
2. **Acknowledge you may feel stressed**, even if the change will be good.
3. **Identify some positives** that will come from this change, such as gaining new skills or meeting new people.
4. **Take steps to incorporate small changes** into your life. Plan and implement changes to find some benefits that you value.

5. **Maintain key parts of your regular routine**. Something as simple as walking the dog can help you anchor yourself.

6. **Maintain healthy eating habits.** Controlling your food intake may keep your weight down and increase your enjoyment of small aspects of your life. Be conscious that increased use of alcohol as a form of self-medication can lead to addiction and additional health problems.

7. **Keeping up your exercise** will assist in maintaining your health and keeping depression at bay.

8. **Stay in touch with friends and family.** With the help of positive friends and family most problems will be easier to solve, but be open to seek help from a professional counsellor if necessary.

9. **Be careful with use of social media:** don't use it as a forum to vent your anger in case you say something you may regret later. If you experience major frustration, it's better to express your feelings to trusted friends.

10. **Remember, you don't have to be perfect all the time**. Be kind to yourself while you transition to this new situation.[1]

Sometimes we resist change because we fear the consequences that it can bring. To deal with fear, we need to understand what we are afraid of. Retirement has many implicitly fearful aspects, such as its association with declining health, reduced financial capacity and irrelevancy.

Acknowledging frailty and death as an inevitable part of everyone's lifecycle may be the most difficult challenge of retirement. Some people want to work in their business forever, some dress up like their grown children, while others become gym junkies to ward off physical decline. These steps may be acceptable in our modern culture that worships youth and beauty. But we must remember the inevitability of change: as the beautiful rose eventually withers and dies, so must we. In accepting our mortality, we allow ourselves to feel empowered, to make the best of our own situation and to make the best contribution that we can to those we care for.

A few facts and figures about the working population

Like many developed nations, Australia has experienced a dramatic shift in the make-up of its population. According to United Nations figures, Australia's older age group is the highest proportionally it has ever been in its history.[2]

This rate, representing a combination of reduced fertility rates and increasing life expectancy will continue with profound effects on the economy. For example:

- Older people have higher accumulated savings but are more risk averse so they tend to spend less on consumer goods, which tends to reduce the inflationary effect on the economy.

- Older people are more reliant on publicly-funded services such as health care and pensions which requires higher rates of taxation on younger workers.

- Currently the over-65 age group represents 15% of Australia's population but by 2056, the over-65 cohort will represent 22% of the population. Like other countries, government policy will continue to strongly encourage self-funded retirement and minimise access to pensions.

- Because women have a longer life expectancy, they comprise just over half of the 65-84 age group and make up 63% of people aged over 85 years.[3]

A 2016-2017 survey by the Australian Bureau of Statistics (ABS) of Australia's 3.6 million retirees[4] showed that overall, the average man had retired at 58.8 years and the woman at 52.3 years. It is likely that women were able to retire relatively early because they were still supported by their husbands and could access the pension at 60.

However, of recent retirees (those retired in the past 5 years) their average age at retirement was 63.6 years for men and 62.1 years for women. This indicates that the actual retirement age is steadily increasing, for both men and women.

Working intentions prior to retirement

In an ABS study[5] of 949,300 people working full-time, 65% intended to continue working for their current employer until they retired with some intending to take on less demanding duties over time.

The remainder either intended to find an alternate employer who could offer part-time work, or find work on a contract basis, or become self-employed.

A significant portion of the interviewees in this study could not say at what age they intended to retire but most intended to retire at 65 years or over. These interviewees nominated financial security as the main reason for continuing work beyond the age of pension eligibility.

However, when they actually did retire, most did so as soon as they reached the age of pension eligibility. Others retired when their own health or the health of a family member required it, or when they lost their employment.

Comparing the pre-retirement intentions with the reasons for actual retirement, it still appears that financial security was not the factor that ultimately determined the retirement date. Rather, interviewees took retirement as a logical choice once they had reached the eligible age for a pension. Changes to an individual's health were also are a significant catalyst towards retirement.

We wait for our pension before retiring

The trend of increasing the pension eligibility age began over 50 years ago. It is only because some groups within our community have greatly resisted the idea, that the age for pension eligibility has not yet been increased to 70 years.

Working longer has become a reality for most of us. Most women must continue to work, firstly, to become eligible for the age pension and secondly, to build up their superannuation entitlements while they still can.

Governments have responded to our lengthening lifespan by increasing the age when we become eligible for the age pension as follows:

If you were born between	You qualify for age pension at age
1 July 1952 to 31 December 1953	65 years and six months
1 January 1954 to 30 June 1955	66 years
1 July 1955 to 31 Dec 1956	66 years and six months
From 1 January 1957	67 years

*Source: The Department of Human Services

The federal government introduced compulsory employer superannuation contributions[6] in Australia in 1992 at an initial rate of 3% of an employee's wage, rising to 9% in 2002 and now 9.5%.

Consequently, women over 40 can expect considerably lower superannuation balances than Gen X women workers who have had the benefit of higher contribution rates in the past 15 years and can expect to see their employer contribution rate rise to 12% in July 2019.

Some employers have a far more generous scheme, contributing 17% of their employees' salaries, however many independent contractors or self-employed individuals will be lucky to have put aside even a fraction of that amount.

In order to be confident of enjoying a reasonable standard of living in retirement, we need sufficient superannuation, to supplement the age pension when we stop working. Of course, many retirees continue some level of paid work, as discussed later in this chapter.

Your working identity

As can be seen from the ABS study, approximately 50% of current employees over the age of 45 years are expecting to retire later than the previous generation of retirees, namely between 65 and 69 years, influenced by the later availability of the age pension.

While there still remains a group who intend to retire between 60 and 64, the number in this group has fallen, balanced by an almost equivalent group who intend to work to 70 years at least.

Significantly, in the ABS study, 40% of older workers were unable to indicate when they intended to retire. Whether they wanted to avoid thinking about this issue, or whether they recognised that the decision may be out of their control was not clear.

However, this group demonstrated the great uncertainty and reluctance that can arise in this later period of employment. The benefits of working can be easily identified, for example:

- Income
- Social status
- Personal identity apart from your direct family
- Participating in a forum in which to contribute your personal skills
- Acquiring and developing competence in an area of knowledge
- Social context through colleagues and friends made in the workplace
- Structure to daily life
- Long-term economic and social security

These very powerful benefits can give us a stable and comfortable life. In our life history, our employment gives us a sense of identity and belonging and has to some extent at least, made us the person who is reading this book today. Whether you are a physio, a caterer, or a teacher, after 30 years' experience in your field you have acquired expertise and the associated status that accompanies your experience. A regular income allows you to plan for the things you either need or would like and enables you to cope with unexpected expenses or additional activities.

This substantially middle-class scenario also applies for women working in sectors such as retail, hospitality or administration in that they continue to work because their skills are flexible and adaptable to many workplaces. However because women in these sectors also have lower incomes, they will more likely continue to work until they reach eligibility for the age pension or beyond, to supplement their superannuation payments.

Both professional and skilled workers will likely continue working into retirement on a contract, part-time or casual basis. For full-time employees these alternate employment styles may represent a gradual transition to retirement, while long-term part-timers probably *need* the income.

CASE STUDY

Born in France, Angelique moved with her Australian journalist husband to Melbourne and began a career as a high school teacher. On her retiring after 30 years' service, they moved to Sydney to be closer to their children. While her husband started writing his dream novel, Angelique brushed up on her French language skills, firstly completing a translating course to get her professional qualification and then completing a course to enable her to work as an interpreter in the court system. She put herself on the register of both a private service and a government department and has been in steady self-employment for the past 5 years.

As an experienced court interpreter, Angelique has had some demanding but fascinating assignments, such as working in North-West Australia for three weeks. But she is also able to manage her commitments to suit her own needs and schedules a four week break every year to take an overseas holiday.

Despite now being in her early 70s, Angelique still enjoys the unpredictable demands of her work and does not intend to slow down for a few more years.

Having to work because you're paid less than a man

For full-time work, Australian women earn on average 15.3% less than men. In actual dollars, that translates to $27,000 per year less than men averaged across all occupations and employment categories.[7]

Female-dominated industries such as childcare and aged care are lower-paid. In other industries, even where men and women have the same roles, women still earn around 20% less than men. Obviously, a lower wage means a lower employer contribution to a woman's superannuation.

Having a higher education does not protect women from the wage disparity. A survey by the Workplace Gender Equality Agency[8] showed that women in the finance industry and in professional areas were likely to have an even larger wage gap than occupational sectors such as manufacturing or retail.

A report by the Senate Economics Reference Committee examined gendered inequality in women's pay structures and its impact on women's superannuation benefits. Entitled, *"A husband is not a retirement plan: Achieving economic security for women in retirement"*,[9] this comprehensive report observed that gendered inequality is inherent in our income system: it cannot change without direct government intervention.

Women still continue to be under-represented in senior leadership roles such as CEOs, on boards and in parliament, despite educational achievements and opportunities.

Because women tend to be employed in industrially segregated workplaces (i.e. the majority of pre-school carers, nurses and librarians are women, while most geologists are men), they are more likely to work part-time for greater periods, or take leave from paid employment to take on full-time caring roles.

Consequently most women will find themselves significantly financially disadvantaged compared to men at the end of their working life, with a much lower accumulated superannuation balance being only the first major disadvantage of being female.

Women are also more likely to be reliant on welfare for more of their retirement years because of their longer life expectancy. Retirement can be a treacherous period for a woman renting in the private property market, because her income will typically not increase sufficiently to meet rising rental costs.

Continuing to work for as long as possible, whether full-time or casually, becomes necessary to avoid the challenges of what might be a long and difficult time. Unfortunately, research seems to suggest that the higher a person's educational level, the more easily and more likely that she will be able to find work and to continue working longer than a less qualified woman.

Whether you a high-flying manager or the lowest paid employee, planning for a time when you are no longer either willing or able to work full-time is essential.

As stated at the beginning of this chapter, retirement is more than opting out of nearly a third of your life. For most women, this means securing your financial future by exploring as many alternative income-producing possibilities as you can find.

Retiring when self-employed or a business owner

For those who run their own businesses, retirement is a more complicated step than simply deciding to close the door. You need to start planning for this step at least a year in advance because you have staff, clients, providers and possibly landlords that need to be advised that you intend to close.

If you give yourself time to develop a retirement strategy, you will have more options on how you retire. Running your own business means you have taken on responsibility for others and have used your energy and ideas to create a money-making enterprise over many years.

Now, will you just give it all away? It's going to be difficult for you to give up your life's work, but even more difficult for your staff who need to find other jobs that suit them as much as working for you.

What will happen to your office fitout, to your records, to your clients? To some extent, these things depend on your particular industry, whether you carry stock and the usual practices in dealing with customers.

Assuming you don't have a family member who wants to take over your business, decide how ideally you would like to wind things up.

Here are a few options to consider:

Selling your business: you need to enlist an accountant to put a value on your business, to prepare at least three years of financial statements and a lawyer to prepare a contract for sale. You could approach a business broker to see how you can market your business. If you are relying on a sale to fund your retirement, you might need to lower your expectations because it can be difficult to find a buyer at times.

Merge your business: find a partner who wants to take over your business. She might even want to retain your services for a time to ensure continuity with clients.

Keep your business: move to a completely online presence and change how you keep it growing. With this option you may not need the same number of staff, so you still need to plan for closure of your working space.

Close the business: do you have to advise your licensing body, your landlord, and other suppliers? You will need to prepare tax records and close off websites, domain names and your ASIC registration.

Hopefully while you have been making super payments for your staff, you haven't forgotten to put money into your own super as well. It's a fact that many small business owners do not put money aside for their own super, expecting that the sale of their business will provide sufficient funds for the future.

Remind yourself, that you don't want to be working forever and early contributions will reap significant benefits.

Age discrimination

Let's be blunt about this. Discrimination on the basis of your age is as real as the lines on your face. Any mature-age person who has applied for numerous jobs for which they are well qualified, will tell you that once they got to the interview, the unspoken fact was that despite their obvious skills, their age was the barrier to their employment. Of course, it is unlawful to discriminate against a person on the basis of their age as stated by the *Age Discrimination Act* 2004 (Cth) but in a survey conducted by the Australian Human Rights Commission (AHRC), 27% of all participants aged over 50 years, reported they had experienced discrimination.[10]

The most common negative assumptions related to the older worker's skills and learning capabilities are the limited opportunities for continued training and career progression. Often older workers were also subject to a subtle but ongoing pressure to "make way" for younger workers to take their positions. In the AHRC survey, over two thirds of the retirees attributed their retirement to involuntary factors such as "having no choice", redundancy or dismissal. Women workers often reported disguising their appearance with hair dye and younger-style clothes to avoid discrimination. Similarly, older workers looking for work stay on income support longer than younger job-seekers.[11]

Involuntary retirement

Older long-term employees are more susceptible to unexpected events, forcing them to leave permanent employment far earlier than intended. Employers consider any worker aged over 45 years an 'older worker'. A report prepared by the Australian Centre for Financial Studies[12] suggested that up to 40% of older workers can be considered to have been involuntarily retired due to factors such as age discrimination, ill health, job type, low levels of education, poor English proficiency and caring demands. The result: lower superannuation balances.

Where a male partner retires earlier than the woman, this can in itself cause difficulties in a long-term relationship. Numerous studies have found that many men find the transition to retirement more difficult than women because of their perception of loss of their provider role and their financial independence. In contrast, often the working woman decides to leave her employment early to assist her male partner adjust to a new lifestyle or to assist family members to care for grandchildren. Reinforcing gender stereotypes, this sacrifice may enable an easier transition, albeit with a financial impact on the woman.

CASE STUDY

As a highly experienced teacher, Helen had taught in a selective high school for 8 years in one of the most challenging and rewarding periods of her career. She intended to remain there until retirement. However a new principal commenced and he soon embarked on a course of undermining and bullying a number of teachers. Helen was a particular target. After nearly a year of such conduct, Helen took stress leave and eventually resigned when her health could no longer cope with a return to the school environment. It took some years before Helen's natural optimism began to resurface. She now tutors students from home.

Exploring retirement options

Ideally, planning for retirement should begin at least 6 months before your intended date. You actually have a lot of thoughtful work to do before the big day. A good place to begin would be thinking about work and your financial future. Do you enjoy working? Would you like to continue working but reduce the actual hours, or change your employer and do less hours?

Once you are over 60 years, the Tax Office can consider leaving an employer as an act of retirement, enabling you to access your super. But if you wish, you are still able to continue working, either full-time or with reduced hours with another employer as a step in your transition to retirement.

Reducing your actual work hours is an option that suits many people and many employers are happy to accommodate good employees by enabling that process. But as this case study shows, part-timers may be more vulnerable in that employers can more easily make them redundant.

CASE STUDY

Fran worked on a three year contract with a training provider. It was her second such contract but she recognised that her involvement with her meditation group was beginning to require more of her time and energy. She asked her employer to reduce her working hours. As they were already restructuring staff responsibilities, they easily agreed. Six months later Fran's position was made redundant.

As this was not unexpected, she negotiated a good payout package and concentrated on helping her group. She located premises for meditation meetings and with the assistance of an IT-savvy member, developed a new website for the group. She designed and printed advertising flyers and personally letterboxed cafes in the local area to increase group membership.

Two years later the membership is growing because of the speakers and workshops that Fran is organising. While Fran does not have a salary, she does have the satisfaction of using her skills to develop a project to which she is strongly committed.

Checklist before you decide to retire

1. **Choose a retirement date** and stick to it.

2. **You don't have to stop working** once you retire. It is well worth looking around to see if there is other work you would like to do.

3. **Formally advise your superannuation fund** of the date. Make an appointment to see your financial planner but before you go, make sure you have a list of the financial goals that you want to achieve. Do your own research before you see the planner to be ready with your important questions. Financial planners often make recommendations that best benefit themselves rather than you, so you need to be clear about your own goals.

4. **Distance yourself** from your current employment issues, whether they are internal conflicts or future events. Open a new email account rather than continuing to check your old work emails.

5. **Engage with your current colleagues** and make sure you have all their contact details. Plan for future catch-ups as you move to your new life, by attending gatherings such as drinks after work or occasional lunches.

6. **Talk to people** you know about their retirement experiences. Go to free information seminars such as those run by a super fund, employee assistance program or Seniors Australia.

7. **Plan to reward yourself** with a nice getaway trip shortly after you have left work. You deserve it after working for many years and fulfilling your family obligations.

8. **Consider your wardrobe** – buy a few good pieces for your new, more relaxed lifestyle. Do a more thorough cull of your wardrobe when you have actually resigned and recycle those office clothes.

9. **What do you love doing?** Golf, quilting, or playing the guitar – sign up for a workshop to improve your skills. If there is something you have always wanted to do – learn another language, study ancient history – sign up for a course before you have left work to get you interested in a new subject.

10. **Join up** – a charity, a local group, a book club – before you leave work and stay in touch with the new group until you have time to be more actively involved.

Working options

So you have decided that it's time to leave your job but you don't want to stop working entirely. One of the advantages of being retired: now you can have more balance between me-time and working-time. You can officially retire by reaching retirement age or finishing working for your employer and informing your super fund. However you can also continue to work, either full or part time for another employer. Eventually you are likely to stop working completely but 'bridging jobs' can be a good transition option. If you decide to take up options such as self-employment or setting up a new business, you should seek the advice of your accountant to advise you of the associated taxation and record-keeping duties.

Assuming you have reached preservation age[13] (being over 55 years and having retired) you can access your superannuation benefits to provide a financial "cushion". Here are some alternate working styles where you are not completely reliant on earned income:

Part-time or casual work with another employer: A part-time worker usually works less than 30 hours per week on a regular basis and has paid annual and sick leave. A casual worker is employed on an irregular basis, sometimes at call or on a seasonal basis but they may actually work more hours than a part-time employee. A casual worker may have a higher hourly rate than a part-time worker but will not be paid annual or sick leave.

Legislation and award definitions for pay rates and conditions apply in these roles. Part-time positions can provide a structure for your week, some additional income and opportunities for new work friendships, while allowing you to maintain your own interests.

You must earn over $450 per month to be eligible for employer contributions towards your superannuation benefits. If you have officially retired, you can continue to contribute to your super until the age of 75, provided you have worked at least 40 hours over 30 continuous days in any year.

Consultant: If you have developed expertise in your field, you can become a consultant to your previous employer or charge out your services to other businesses. You are likely to be responsible for payment of GST and superannuation.

Contract work: This term often applies where payment relates to completion of a project, or for work performed over a fixed period. You should negotiate the terms of the contract including the rate of payment but it will rarely include any leave payments or superannuation.

Starting a new business: Probably the most adventurous of these options and the one that requires the most effort and commitment. Being your own boss allows you to work as much or as little as you want.

At the most basic level, this could be a simple setup using a particular skill to market or create and sell certain products. It must be more than a hobby to have any taxation advantages.

Alternatively, if you already work in an area that you know well, you may see a need for a new service or a product. You may want to develop your hobby into a money-making enterprise, for example by reviving artisanal crafts such as bookbinding or cheese-making.

Or you can have a business that is completely on-line, such as digital illustrating that you do from home, or you can work remotely and report into a central office.

In any case, it can be a very exciting time as you develop new skills in areas such as social media marketing and website development to promote your business. Some points to consider before becoming a business owner:

- You should register a business name/company and obtain an ABN.

- You intend to make a profit even if you are unlikely to do so in the short term.

- If you operate from business premises, you have the requisite license or qualifications.

- You will have opened a separate business bank account and will keep business records and account books.

- You have consulted an accountant on how to structure your business. The Australian Taxation Office (ATO) website lists relevant factors to be assessed, including whether a portion of your home could be regarded as business premises. A good accountant can save you money and tears in advising you about your tax liabilities.

Some income-generating alternatives

Making good use of your money through investments and financial planning is covered in more detail in **Chapter 4 Financing Your Retirement**. In this section I am suggesting other options for increasing your income sources which do not rely solely on having a job, but propose alternative methods of using your existing assets.

Many older people are described as being asset-rich but cash poor. For example, they may live in large but empty houses while there are students or low income earners who would gladly rent out part of their homes. Here are a few suggestions on how to earn some additional income using your existing assets. However, be aware that there may be taxation issues if the ATO considers your activities to be a business.

Making a sea change/tree change: Around 30% of retirees move house at some stage. Of those, many seek a quieter lifestyle that emphasises community, warmer weather or an ocean view. Having less expensive housing and associated costs no doubt attracts many people even at the cost of moving away from friends and family. If you intend to take this route, do so while you are a relatively young retiree. You need time to integrate with the broader community through work and voluntary activities.

CASE STUDY

Ellie and Maxine retired in their early 60s. Ellie was a high school teacher who was burnt-out by inner-city students while Maxine was an airline steward who was happy to settle down. They decided to move to a NSW north coast city which was well equipped with hospitals and schools and was close to some of Ellie's family members. They were able to buy a comfortable modern house on a small acreage for half the price of their small inner city terrace with some funds to spare. Ellie began part-time teaching while Maxine found work as a casual postie and was soon a familiar sight in the local area. Three years later, they are involved in a number of community groups and have no thoughts of leaving.

Bed and breakfast: More suited to those making a sea change/tree change – buying a larger property in a beautiful location with separate accommodation and renting it out for luxury holiday lettings. This option includes providing a daily breakfast and suits those retirees who enjoy providing a "bespoke" hospitality service.

Student lodgers: This option can be very suitable if your home is within a convenient distance of an educational institute. You can have a steady income providing breakfast and dinner to international students who share your home. An ensuite bathroom is an essential requirement for your lodger, but a separate entrance and sitting area can give you some privacy as well.

AirBnB: Ignoring the more controversial aspects of this "online marketplace", this option will suit those with a larger house and a separate studio, bathroom and kitchenette for short-term stays. This business requires some effort in advertising and maintaining the property, but can generate good income with a larger property. Not recommended for strata apartments as many owners' corporations do not allow this accommodation service.

Garden flat: You need to meet council requirements for land size and usage but building a garden flat in your backyard can provide a steady income with little interruption to your lifestyle or privacy. It may also have a good effect on resale of your property.

Investment property: Buying an investment property requires a careful weighing of many factors. Generally a retiree should not consider a negatively-geared property because they need a positive income flow to support their lifestyle.

In my view, any property purchased needs to have a relatively low mortgage with a focus on income generation rather than an expectation of capital gain that depends on selling into a rising market.

You should not consider property to be an entirely "set and forget" type of investment even if you have a managing agent, which I would strongly recommend. A capable agent will ensure the regular collection of rent, maintenance of the property, and will resolve tenancy issues. Even so, you should make it a rule to inspect the property every six months. Making any minor improvements suggested by the agent will keep the property looking good.

Given the high property prices in capital cities relative to income generated, investors can find solid income returns in buying reasonably priced properties in larger regional cities which have a well-developed infrastructure.

Volunteering can be rewarding

Once you break free from the requirement to put most of your time into earning an income, many options arise to follow your own interests. Volunteering – that is, work without receiving an income - benefits both the individual and our society. Taking up volunteer activities offers one of the most worthwhile aspects of the retirement phase when we have both skills and time to contribute to improving the lives of others.

In fact, many of the things we take for granted in our society actually reflect the unrecognised work of volunteers. For example, the 2018 Commonwealth Games at the Gold Coast, Queensland, relied on 15,000 volunteers to assist with staging events in four locations over 11 days.

Most volunteering examples receive less attention but contribute just as well. For example, helping at charity fundraising events such as marathons and walks, or assisting emergency services workers at festivals.

For you as an individual, there are considerable benefits in volunteering such as:

- Increased self-confidence and self-esteem.
- Acquiring new skills and knowledge.
- Meeting new people.
- Making a difference to others on a regular basis.
- Promoting your personal values and interests.

CASE STUDY

As a civil engineer, Terri could see her retirement date coming up. She decided she needed to plan for this new phase of her life, or she would be very bored. She had always been a bit of a country music fan and had an extensive collection of CDs. She saw an advertisement in her local paper for an eight week training course for radio presenters. At the end of the course, the community radio station offered her a weekly presenter slot to play and talk about country music.

Some years later, Terri presents her own radio show twice a week, gets to meet up-and-coming Australian musicians and goes to as many music festivals as she can manage. "Best thing I ever did!" she comments about retiring.

Most organisations want a certain level of commitment from would-be volunteers about the amount of time they have available. You should be prepared to take a serious approach to taking on a role because staff and clients will depend on you to deliver a service.

Before applying for a volunteer position, many organisations will require you to obtain a Working With Children Check (WWCC) through the NSW Office of the Children's Guardian (valid for up to 5 years) or equivalent in your state, or a National Police Check. Both are relatively easy to obtain.

There are many types of organisations advertising for volunteer positions, from well-known service organisations such as Meals on Wheels and charities like St Vincent de Paul, to small community groups, hospitals and special interest groups. Consequently volunteer roles exist with a continual demand for a wide range of skillsets.

Many organisations seek specialist skills and experience such as accounting, legal and marketing for board of director roles which manage most not-for-profit (NFP) organisations.

Online sites to find advertised volunteer vacancies include:

- The Centre For Volunteering – www.volunteering.com.au
- Volunteering Australia – www.volunteeringaustralia.org
- VolunteerMatch – www.probonoaustralia.com.au/volunteer
- GoVolunteer – www.govolunteer.com.au

Note that some of these volunteer positions are advertised across a number of sites at the same time.

The unpaid economy

Numerous surveys over the past 10 years by many agencies have estimated the value of formal and informal volunteers to the economy.[14] Measuring volunteer participation is important:

- First, because not-for-profit organisations are able to put a value to work undertaken if they had to pay for an employee;
- Second, knowing the hours contributed by a volunteer recognises that there is an economic value in the activities they do, and
- Third, measuring the contribution of unpaid workers quantifies their value to the economy of society which for many decades has been unrecognised.

Summarising some of the key points from the research:

- If an organisation had to pay a volunteer, the average hourly pay for a volunteer is estimated at $31.50 per hour;
- In 2010, 49% of people surveyed provided informal assistance to another person;
- In that survey, 43% of people aged between 55-64 years provided assistance, while 31% of those over 65 years provided volunteer assistance. But more strikingly, the younger age group averaged 80 hours per year assistance, while the 65-74 age group provided an average of 104 hours per year assistance to others.

- In 2010, the volunteer sector contributed $25.4 billion to the Australian economy.[15]

- In another study by Giving Australia, it was suggested that volunteers had contributed 932 million hours in the past 12 months in three major areas: religious causes, health and social services.[16]

Dr Lisel O'Dwyer, Flinders University, in her 2014 study, suggested that the economic contribution by volunteers was worth more than the mining sector and was valued at about $290 billion.[17]

4

Financing your retirement

"All my life I've believed that men and women have equal capacities and talents ... consequently there should be equality in life's chances."

Julia Gillard, former Prime Minister

If you were guaranteed that you would have the same money and lifestyle as when you were working, you would worry far less about retirement and managing a comfortable lifestyle until you died. But retirees have good reason to be worried about having enough money to last through retirement.

Reflecting on your finances

You may be fortunate in coming to your post-work life with a healthy super balance, but for many people it can be a rather sobering moment to realise that we will need to work longer or will need to rely on the age pension to make ends meet. As always, there are many options available. Some of us will become Ms Frugal, others will become Ms Creative – it's going to be your call.

But the fact is that retirement inevitably represents a reduction of income and lifestyle, unless you have been able to make very large additional contributions over the years. Most people would be pleased to live on 75% of their pre-retirement income. However actual superannuation pension figures show that many people will not be able to achieve even half of their desired lifestyle without the assistance of the age pension.

Furthermore, lifestyle statistics assume that retirees will own their own house by retirement and that housing costs will form a relatively small portion of the weekly expenditure. While this may be true for approximately 75% of the baby boomer generation, it is far less likely for Gen X and Y workers who will struggle to repay large mortgages in capital cities as they approach their retirement years.

Besides the following general comments about managing your finances more effectively, I also recommend you consult a qualified financial advisor about your personal situation.

Setting your goals

This book can make suggestions and provide information, but you will need to set your goals for yourself. However, I suggest the following as a generic outline:

- Reduce expenditure.
- Pay off or substantially reduce your debt before retirement. After all, it will be harder the longer you wait.
- Review your superannuation. Yes, you should have checked before now (good on you if you have!) but better now than not doing it at all.
- Think about your housing options – you might be far better off if you lived somewhere else – maybe by downsizing, by moving out of the big city, or some other change in living arrangements.

Keep reading this chapter for more on each of these.

Preparing a pre-retirement budget

One thing that no one likes doing is working out how much you are really spending. Suggesting that you have a serious look at your income and expenses is not to embarrass you, but rather to encourage you to think about saving, one smashed avocado[1] at a time.

If you haven't looked recently at ways to reduce your debt, now take the opportunity to plan for the next phase of your life.

There are two aspects to improving your financial position: One, reduce your debts. Two, increase your savings. Most people need to do both.

Credit card debt, as the most easily available and expensive debt, can negatively impact your credit rating and limit your savings capacity. Your retirement date may be clearly in view, or off in the distance. Either way you should make improving your financial health one of your highest priorities.

Keep a money diary

So for the next month, keep a **money diary**. Note down all money coming in and going out including those quick coffees and after-work drinks. In many cases, you can just get a receipt on your spending, or put it on a card - that reduces the amount of times you need to pull out a notebook. At the end of the month review your spending and allocate your expenditure into **fixed** expenses, **discretionary** expenses and **unexpected** expenses.

Fixed expenses include: your mortgage/rent repayments, energy, phone/mobile, insurances, petrol, credit card repayments, public transport.

Discretionary expenses include: coffee, movies, clothes, dinners, self-improvement, education, gym membership, yoga class.

Unexpected expenses include: car repairs, family gifts, emergency dental visit.

Review your spending

Having examined your month's figures, you should be able to say how much you need each week to meet your essential expenses and how much discretionary income you actually have. Now, imagine that you no longer have the income to cover your discretionary spending – how would you manage your current lifestyle?

Your pre-retirement plan should include achievable and realistic goals and the first step should be reducing any outstanding debts such as car loans, credit card balances and mortgage repayments. Paying out your expensive debts first and making more than the minimum repayment is your highest priority. You then need to increase your investments such as savings, term deposits, superannuation or shares.

In your pre-retirement planning, also take the opportunity to investigate ways of reducing fixed expenses such as energy, internet and phone costs. With market competition, you will find alternate providers who can offer a much better deal. Shopping around to reduce your private health insurance costs can also represent a significant cost reduction. If you have not reviewed these costs recently, it is highly likely you can make some savings without reducing your health coverage.

Pay yourself first (otherwise known as saving)

So, reflecting on your month – what did you pay yourself? Regardless of your actual income, it is more than likely that you did not pay yourself anything. Paying yourself is a way of saving to give you a resource to meet unexpected expenses and for future treats such as holidays. My suggestion is that you automatically debit 10% of each pay into a special account, whether that is your loan offset account or a savings account. Don't touch that money unless it is an emergency or when it's time for that holiday. Or you could just put it into your super fund because it is going to give you a much better return than any bank account. But more on this later...

Other advisors suggest that you live on 60% of your income and save 40% for various purposes (such as the Splurge account).[2] Do it, if it works for you, but my view is that 10% is a far more achievable amount to put away. You need to be disciplined about saving: an automatic debit means any temptation is simply removed from your available funds. This way you set yourself up to achieve your goal of financial security, without stress.

Reduce discretionary spending

What about those discretionary expenses? If you want to get serious about saving, you can really make a change in this area. Look at those impulse clothes purchases when you were feeling a little down, those random coffees and magazines, those expensive (and not-so-good) take-out meals when you didn't feel like cooking. Small purchases can add up to a big chunk of your available funds – what do you have to show for them? Not much, except your credit card debt has increased again.

By the time most women reach their 50s, they know what styles suit them. Purchasing clothes relates more to changes in fashion, keeping up with friends or continuing to make a good impression. If you have been working, you probably have a different outfit for every day of the week. Even if you haven't been working, you probably own a reasonable range of clothes and it is highly unlikely that you really don't have a thing to wear! If you have a special event, you might consciously want something new to wear, but the chances are that months later, it is still sitting in the wardrobe waiting for another event, possibly never to be worn again.

There are numerous psychological studies related to the reasons behind impulse purchases – unhappiness, boredom, stress – but none of these relate to actually needing more clothes, shoes or makeup. Studies also point to the short period of happiness from spending, followed by anxiety or guilt about increasing your credit card debt. You probably face more risk of emotional spending when doing online shopping because of the sheer range of products that are available at any time and the ease of ordering.

I am as guilty of using retail therapy as an emotional boost as anyone. However, let's recognise the symptoms of being an emotional spender. Here are some suggestions to resist those impulse spends, whether online or in the shopping mall:

- Delay your purchase – think about it for 24 hours and then decide whether you really still like, need or want it.

- Avoid going to shops or online sites that appeal to you.

- If you are having a bad day, meet up with a friend and talk about it rather than wandering around the shops by yourself. Buy yourself a special small coffee, a fancy cocktail or a new book as a substitute for those new shoes. You'll still feel better but save heaps.

- Keep focused on the big picture – put your credit card statement up on the fridge where you can see it and remind yourself of your true financial goal.

Understand and accept that buying things cannot solve underlying unhappiness. You might feel good about your purchases for a while, but then the pleasure fades and you are back to where you started, but with less cash. If you constantly use retail therapy as a substitute for real happiness, counselling can provide a more effective solution.

Reflect about the things that you have bought in the last few years. How many are you actually wearing or using? Maybe you decided to cull your wardrobe and put out a bunch of other things in the council clean-up. Where does all that stuff go? Well, some of the better clothes might be recycled in charity shops but 85% ends up in landfill.[3] Australians and Americans are the biggest consumers of new textiles and this figure steadily increases with the rise of cheap imported fashion products. Only about 15% of those discarded clothes can be recycled.

Buying less stuff is good for the environment and your pocket.

Fast fashion tempts us, but in reality those synthetic clothes take a long time to degrade once they are in landfill. Buying clothes should be an ethical and sustainable decision that reduces our carbon footprint.

For some, that's like other lifestyle choices such as eating less meat, or using fewer plastic bags. In time, your retirement wardrobe will come to reflect your new volunteering and active leisure interests, with less use for corporate jackets. Recycle those suits while they are still fashionable and give yourself some space for the new you that is developing.

The old adage of – one item in, one item out – still holds good for modern girls.

WHAT IS YOUR MONEY TYPE?

This exercise offers a not-too-serious look at the kind of relationship we each have with money. Our financial habits have developed from our family experiences, things we have been told and our own experiences with either making or spending money. There are a number of models, but broadly, each category has its positives as well as its negatives:

Amasser: You enjoy making and spending money and equate having money with your self-worth and power. You enjoy making financial decisions and can be overly concerned with details. Lack of money can lead to feelings of failure and depression.

Avoider: You don't like dealing with the details of either making or spending money. You can be unaware of your income or expenses and leave doing your tax return until the last minute because the complexity can seem so overwhelming.

Hoarder: You like to save money and do not like spending it on frivolous and unnecessary expenses such as gifts or holidays. Having money represents financial security even if it is at low interest. You avoid risky investments that might fail and affect future security.

Money monk: You believe that money is a corrupting influence and you would become anxious if you suddenly inherited a fortune. If you were going to invest, you would only choose ethical, socially responsible investments.

> **Spender:** *You enjoy spending money on yourself and others because it boosts your self-esteem. You find it difficult to save for long-term goals. You are likely to have high debt levels. Any change in your income could cause a crisis unless you find a new income-generating strategy.[4]*
>
> *Even though you might think that some categories would be better suited to the reduced income of a retiree, each category type will need to make some changes to their attitude and lifestyle to ensure they retain a reasonable quality of life as well as their income.*

Balancing debt and income

Credit cards

In November 2017 Australians had over 16 million credit cards with an average debt balance of $3,128.[5] Approximately 80% of Australians over 55 years had at least one credit card and nearly a third of those had two cards. In 2016, Australians owed $50 billion on credit cards and were paying interest on $32 billion.[6] This figure has remained relatively constant over the past three years.

Credit cards can be both useful and dangerous to your financial situation, so you cannot be complacent. They harness the power of compound interest – it works both ways! When you save regularly, compound interest increases your savings with no additional work by you, except finding the highest paying account. But if you have a debt, whether a loan or a credit card debt, compound interest steadily increases at a much greater rate than your savings. Paying it off slowly may mean wasting money paying off the accumulating interest. You certainly need to pay off credit cards at a faster rate than increasing your savings options.

If you have credit card debt, paying this off must be your highest financial priority. Once you have cleared the debt, consider replacing it with a debit card that uses money from your own bank account. To reduce the temptation to spend, paying with actual money rather than virtual money can help deter frivolous spending. Then if it's not in your pocket, you can't spend it.

With the high cost of interest and bank charges, I recommend reducing the number of accounts and credit cards that you have. Just remember, most credit cards charge an annual fee. Even if you always pay your balance, chances are that every now and again you won't and then you will get charged with interest ranging from 17% to 20% or more. That's a good reason to switch to a debit card.

For some people, high interest debts have reached crisis point. Financial advisers frequently provide advice about how to deal with high interest debts such as large credit card debts, personal loans or car loans. I recommend the following:

Step one: rank all your debts according to the interest rate. The highest interest debts (usually credit cards) **must get paid off first**. Personal loans will have lower interest than credit cards. In turn, a home loan has lower interest than a personal loan.

Step two: use all available spare cash to pay down the highest interest debts as soon as possible. If you have existing redraw equity on your bank loan (great if you've got it), use that as necessary – the higher cost of credit card or personal loan interest means you will be better off using it to clear those debts.

Step three: if you still have substantial remaining credit card or personal debt, consider renegotiating your home loan to a lower payment so that you can put more onto the high interest debts. But **be careful** – accepting a higher interest rate on your home loan could lead to a much worse long-term result. Don't do that!

Often people have savings accumulated that accrue 4% interest while having loans payable at 12%. You do the maths – pay out those high interest debts however you can and as soon as you can. **And do not incur more debt!** You can live with that old car for a bit longer and if you do need to buy another one, do the research to find the lowest rate of interest.

Bank accounts

Approaching pre-retirement, why not review your banking choices? Despite all the marketing hype, most people still bank with the bank they had at school.

People resist changing banks even though they treat us so badly. But when you are in review mode, you should be able to find a bank or a credit union that does not charge fees for keeping an account, offers you good rates of interest on term deposits and importantly, communicates with you as if you matter.

Many banks offer a good rate of interest on a loan or on an account, but also charge high fees which easily eat up any interest payments. If you bank with one of Australia's "big four" banks (Commonwealth, Westpac, ANZ or NAB), you are probably paying some substantial bank fees. Believe it or not, some alternatives bank institutions don't take so much out of your pocket. Ask yourself what you need from a bank.

If you really, absolutely need to have a local bank branch you can walk into, then that will be an important factor. But for most people, that now matters very little. In my case, I pay my bills through internet banking and get cash from a supermarket or an ATM (auto teller machine). That means I have a lot more choices than staying with the nearest bank branch. Remember also that some banks allow you to deposit money at post offices.

I am a fan of non-bank institutions, such as credit unions that have lower transaction fees. Credit unions (some are now called mutual banks) redirect money that would otherwise go to paying shareholders into better services. If you want additional choices, you can also look at smaller banks like Bendigo Bank or Me Bank, to name just a few.

Many people don't realise that sticking with their current bank costs hundreds of dollars a year. You can save real money here but only if you overcome your inertia. If you have already made the change, good on you!

Paying off your home loan

Chances are that you the reader of this book will be a person of mature years – unless you just happen to be an extremely forward-thinking Millennial! In either case, my advice is the same – owning your own home is the best investment you will ever make. The financial and emotional security of owning your own home outright in retirement should not be underestimated. In my view, discharging your home loan should be the very first goal of a retiree even if it is necessary to use part of your superannuation entitlements to do so. (Unless you have a credit card debt backlog, which you must deal with even more urgently.)

Besides having an asset that appreciates in value over time, your home provides a social framework and stability. There is no doubt that the age pension favours homeowners over renters, in that homeowners have an asset that is exempted from being included as an asset while you are living in it and exempt from capital gains tax if you sell it.

This book cannot cover every financial situation, but mature workers frequently face the common dilemma of either not receiving approval for a loan or continuing to pay off a home loan that looks like it is taking forever. This can arise from divorce, losing employment or other crises. Applying for a new loan or refinancing an existing loan in your later years can be very demoralising.

In general terms, the over 65 years' age group who are outright owners of houses have the lowest level of indebtedness. However if you are close to retirement and still have a very large mortgage, it is time to consider these questions:

- If I was not working and earning as I am today, could I afford to live in this house?
- If I paid out my remaining mortgage with some of my super, would I have enough income to live a lifestyle similar to my current one?
- Am I willing to downsize to a smaller property in a similar area, that I can either own outright, or have a greatly reduced mortgage?

Answering these questions as you are about to retire may be uncomfortable, but might give you more future security. The average Australian borrower has a mortgage of $393,200. Freeing yourself from the burden of making large mortgage repayments, with fluctuating interest rates, gives you financial peace of mind.

While you will pay costs associated with downsizing, such as agent's commission, stamp duty, legal fees and removalists, these costs will hurt far less at the start of retirement than at the end. Changing homes also symbolises the transition from the obligations of parenthood and work, to the more independent lifestyle of a retiree.

Australia has one of the highest personal debt levels in the world. It has more than doubled between 1995 and 2015 according to OECD data. The average Australian household owes $250,000, with 56% of that figure is for housing loans.[7] While some economists classify housing investment as "good debt", it nevertheless represents a significant risk if the economy should experience a downturn and people are likely to become unemployed.

Remember the aim of pre-retirement is to be **debt-free** before you actually retire.

So what if you have reached your middle years and you don't own your home? For whatever reason, whether because of a relationship break-up, you have had a period of unemployment, you have moved around or it was just too expensive, when you get close to retirement you should be serious about buying yourself a home. Remind yourself about all the bad things about renting – your landlord decides to sell, the rent goes up every year, things don't get repaired – and say, *I've had enough, I need my own space.*

Unlike the European experience where renters have long-term and affordable housing, in Australia being a renter puts you into a very vulnerable position, especially as you get older.

Once you are 65 and have access to your super, you may not have enough in your super to buy a property in a capital city. But that still leaves a whole lot of country living available to you. Housing prices in regional cities are a fraction of capital cities and they have the added benefits of less traffic, access to nature, and a closer and more involved community. Larger regional centres often have relatively healthy economies based around education, hospitals and government departments.

It's a big step to move out of your home town, but not paying rent, or not making big mortgage repayments on your own home has huge benefits in the long-term for every retiree. If you keep paying the rates and water bills, you will always have a roof over your head. Also if you really need a bit more cash, you can rent out a spare room or the garage.

Re-thinking insurance

It's so much part of the furniture that you probably don't even think about it until there is an event. That is, when something happens like a car accident and you contact your insurer and make a claim. But when you think about it, you are likely to have insurance for your car – 3rd party and comprehensive, for your house – building and contents, and for your health – hospital, plus extras. You might also have life insurance and income protection. More than likely, you are making a significant contribution to the insurance industry and you just put the payments on auto-pay without a second thought.

But insurers are also seriously competitive and perhaps it's time you reviewed how much you could be saving. This can be done without leaving your computer by checking any number of comparison sites.

Australians are fortunate that they have a universal health system, Medicare that is available to all, both for hospital treatment as a public patient and for visits to general practitioners (GP). However it is not entirely free. If you go to a GP who "bulk bills", there will be no charge but many GPs charge a higher fee. Most specialists also charge higher fees that continue to increase faster than the Consumer Price Index.

Medicare (a government entity) pays doctors, hospitals and allied health professionals for the services they provide based on a schedule of fees. However this repayment is very low, with most doctors charging a higher fee. The difference between those amounts ("the gap") is payable by the patient. Public hospitals provide free emergency care to anyone requiring immediate treatment, but elective surgery remains subject to availability of staff and beds with a wait of months or even years. Private hospitals can provide much faster treatment but usually at a much higher cost.

To meet the additional demand for services and associated expenses, Government policy encourages Australians to take out private health insurance by imposing a levy of 2% if they do not have hospital cover by the age of 31, with rebates to people who do. In 2016, approximately 11 million (45.6%) Australians had private health insurance for hospital treatment[8] entitling them to shorter waiting periods for surgery, better accommodation and sometimes better facilities.

Nevertheless, private health insurance does not cover the entire cost of a hospital stay or surgery and out-of-pocket expenses, such as medicines, anaesthetists and even MRI scans. Consumers continue to pay a significant portion of their medical expenses even when they have private insurance. A 2015-16 report by the Australian Institute of Health and Welfare showed that of the $10 billion spent on dental services, consumers paid for 58% and private health insurers paid 18%.[9]

Patients over 65 years account for 41% of all hospital admissions[10] and make the most claims for hospital, medical and prosthetic treatment.[11] However, claims for allied health services such as dental, optical, physiotherapy and similar treatments are spread over all age groups. Low income consumers and pensioners with chronic conditions who rely solely on the public health system often cannot self-fund the gap. Many suffer either crippling expenses or conditions that remain untreated until an emergency arises.

Despite federal government assurances of changing the existing system to being simpler and more accountable, little practical progress has occurred to date. Many online sites enable you to compare confusing health insurers' premiums, although they may leave out some options that you really need to know. Your first step should begin by establishing your own needs, taking into account your age and family history. Choose whether you would rather have extras such as optical and dental costs covered, or your hospital treatment covered with a lower excess payable, or both.

Reviewing your private health insurance, or even deciding to abandon it completely are appropriate options to consider when you leave the employment landscape.

Be sure to check which procedures are covered by each policy and how much the insurer will pay, as these can vary substantially. Check that your insurer provides coverage for the most common procedures such as joint replacement, cardiac surgery and cataract removal. Some insurers also offer a specific seniors hospital policy which can include cancer and stroke treatment and palliative care.

In conclusion, either go the private insurance route with cover that you can afford and meets your needs, or go the public route. Going public will also require that you seek out medical specialists who will bulk bill (a tiny number will), or who are accessible in a public hospital. You may still need to partly fund your own medical expenses, but it may be less than paying your insurance premiums.

Events that disrupt your financial plan

As John Lennon said, *Life happens while we are busy making other plans.* Major disruptive events in your life can negatively impact post-work financial plans, for example:

- Your partner loses his job;
- Family illness or death;
- Separation and divorce.

Of course, you will find a way to cope and manage those changed circumstances, but I strongly suggest that you take a selfish attitude to ensuring that you get the best financial result for yourself. You need all the resources you can muster at this point in your life, even if that means going back to work for a while. Get professional advice to support your mental health as well as your financial health and be kind to yourself.

Even Superwoman occasionally has some down time.

Experiencing separation or divorce can be especially damaging for a woman after a long-term marriage. The financial loss may include no longer having the family home, but also losing financial resources such as savings and investments, which had previously cushioned a lifestyle.

There is also the emotional and psychological impact of losing trust in your closest relationship, unexpressed hostility and the breakdown of the family structure, which may affect children and other family members as well.

No matter how welcome a divorce may be, its effect on your wellbeing and finances should not be underestimated.

How much do you know about your finances?

- Recent research by UBank[12] made some interesting findings:
- 86% of Australians don't know their monthly spending;
- 59% of Australians lose sleep or are stressed about their current financial situation;
- 20% of Australians say they have full control of their finances;
- 82% of Australians don't know their exact home loan rate;
- 22% of Australians knew how much they owed on their credit cards.
- To get more control:
- Visualise your savings goals.
- Get into the habit of saving, don't make it a chore.
- Using cash rather than a card to pay for items will reduce your urge to spend.

Making better investment choices

Purchasing an investment home

Aussies love to invest in bricks and mortar and about 8% (2.03 million) of the population own at least one investment property.[13] Of those investors, approximately two-thirds of the properties were negatively geared, that is, the income made was outweighed by the costs incurred in maintaining the property.

In plain terms, despite the very low loan rates of the past few years, rental payments did not cover the costs of having a property and investors relied on capital gains on the sale of the property to make up the shortfall of income received. Depending on the individual case, this may have been due to low returns or alternatively, a deliberate investment strategy to minimise taxes on other income.

Is it a good idea then, buying an investment property if you are likely to be paying the gap in income received? If you want to reduce your total (high) income through deductions and losses, then negatively-gearing your property investment is ideal, but most retirees will want to ensure a steady income-positive stream.

If your investment generates a positive income, an investment property can be a worthwhile income source, particularly if it is in a desirable area with high capital growth. Even when there are vacancies, rental property gives a relatively stable and rising return irrespective of economic fluctuations.

While in some cases you might save money by personally managing the asset, I recommend using a (tax-deductible) real estate agent to deal with tenancy issues.

Professional advisers either love or hate investment property. Personally I find property reassuring. I would not suggest that it's a get-rich quick option but generally the right property will give a better return over time than the average bank account.

Putting extra money into your super

Contributions to your superannuation are either compulsory or voluntary. If you earn over $450 per month, employers must automatically pay the equivalent of 9.5% of your salary and deposit it into a superannuation fund of your choice.

But you can also make voluntary contributions. One of the most tax-effective means of saving is to make additional contributions directly to your super fund. Since 1 July 2017 workers under 65 can directly contribute up to $25,000 each year into their super fund which includes employer contributions. The government taxes additional amounts made by the employee at 15% when they are withdrawn, and at 15% while in the super system.

"Salary sacrifice" means debiting an amount from your pre-tax income that is paid into your super fund. In other words, the deduction happens before you receive your net pay from your employer. The best way to do this is through an automatic debit on your income. You will need to ask your employer (in writing) to make this deduction, which would usually be in addition to existing compulsory super payments. The deduction reduces your taxable salary and lowers your overall marginal tax rate.

Be aware however, that funds paid into super become a long-term investment that you cannot draw upon until you retire or start a transition to retirement pension. Don't put your additional money into super if you need ready access to cash or still have a relatively large outstanding mortgage which would benefit from having additional payments made into it.

Most super funds offer a free annual session with an investment advisor. In addition to keeping track of your super investments, using this service will usually allow you to ask questions about other financial issues which may concern you.

Investing in shares

Approximately 37% (6.7 million) Australians invest in shares or similar commodities, not including institutional investors such as superannuation funds. The 2017 ASX Investor Study[14] found that as a demographic group, retirees invested in shares as a means of accumulating wealth and supplementing their income, with 60% of them seeking a stable source of income. By and large, share market investors are better educated and have higher incomes than the average population. Notably, there are fewer female than male investors.

Dabbling in the share market is not for everyone because of the occasional volatility of the market, but if you are looking for a long-term growth plan, investing in shares can be more effective than an average savings account. Buying shares means buying into someone's business and receiving a dividend when it makes a profit. Most investors rely on professional advice in choosing stock but with the ease of online trading, younger investors are increasing their participation in the market without specific professional advice.

While the Global Financial Crisis in 2008 dented investor confidence, by November 2017 Australian share prices continued their upward path and despite occasional rocky patches, Australian shares still average around 3.3% dividend per annum. This compares with bank interest of somewhere between 2-2.5% per annum at present.

Giving advice on share market investing goes beyond the scope of this book. If you are not sure whether investing in the stock market represents a good choice you can do your own research or attend investor information sessions to make an informed decision.

Getting rich really quick

You might get an offer to invest in a scheme, by email, by phone, in a brochure or through a friend. The offer emphasises that the information is only available to a select few, but you need to make a decision right away to get a really amazing rate of return. You show some interest and the offerors become very persistent, calling you and then threatening you if you try to get out of the deal. Stop talking to your callers and contact the Australian Securities & Investments Commission to find out if it is a legitimate offer. In 2016 there was a 40% increase in reported scams so it's worthwhile to make a call before you invest even a dollar.

> ### CASE STUDY – OUTLINE OF A 'PONZI' SCHEME[15]
>
> *In January, the promoter convinced Katie to invest $100,000 in his scheme. The promoter then paid Katie $10,000 each month using Katie's own money. As Katie receives $10,000 each month she doesn't suspect any problems. Then she recruits friends and work colleagues to invest in the scheme as well.*
>
> *After three months, Katie's neighbour Adam decides to invest $100,000 after hearing about Katie's great returns. After both Katie and Adam have invested their savings, the returns continue to come in April. But in May they don't hear anything from the promoter. They try to contact him but his number has been disconnected.*
>
> *The promoter has disappeared leaving two devastated people in his wake. Katie lost $70,000 and Adam lost $90,000. The promoter got $160,000 of Katie and Adam's money out of the scheme. This example has only two victims but in reality such schemes can have hundreds of victims. Even if the police catch the promoter, Katie or Adam will probably never have any of their funds returned.*

Complex investment products

Potential investors can be tempted by complex investment products such as agri-business schemes, future and options, hedge funds and hybrid securities and notes because they appear to offer high returns very quickly. Even if they are legitimate schemes and you are an experienced investor, you can easily lose a lot of money without professional advice.

Making a complaint about a financial product

The Australian Financial Complaints Authority (AFCA) was established in 2018 to replace the Financial Ombudsman Services, the Credit and Investments Ombudsman and the Superannuation Complaints Tribunal to provide a dispute resolution service to deal with complaints about financial products and services. It will investigate complaints about:

- Credit, finance and loans
- Insurance
- Banking deposits and payments
- Investments and financial advice
- Superannuation

While you should first complain to the relevant financial organisation, you can also call **1800 931 678** to discuss your options. This authority can make determinations which are binding on financial organisations but cannot impose penalties.

Why your super is just super!

Like the Magic Pudding that keeps on giving, compulsory superannuation has completely transformed the retirement phase for retirees over the last 20 years. In 2017 public sector, industry, corporate, retail and small funds held $2.5 trillion of superannuation assets – the highest figure ever recorded.[16]

The five year annualised return on revenue across all investments held by super funds was 8.5% for 2017 – a healthy figure compared to interest rates on bank accounts. Obviously in some years, super investments can have negative returns but in the longer term, institutionalised investment has been a very successful savings plan for Australian workers.

Because of the importance of super for every retiree, the second half of this chapter focuses on understanding how to get the best result out of your superannuation income.

Superannuation in context

There are two aspects to funding the post-work stage of our lives. First, there are **government-funded pensions** that the German Chancellor Otto von Bismarck first introduced in 1883, available to all people over the age of 65 years to assist them if they were unable to work. That age was chosen because it was anticipated few people would reach that age to take advantage of the benefit. Similarly, in 1909 Australia introduced the age pension but only 4% of the population lived long enough to be able to claim it.

The second type of funding is **employee-funded saving** for the post-work stage, either through employer or employee contributions. In 1862 the Bank of NSW introduced the first superannuation fund for its employees. In the USA, old-age insurance was introduced in 1935 with a view to encouraging older employees to make way for younger staff.

Until 1992 when the Superannuation Guarantee Scheme was introduced in Australia, saved superannuation could be withdrawn from a fund on changing employment, with the emphasis very much on providing a lump sum towards paying out a mortgage or taking a holiday. People at that time expected to rely mainly on the age pension for their financial support for when they ceased employment. However over the past century, by virtue of health and social improvements, people are living some 15 to 20 years longer than their retirement day. This longevity represents a significant imposition on public funds, even where the government sets the actual level of pension payments below the poverty level.[17]

Reflecting these changes, Government policy since 1992 has shifted towards ensuring employers contribute to their employees' super funds with a prohibition on employees withdrawing funds until retired (there are rare exceptions) but permitting tax-free withdrawals after a person reaches 60 years. Being solely reliant on the age pension basically means living on the poverty line, because you will be living on less than 50% of the median adult wage. In 2016 the median gross Australian household income was $1,616[18] per week. The weekly pension rate for a single person (in 2018-19) was $768 per fortnight or around $20,000 per annum – less than 25% of the median weekly income. If you are still paying rent or paying off your mortgage, you will be struggling to survive.

Contributing to superannuation personally, or through your employer, offers the best antidote to pension poverty.

Government policy has deliberately reduced reliance on the age pension by compulsory employer superannuation contributions for workers. Where retirees have accumulated large superannuation benefits their access to a full pension is limited or completely excluded. But government policy has also restricted any increases to pension levels with dire consequences for people totally reliant on the pension. People with disabilities or little work experience during their life will retire with small accumulated super benefits and face ongoing hardship.

Research shows that in general, women will more likely live in poverty than men.[19] Given that women will less likely accumulate much super because of their lower wages and interrupted working life, they remain far more vulnerable to live in poverty in later life.

Pre-retirement superannuation planning

You should be thinking about your super well before your planned retirement date. The earlier the better. Many people think that a quick trip to the financial adviser just before the big date is enough, but if you haven't thought about what you need, you probably will not be getting the best value from the adviser either. Being prepared is the best way to ask the right questions before making any significant financial decisions.

Your pre-retirement superannuation checklist:

1. **Have you located all your super?** Use ASIC's **MoneySmart** site to find lost super: www.moneysmart.gov.au/tools-and-resources/find-unclaimed-money

2. **If you have several super accounts**, roll them into one account – preferably the fund with the **lowest management fees**. A difference of 1% in fees could make a 20% difference in your final balance over 20 years. You will need to formally notify each fund if you intend to do this. Also find out if you are paying for advice fees when you are not actually receiving advice. When you "roll over" your money from one fund to another one, you are not making a withdrawal –

it goes directly to the next fund. Warning: some funds take a long time to do a rollover, so they can keep your money a bit longer.

3. **How much will you need in retirement** to maintain your current lifestyle? Assuming you own your own home, you will need around 67% of your current income. What changes can you make to keep the important things part of your lifestyle?

4. **Are you able to salary sacrifice** additional contributions into your super now?

5. **Are you likely to need to access your super before retirement** (called 'early release' of super) on such grounds as severe financial hardship, permanent or temporary incapacity, or a terminal medical condition?

6. **Are you thinking about reducing your work hours** and relying on a "transition to retirement" pension to supplement your income?

7. **Do you have a "defined benefit" fund?** This is more likely if you have been a public sector employee. Other funds cannot be rolled into this fund. If you hold membership in one of these funds, stick with it – they offer unrivalled benefits, typically guaranteed lifetime indexed pension benefits as well as a lump sum benefit. But don't expect to join one now – these funds have now been closed off by Federal and State governments.

8. **When did you last review the growth strategy** for your super benefits? Every fund has a range of options, from conservative to balanced to growth, depending on your risk profile, which leads to a variable result in the growth of your super income. Questions for you might include what types of shares does your fund invest in? Are there more ethical share choices?

Choosing the "conservative" option means that your returns will be more consistent but lower on average. Choosing "growth" means that your returns will be higher on average, but more variable. In some years your growth investments may actually make a loss. If you expect to keep most of your funds in super for, say, over ten years, then you would probably invest in growth investments, with higher long-term returns.

However, if you expect to retire in say two or three years, you would more likely invest in conservative investments so as to not risk losing capital, with more consistent and certain (but somewhat lower) returns. Remember, none of these companies will guarantee the outcomes you want, even if that's what they achieved in the past.

9. **Do you know how your financial adviser is paid?** Is she/he paid for recommending certain products? The role of the financial adviser has increasingly come under scrutiny but they should be able to advise you about all the super options, about investing opportunities and help in navigating the tax rules.

10. **You should also review personal insurances** such as trauma, life and income protection in your super fund because they can become increasingly expensive as you get older. Paying for insurance through your super fund has the tax benefit of reducing your taxable income.

11. **How well is your super fund performing?** Performances vary from year to year, so you should be looking at your fund's returns over the past five years and comparing them with other funds before you finally decide whether to change funds.

12. **If you are still working part-time**, you may be eligible for the government super contribution of $500 if you make your own extra contribution of $1,000 each year.

Reviewing your super fund – especially check the fees

You may be absolutely sick of hearing people talk about super and hate the thought of receiving one more letter from your super fund, but this is something you cannot ignore because it may result in your having less retirement dollars.

If you look at the super fund options available to you, they all seem to have glossy publicity showing carefree people on holidays who look how you imagine you would like to feel. Ignore all that. The key factor is the **fees** the funds are charging to manage YOUR money. There are some *large* differences in fees charged by different funds. ***Choose a fund with low fees.*** Here are some clues:

- Funds owned by or associated with banks usually charge higher fees.
- "Industry superfunds" owned by their members charge a lot less in fees.

You might find one of the super comparison sites on the internet useful such as the **Moneysmart** website. It is a good independent place to start as it's operated by ASIC (Australian Securities & Investments Commission) but also sites like Canstar have a good site for comparing fees and performance of super funds.[20]

If you have not specified a superannuation fund, **MySuper** has become the default low cost super fund into which employer contributions can be paid.

Over 100 super funds have created this new product which has a single diversified investment option, a minimum amount of life insurance cover, and standardised disclosure of fees.

You can also invest in "ethical investment" choices for your super, that don't invest in tobacco, coal mines or other undesirable investments. Some of these have a strong record, making them worth a look – companies like Australian Ethical Investment or Future Super.

In general, many ethical investment options outperform the rest of their market sector. However, as always, do your homework before you invest your money.

Self-Managed Superannuation Funds

It is beyond the scope of this book to do more than mention Self-Managed Super Funds (SMSF) as a super fund option, but the fact is that currently there are nearly 600,000 such funds in Australia.[21]

Basically a SMSF is a do-it-yourself super fund in which the members are also the super trustees. They have steadily gained popularity because they give individuals the ability to control the investment strategy of the fund.

While nearly half of all existing SMSFs have assets of less than $500,000, this option is best suited for larger balances and for people who can comply with the more onerous reporting responsibilities required. Professional advice is an absolute necessity for this long-term commitment.

Transition to retirement (TTR)

Deciding whether to take up this option depends on your particular circumstances: whether you need to accumulate more savings or whether you want to wind down your work hours to develop other personal interests. Here is a brief outline of how the Transition to Retirement (TTR) scheme works:

- You decide you want to reduce your working hours to three days per week but want to maintain your income.

- You have reached preservation age (between 55 and 60 but less than 65) and can access your super. You advise your super fund (usually by contacting their financial adviser who will set up the account).

- The fund will set up a fund-based pension account, but will keep your super accumulation account so you can continue to contribute to your super.

- If you are under 65 years, you must draw between 4% and 10% of your pension account annually. You are not able to withdraw a lump sum. The earnings on your pension account will be taxed at 15%.

- Under 60 years, your TTR pension income will be taxed at your marginal rate but you will receive a 15% tax offset. Over 60 years your TTR pension income will be taxed at 15%.

> ### Case Study
>
> *Susan, an admin assistant, has just turned 60 and has a super balance of $160,000. She earns $50,000 a year before tax.*
>
> *Susan decides to work 3 days a week so that she can ease into retirement. This means her income from work will drop to $30,000 a year before tax. Susan can afford to reduce her take-home pay a little bit but wants to use her super to soften the drop in pay.*
>
> 1. Susan transfers $155,000 of her super to an account-based pension.
>
> 2. She draws a pension of $9,000 each year, tax-free.
>
> 3. Susan's take-home pay only drops by around $5,000 a year.
>
> 4. Her super continues to grow by $3,615 as she is still working part-time.
>
> 5. She saves around $6,400 each year in tax.

Disadvantages of Transition to Retirement (TTR) pensions

- They can reduce your available super balance on retirement which can impact smaller super balances.
- TTR is not available for defined benefit funds.
- There is a cost in receiving the financial advice to set up a pension-based account.

Deciding to retire

As was pointed out earlier in this book, people finally decide to retire for a number of reasons, sometimes voluntarily and sometimes involuntarily which affects their individual experience.

You cannot access your superannuation funds until you have reached preservation age which ranges from 55 to 60 depending on your date of birth.

Date of birth	Preservation age (years)
Before 1 July 1960	55
1 July 1960 – 30 June 1961	56
1 July 1961 – 30 June 1962	57
1 July 1962 – 30 June 1963	58
1 July 1963 – 30 June 1964	59
After 30 June 1964	60

Once you have reached preservation age or are over 60, you can access your non-preserved[22] super when you leave your employment either as a lump sum or as a pension. You must formally advise your superannuation fund that you have retired before you will be able to access your benefits.

Note that some situations which can trigger release of super funds without requiring the above conditions. In emergency situations such as temporary or permanent medical incapacity, terminal illness, or severe financial hardship, you can apply to the Australian Prudential Regulation Authority under the early release of superannuation scheme without meeting age or work restrictions.

If you are 60 years and have left your employer, you can continue to work in another role and access your super. Once you reach 65, you can access all your restricted or preserved benefits. Once your super is converted into an income stream (i.e., a pension), you must draw down a minimum amount each year depending on your age.

Between 55-64 years, you must drawdown at least 4% of the account balance at 1 July and between 65-74 years you must drawdown at least

5% of the account balance. All super pension income is exempt from tax even if you are under 60 years.

How much super will you need?

In December 2017, the Association of Superannuation Funds of Australia (ASFA)[23] once again announced the yearly income figures that they believe defined either a modest, or a comfortable retirement, **assuming that you own your home**.

A "modest" lifestyle, is somewhat better than living solely on the age pension with an occasional holiday, while a "comfortable" lifestyle includes an occasional overseas holiday, being able to buy some new items and keep a house in reasonable repair.

As long as you own your own home and are in reasonable health, ASFA suggests that a single person needs $44,011 per year and a couple needs $60,457 to be "comfortable".

A single person with an income of $24,506 and a couple with an income of $35,189 are able to achieve a "modest" lifestyle. Without access to an age pension "top-up" both groups of retirees will lead fairly restricted lives.

If you are living solely on the age pension, a single person receives $21,222 and a couple receives $31,995 which means you are unlikely to own a car, to have private health insurance, are likely to restrict your heating in winter and to not be able to afford to repair your house. If you do not own your own home, you are likely to spend around 40% of your pension income on rent.

To be able to achieve a comfortable lifestyle in retirement a single person needs $545,000 in super benefits, while a couple needs $640,000. This model assumes that their super will return a 6% investment rate and retirees will draw down all their capital and receive a part age pension over the course of their life. Retirees in their 80s and 90s generally have lower financial needs because of their less active lifestyle.

How much super do you have?

According to ASFA[24] average superannuation balances in 2015-16 for retirees were $270,710 for men and $157,050 for women. To some extent super balances have been affected by contribution caps which have limited the amount that individuals can contribute to their funds.

More tellingly, the median figure for superannuation assets (that is 50% of the population) is $110,000 for men and $36,000 for women at retirement, reflecting the effect of the earlier non-compulsory period of super. Look at the difference between the *average* balance for women of $157,050 and the *median* of $36,000. Which one gives a better idea of the balances of most women?

The median, not the average, because the super balances of a smaller number of better-off women have pushed the average right up. The median shows that most women have far less than what they need. Hopefully, because of compulsory super starting in the 90s, the next generation of women will have more super to retire on. Sorry, but that may not help many readers right now.

Significantly, the ASFA report comments that many recent retirees (those aged 60-64) will substantially rely on the age pension throughout their retirement, given that their super balances are significantly lower than what is required for even a modest lifestyle.

Over time, it can be expected that the financial position of women at retirement will improve as they benefit from making compulsory contributions. However, as they also are the most casualised workforce, it may not be as much of an improvement as hoped. Even as recently as 2015-16, approximately 27% of men and 32.7 % of women reported a nil superannuation balance.

While women's superannuation balances have grown over the past two years, overall they are still likely to spend more time out of the paid workforce, as well as having lower paid jobs. Without the benefit of the age pension, women remain greatly disadvantaged and likely to outlive their super entitlements.

Super and housing

As quoted above, the previous ASFA estimates have long assumed that at retirement, retirees will own their homes. Alternatively if they are renting, the assumption requires that they will be renters in public housing with low, fixed rate rents. As homeownership affordability in Australia declines, there is an ongoing impact on retirees who erode their super balances to pay out their mortgages or use their super savings to pay private rentals.

In its report prepared by economist Saul Eslake, the Australian Institute of Superannuation Trustees[25] described outright home ownership as declining from 61.7% in 1996 to 46.7% in 2013-14 as a consequence of significant house price rises and increases in mortgages. Coupled with reduced availability of social housing, there are 8% more older households (aged 45 +) now renting who can be expected to continue renting in the private sector than in previous decades.

The report concludes that where once home ownership was "the fourth pillar" of our retirement system, that assumption is no longer likely to be valid. Retirees will be forced to rely more on the age pension to meet housing costs. In addition they will be unable to meet an accommodation bond from the sale of their home on entering aged care, putting even further pressure on public spending.

Using the equity in your home

One recent government response to the lack of affordable housing for families has been to offer an incentive to older persons to sell their family home. Retirees over 65 years who have owned their home for at least 10 years are able to release the equity in their homes and make a "downsizer" contribution to their eligible super fund of up to $300,000. By selling their home and buying a smaller and less expensive home, the downsizer[26] can use the surplus funds from their sale to make a non-taxable superannuation contribution to be able to continue to self-fund their retirement.

Having sold their home, the downsizer has to formally advise their super fund and make the payment into their fund within 90 days of the sale. The government hopes that this incentive will increase the availability of established housing for younger families as well as encouraging the financial independence of retirees.

Alternatively, if you are over 60 and own your home, a reverse mortgage can provide you with cash flow for a specific purpose such as doing major renovations, undertaking major medical treatment or as a loan to enter aged care. Effectively, a bank or other financier uses the security of your home to lend you an amount which is repayable either on sale of the property or on your death. Before deciding to enter such an arrangement, you should seek professional advice because these loans are usually at a higher interest rate than an ordinary loan. Over time, they can seriously damage your equity in your home.

Payment of death benefits

Assuming you belong to a regulated super fund, you should have made a binding nomination which is valid for three years. That is, you have nominated one or more persons to receive a lump sum death benefit should you pass away. If that person is a dependent, that is, a spouse, or a child, or a person living in an interdependency relationship with you, that person may receive a lump sum payment as determined by the trustees of your super fund that is tax-free. Beneficiaries who are not dependants may be liable to pay tax. If you do not give clear instructions to your super fund, they may make their own decision in a way you may have not wanted.

Putting your wishes in your Will may not be not enough. Be aware – your superannuation benefits do not form part of your estate unless you specifically include it in your Will. So, you should ensure that your binding nomination (i.e. instructions to the super fund) remains up-to-date. Where you have made a binding nomination, the trustees of the superannuation fund must pay out the death benefit as nominated, while in a non-binding nomination, the trustees have a discretion as to whom the benefit shall be paid, which may be to a beneficiary or to the estate.

5

Housing options

"In life we may live in many different homes, but where we are loved and feel safe that is the place where we are at home with family or friends."

Catherine Pulsifer, author, *Inspirational Words of Wisdom*

When contemplating your retirement future, you can expect changes, regardless of your individual circumstances. These changes may affect:

- Your income level;
- Your family size;
- Your day to day activities;
- Your family relationships.

In consequence, you may involuntarily spend a lot more of your day at home, no longer a slave to the daily commute and the office routine. How does that feel for you?

Initially, some readers will no doubt be pleased to have more time for the garden, for fixing up the house and for children and grandchildren.

Your home, your community and your neighbourhood will move more to the centre of your life. Others of you will be thinking about becoming 'grey nomads' or going on a long overseas trip – so home is really a temporary camp for now. Some might even decide to sell their house with its big mortgage and buy a campervan that will become their full-time home.

For those living in an apartment, your neighbours' choice of loud music may prove a daily challenge, prompting you to complain to your strata block owner's corporation.

Consequently you may find yourself a member of that committee, being regularly called out to inspect the leaks and the noise. When you're a retiree, everyone thinks you have the time to deal with all those annoying complaints that someone needs to fix.

This chapter examines a range of housing options for retirees, beginning with options for those who want to downsize or change their location. I then explore housing options for older retirees such as retirement villages and residential aged care.

If you are considering these options for yourself or for a family member, you will need more specialised professional advice to ensure that you fully understand the aged care system,[1] because each person's requirements are likely to need more than the general material offered here.

Home ownership: Australia's "fourth pillar"

Housing can be seen as representing the fourth pillar of Australia's retirement security system.[1] (The other three pillars are the age pension, employer contributions and voluntary contributions to superannuation.)

While the official three pillar government policy only takes into account raw financial contributions as elements of the social security system, a concept such as the poverty level is meaningless without taking into account an individual's living situation.

Apart from its economic advantages, home ownership links closely with many aspects of personal wellbeing, by supporting:

- Personal security and independence;
- Continuity of life experience in a neighbourhood;
- Ability to accumulate assets over time;
- Development of family and social connections.

A person growing older will likely experience more social isolation, particularly if living alone with increasing physical incapacity. You can greatly improve your individual wellbeing by connecting to the wider community through formal community agencies and maintaining family relationships. However, those with a low income, poor health and reduced physical stamina (perhaps because they are unable to afford medical care) often do not frequently participate in social activities.[2]

Home ownership vs rental

Australia's very high home ownership rate compares favourably to many European countries. Owning your own home effectively provides a safety net that reduces pressure on a government to fund an increased age pension and more social housing.[3] In contrast, people in countries like Germany, Austria and the Netherlands, large (40-60%) portions of the population live in affordable, secure, private rental accommodation. Their national governments support this approach with strict protections for private renters, an adequate age pension, and other supportive economic policies. These entirely different approaches have different advantages. But recently, Australia's rate of home ownership has been falling, without the support policies implemented by those countries in Europe.

The 2016 Census showed a general decline in younger age groups owning homes since the previous Census, although home ownership in the over-65 age group remained at 84.5%[4] which was much higher than the 67.2% ownership of all households. Of all homeowners, only 31.2% owned their property outright.[5] If this trend continues, many future retirees will come to the end of their (longer) working life still owing a substantial amount on their mortgage. Consequently, even though future retirees can expect to have larger super balances, their available balance will likely be reduced by the need to pay out their mortgage. At this stage, future retirees can still expect to substantially rely on the age pension in the longer-term.

About 15% of older Australians remain renters in the private rental market. But in contrast to the European examples above, this group remains "highly vulnerable and economically disadvantaged"[6] and rely on the landlord's disposition in setting the rent and repairing the property.

As a result, older private renters will most likely suffer housing stress (i.e. spending over 30% of their household income on housing) and be at risk of poverty and homelessness.[7]

When a person entirely depends on the age pension while living in private rental accommodation, they will likely subsist on the poverty line.[8] In contrast, a person living in social housing or in their own home is better off both financially and psychologically, even though their actual disposable income may not be very different.

Maintenance costs for a free-standing house can be very expensive, while owners of apartments can be affected by very variable strata levies, sometimes leaving them just as financially stressed as renters. However, homeowners have the advantage of controlling their own property, giving them far greater stability than a renter.

Housing for different stages of life

In its 2015 Report, the Productivity Commission[9] identified three life stages for housing:

Active	60-75 years: comfortable in a standard dwelling
Passive	65-85 years: need to "right-size" when a standard house becomes difficult to maintain
Frail	75+ years: growing need for assistance in daily life.

Surprisingly, the Commission report found that most people stayed in their home until they reached 90 years. Retirees who intended to down-size to smaller or more "age appropriate" housing tended to do so before they reached 70 years. Reasons for *not downsizing* included not being able to find suitable properties in a particular location and the expense of finding a suitable property.

Downsize, right-size or upsize – which is right for you?

Let's start with a few definitions:

> *Downsizing* – *to make smaller. Often used in other contexts such as reducing the workforce. In relation to housing, it means moving to a smaller house such as a townhouse or an apartment.*
>
> *Right-sizing* – *to reduce to an optimum size. Possibly a more recent version of downsizing but choosing a property that is more appropriately equipped or located for an older person, not necessarily smaller.*
>
> *Upsizing* – *to increase house size. Choosing a larger property which has the benefit of being exempted from capital gains tax but can be divided and a section used for rentals. In some cultures buying a larger property that can be shared by all the generations within a family can be a more efficient way of meeting various/intergenerational needs. Adult workers can go out to work, knowing that young children will be cared for. In turn, as parents begin to age, they will be cared for by younger family members.*

A smaller property may not necessarily be a less expensive property, with strata properties often carrying ongoing substantial levies.

When planning for your retirement future, the question of where you will live for the last third of your life probably doesn't rate as the first item on your to-do list. Most older home owners, even with a very low personal income, resist moving house because of their emotional attachment to their home and its location. They may also want to leave it as an inheritance for their family.

Older home owners generally value the location and layout of a large house. They often fear the substantial transaction costs of moving to alternate accommodation. Retirees have generally made little use of "wealth releasing" products such as reverse mortgages which enable owners to top up their income using the equity in their homes, despite their availability in the market.

Many find it difficult to leave because of the longstanding emotional attachment to their family home. Often it takes a major disruptive event to decide to change. While some retirees welcome their new freedom from family obligations by buying a dream unit at a different location like the beach. Others simply want relief from looking after a large home and garden, moving to a more manageable property in the same area.

In my view, the media these days apply social pressure on older people to "release the equity" in their large home by putting their property on the market for younger families.

There are some disadvantages to downsizing however, for example:

- Transaction costs in selling include the agent's commission, advertising costs, removal costs and the stamp duty in buying another property, which in a major capital city like Sydney can be close to $100,000.
- While a strata unit may be physically smaller, the associated costs can be more than those of a freestanding house, for example, strata levies, rates and insurance – for which there is no pensioner discount. Often there are additional mandatory fees payable as well, such as fire safety inspections, lift and air-conditioning inspections, which are unlikely in a ground level property.
- Because owners in strata blocks must contribute towards communal costs, the property may well require a substantial upgrade every 10 years or so, for example, painting of

external areas and major repairs. Such levies can be a burden on retirees with fixed incomes causing a real loss of financial control for the individual.

- If you receive the age pension, there can be negative effects as a result of receiving a cash windfall after the sale of a property and moving into a less expensive property. The additional cash can be treated as an asset which may result in a reduction of your pension entitlements.

- Due to changes in NSW legislation, an owner in an older building complex may possibly be forced to sell their property following a vote to terminate a strata scheme.

Some homeowners will effectively be forced into poverty as a result of the hidden and unintended consequences of apartment living.

So what would be **the "right-sized" home**? This concept is well established in the US with houses being designed to be more eco-friendly, more energy-efficient and having a smaller footprint. Likewise in Australia, the right-sized home deliberately avoids "McMansion" sized houses in favour of smaller housing developments with community title. These schemes usually concentrate on owners having a freestanding townhouse or duplex property with a lower maintenance levy for communal areas. Generally such schemes give each owner a separate lot and title with responsibility for their own insurance and maintenance, but common areas such as bike tracks or a swimming pool having communal liability.

Retirement villages appear to offer alternative affordable and smaller housing options and will be discussed in more detail in the next chapter.

The "upsizing" option might seem an unusual housing choice but some retirees have found that a bigger house (which is more affordable in a regional area) gives them the opportunity to rent out part of the property to backpackers, students or even other family members. This can allow them to create an income stream without losing the capital gains exemption that arises from living in their own home. However the income generated may possibly affect their pension entitlement.

Some baby boomers remain unsatisfied by not only the social but also the financial models offered by conventional housing options. Some innovative developments emphasise maintaining the individual's independence in their housing choices, for example:

- Co-housing – where people live in separate rooms but share communal eating and living spaces;
- Niche retirement communities – for people with shared sexual identity orientations or religious beliefs;
- Eco-villages – where people live on larger blocks of land but within close range of village facilities; and
- Communes – where people of all ages with a shared eco-aware ideology live.[10]

Should I stay or should I go?

When considering whether you should move out of your current home, you are planning to better manage your future health and lifestyle. Here are some questions that can assist you with making the right choice for you:

1. **Access to your current home:** do you have to manage steep driveways to get into or around the property? Could you maintain the garden area yourself or would you need assistance if you were less physically able? Could you install ramps to improve access? There are government programs available to assist you.

1. **Internal access in your current home:** are there steep stairs, narrow hallways or small bathrooms that make it difficult to use your home? Would additional fittings such as ramps, handrails or chair lifts for stairs improve accessibility?

2. **Access to transport:** how easy would it be to manage in your home if you were not able to drive? Are there public transport options nearby that enable you to do the shopping or get into town?

3. **Access to shopping:** being able to do your own shopping connects you to your local neighbourhood and improves your quality of life. Do you need assistance to be able to get

to a shopping centre?

4. **Access to health and community services:** how close is your local doctor or hospital? Can you use community transport services to take you to appointments or take you out for daytrips with an interest group?

5. **Access to your family and friends:** as you get older you are more likely to rely on them for occasional support and social activities. Depending on your own inclination, you may want to be closer to them or you might prefer some distance.

Caring for someone at home

While I have written this book primarily for early-stage retirees, you would be aware that the physical and mental challenges we face in growing older can also apply to younger people too. Disability can come at any stage. Appropriate care and housing for somebody you care for can make a big difference in helping them retain independence and support within your community.

Again, your personal circumstances will make a difference in deciding whether to stay in your current home or move into supported accommodation. If you are part of a couple (or have a companion), you may have the financial and personal resources to remain in an otherwise unsuitable situation. Having a personal support person can delay or manage issues that cause people to leave their homes, such as loneliness, fear for their own safety or fear of falling. Early stage dementia can also increase a person's emotional reactivity and disorientation which can increase their vulnerability to incidents in the home if they have no ongoing personal support.

Whether you become the carer for someone or require ongoing support yourself, you will need to become familiar with the **My Aged Care** website[11]. This website provides extensive information and links in relation to obtaining a Commonwealth Home Assistance Package either to enable a person to remain at home or to move into supported accommodation. It is beyond the scope of this book to give more than an outline of the process but contact numbers can be found at www. myagedcare.gov.au/about-us

Becoming a carer

For most people, becoming the carer for a family member is a gradual process as their physical or mental capacity lessens. But it can also arise suddenly when a person is injured in an accident or suffers a debilitating condition such as a stroke. In either case, you may be eligible to receive a Carer's Allowance provided you are caring for a person who has a disability, is seriously ill or is a frail aged person and that person requires assistance for at least 12 months.[12] In addition, Home Care Packages can provide more specialised assistance if necessary and are outlined in more detail in **Chapter 10 Accessing Support Services.**

Moving in with the family

CASE STUDY

Robyn was a retired music teacher when she decided to sell her large house on Sydney's north shore because it was becoming too hard to maintain. Two of her three children had moved to a north coast regional town and she decided to buy a large house on a small acreage closer to them, but outside the main town. Her son, his wife and their child moved into the home and Robyn built herself a self-contained wing with her baby grand piano in pride of place in the living area.

Right from the start, it was obvious that Robyn could never manage the outside of the property and her son took over the outside maintenance. Soon she relied completely on her daughter-in-law to cook for her and clean the house. Not long after, Robyn was diagnosed with various health conditions that made it impossible for her to drive. She became reliant on someone to drive her to medical appointments and social activities.

I would have liked to say that everything has turned out well, but in fact, Robyn's children began to argue about how her property should be divided once she had passed away. As she is still alive, fortunately we don't know the answer.

This case study illustrates the difficulty that can arise if one child moves into a parent's home and that house becomes their home over time. How do you put a value on the personal support that the child has given the parent, as well as the maintenance and improvements to property that have occurred? Careful estate planning is essential to avoid conflict where other children believe they have a right to an equal share in an inheritance.

Moving in with your kids

An alternative approach is for the parents to either move into their adult child's house or into a granny flat on the property. With this latter option, the parents either make a large financial contribution towards either the purchase of the home or to the building of the flat.

No doubt there are many situations where a parent moving into their child's home can be of great benefit to everyone concerned. Having lived with my own grandmother throughout my childhood, I never questioned her contribution to the family. I have no doubt that without her presence, my mother would not have been able to work, as she supervised us children when we came home from school. My grandmother's life would not have been better if she had lived alone.

This issue challenges our society to rethink our allegiance to the nuclear family. However for many families, this situation would require a more cooperative style of family life to be successful[13].

Clearly, there are some serious risks when the parent sells their main residence to enable the adult child to buy their property or to build a granny/garden flat. Some of the most obvious issues include:

Centrelink/age pension issues: If you sell your home to buy a less expensive home, Centrelink considers the remaining cash to be an asset, which may reduce your pension entitlement. If you sell your home and use the money to assist your child, Centrelink considers that to be a gift to the child. Receiving an age pension can greatly affect your pension entitlement because Centrelink considers the gifted amount as remaining your asset. It also increases its assessment of your income by an amount you are deemed to receive from the asset. Currently you are limited to gifting $30,000 in a five year period without it affecting your entitlement.

Granny flat rules: If you are considering assisting your child with the building of a granny flat, you should be aware of the Centrelink rules that apply[14] to the gifting of any money. In addition, I strongly suggest that if you want to take up such an arrangement, you have the arrangement verified in a legal agreement to ensure that you can continue to live in the flat until you wish to leave.

Effectively, the "granny flat rules" mean that you can only acquire a life estate interest in your child's property and this interest ends when you pass away. A life interest in a property entitles you to live in a property until such time as you wish to permanently leave or die, but it does not give you legal title to the property.

Put your agreement in writing: Whether you decide to make a gift to one child to enable them to purchase a home, or whether you are providing funds to build a granny flat for your future residence, make sure the terms are set out in a legal document not only to protect your interests, but also to prevent future disagreements. Decide whether you are providing a loan that will be repaid eventually or whether it is truly a gift.

Especially in the case of a granny flat, consider all the worst outcomes that might occur if you have a falling-out with your family. For example, your child's family decides to sell and move to another city; they decide to sell and live in another area and the house does not have a separate residence for you; your child's relationship breaks down and the house must be sold.

Alternatively your health could deteriorate to the point where you need to enter an aged care facility and you need to put down a deposit for a suitable facility. Getting legal advice at an early stage will manage everyone's expectations in the future.

Fairness between your children: Making a large gift to one child and not to another is a certain way to cause tension within your family, even where you believe that one child has more need. You should address any such inequities immediately. Options can include making equivalent gifts to all children or by making provision in your Will to create equity between them to avoid future disputes and a family provision claim against your estate.

Caring for ageing parents can be a significant commitment: While parents may initially be in good physical and mental health, over time it is inevitable that there will be some deterioration in the capacity of ageing parents to care for themselves. This may mean driving them to their medical appointments, paying their bills and organising their medication. You should discuss alternative housing arrangements at an early stage before you reach a crisis point.

Making a sea change

Fed up with the traffic in your area? The noise? The pollution? Then you may be ready to make a change – either by moving closer to the ocean, or inland to the hills and open spaces.

There may even be a few readers who want to move overseas to another country permanently for the last third of their life, lured by promises of a very cheap cost of living and being permanently on holidays.

While this may be a good option for readers who are very familiar with another country, for example, having worked there for some time, others may find it does not offer the retirement they were expecting. Issues that can arise include being unfamiliar with another language, living in a more restrictive political system, or poorer quality health services that do not support an older person.

Many people see retirement as a time to fulfil their personal dream, whether or not it reflects a realistic view of their own capacities and needs. Dreaming of surfing and life on a beach may not be exactly the right location if you were recently diagnosed with a melanoma.

Occasionally people move closer to children who have moved interstate, but often factors such as warm weather appear to be a motivator for making a big move. Interestingly, for older people, Queensland and Tasmania remain the most popular relocation destinations, while the Northern Territory and the ACT have the greatest number of older people relocating elsewhere.

Advantages of relocating to the coast or the country:

- More peaceful and quieter lifestyle.
- Healthier environment.
- Lower cost housing and food.
- Owning animals and growing own produce.
- Sense of community.

Disadvantages of relocating:

- Limited public transport.
- Poorer quality hospitals and medical services.
- Poorer quality internet connections that limit easy communications with friends and family.
- Fewer visits by family and friends.
- Difficulty in developing new friendships amongst long-term existing groups.

Suggestions if you really want to make the change:

- Start with a plan about what you would like to achieve and how you can do it.
- Do your research. Visit the area during both holiday times and quiet times.
  - » Try renting in the area for a year before you buy.
  - » Compare property prices in the area, not with the prices in a capital city. Accept that once you sell your city property, it is unlikely that you will be able to afford to buy into the same city area again.
  - » How accessible is the area if your family want to visit?

CASE STUDY

Colin, a solicitor and Carol, a self-employed florist, lived a comfortable life in a large regional city. As retirement drew nearer, Colin decided to leave his legal practice and follow his dream of being a farmer. They sold their home and bought a dairy farm amongst rolling hills, not far from the coast but a further 300km away from their three adult children who lived in Sydney. One son relocated with them. However after a time he left to follow other interests.

Physically, because of the constant work involved, it's been a difficult change for both of them. In addition, Carol has travelled to Sydney many times to assist with family matters and her children have found it difficult to visit their parents because of their work commitments. Colin and Carol have not really made a living from the farm but are relying on their super and savings to top up their income.

They love the new area in which they now live, but will they stay as they get older and find the farm harder to manage? Only time will tell.

Wherever you lay your hat, it feels like home

When discussing post-work life, it would be a gross omission to not mention "grey nomads", those retirees who travel the length and breadth of the country for long periods in their various vehicles – caravans, campervans and camper trailers.

The more moderate nomads keep their city base and only venture out for a few months at a time, but others sell up their homes and invest in a comfortable caravan or campervan to remain permanently on the road.

Exact figures for grey nomads seem hard to determine because of their association with homelessness, but 2006 ABS figures estimate around 2,500 people who meet that description.[15]

Government tourism departments suggest far higher figures based on increased caravan sales and use of caravan parks, but no doubt a robust cohort of travellers shares information and ideas as part of a growing lifestyle. There are a multitude of online and social media sites if you want to find out more and join these self-described geriatric gypsies.

Moving into a retirement village

One of the fastest growing accommodation options in Australia is the over-55 retirement village. Either owned privately or by a non-profit organisation, retirement villages can have many names and even more ownership schemes. For the purposes of this chapter, I will refer to them all as retirement villages but you may encounter them described as lifestyle resorts, retirement communities, rental villages or gated communities.

While they may have similarities in their stated purpose, the actual legal structures in which they operate can differ markedly. Beware: you **must** do your research and get professional assistance before deciding to enter a contract with any provider. Remember you are entering a long-term relationship with the operator of the village which includes payments for services and substantial fees on exiting.

Retirement villages have a lot of appeal for retirees, probably not so much in early retirement but more towards their 70s when people are thinking about downsizing and housing can become more troublesome. Figures for 2013 show that there were 170,000 retirees living in 2,200 villages around Australia[16] with an average age at entry of 76 years.

Advantages of retirement village living include:
- The cost of buying a residence is probably 80-85% that of a comparable residence in the same area.
- An available range of relatively modern, smaller villas or units.
- Living in a secure, well-maintained property.

- Access to communal dining and other services including personal support services, transport and social companionship.

- Your village unit/villa is an exempt asset for the purpose of the age pension, for government-subsidised home care and capital gains tax.

However you should be aware that the types of properties, services and financial arrangements offered vary a great deal, and this book can only outline the most usual arrangements available. Also be aware that retirement village services do not generally include healthcare. If they have an associated aged care facility, there is no automatic guarantee that a resident will get priority access.

You can obtain further information about residential villages, their accreditation and quality standards from the Property Council of Australia – Retirement Living division.[17]

In December 2018 retirement village operators and owners introduced a Retirement Living Code of Conduct, which will come into effect fully in January 2020. Following an extensive consultation period, the intention of the Code is to promote higher standards of marketing, compliance and complaints handling by village operators. An independent review panel will oversee administration of the Code. More information can be found at www.retirementlivingcode.com.au

In NSW, the *Retirement Villages Act* 1999 regulates retirement villages and manufactured home parks. NSW has a mandatory standard form contract of about 20 pages. The operator must provide a disclosure document at least 14 days prior to signing.

Under the legislation, a village operator:

- Must pay for replacements of capital items, for example, a hot water service.

- Must provide a projection table showing fees and capital gain over time as part of their disclosure to a would-be purchaser.

- Can charge a departure fee at a specified percentage on a daily basis, usually a maximum payment of around one third of the amount paid.

- Can share capitals gains or losses with residents.

- Is limited in the cost of rectifying damage to a unit to fair wear and tear.

- Is required to pay a resident their refund in full within six months of moving out, unless the contract permits the resident to set the listing price for sale of the unit and use an agent to sell the property.

Consult a specialist about the legal situation for other states and territories.

Retirement village life

Communal facilities and areas are a feature of retirement village life. Residents actively participate in running their village activities through a residents' committee in conjunction with the operator managers. Actual facilities vary but can include dining rooms, libraries, community centres, swimming pools, bowling greens, hairdressers and professional medical and health services.

Organised social activities are another feature and can include aqua aerobics, "happy hours", craft groups and excursions to places of interest. Some villages also offer a 24 hour monitoring service for medical emergencies.

As might be expected, the cost of entering a village can vary greatly, depending on their location and their facilities. Similarly, ongoing maintenance and management costs also vary between villages, although they can be expected to regularly increase at the Consumer Price Index rate at least. Disputes between a village operator and residents are handled through the NSW Civil and Administrative Tribunal, Consumer and Commercial Division (NCAT) for a nominal fee.

Accommodation options

Retirement villages may be either resident-funded by residents who purchase their apartment or villa. Alternately they may be donor-funded, that is owned and operated by a not-for-profit organisation with entry restricted to disadvantaged people.

Because of the advantages of collective living, retirement villages generally offer a cheaper option than living in a freestanding home in a similar area. However, being close to transport, shops and medical facilities still matters when choosing your future home.

Within retirement villages, there can be a variety of styles of accommodation:

Independent Living Units: Also known as self-care units, these can be either apartments in high-rise buildings or semi-detached villas in garden-style complexes. Usually there are some communal facilities such as recreational areas, buildings and gardens which are professionally managed. Personal or other services require additional payment. These units are suitable for healthy, active retirees who can manage their own needs.

Assisted-living apartments: Also known as serviced apartments, additional services such as cleaning and laundry are provided to these apartments and sometimes personal care. The apartments themselves usually have small kitchenettes but meals can be served in a communal dining room. Usually you need to be assessed as requiring some assistance with daily living before living in these units. Additional personal care services can be arranged for a fee.

Rental units: These are available for people with limited financial resources who have been income assessed and receive rental assistance from Centrelink.

Legal structures that affect occupancy rights[18]

Loan and licence agreement: Resident-funded villages (usually run by non-profit organisations) rely on the resident to contribute to the ongoing costs of a village such as insurance and building and garden maintenance. The resident does not actually own the unit, but rather signs a loan licence agreement, that is, the village is given an interest free loan and the resident receives a licence to reside in the village. These units may then be sold at market value. Personal support services are not always available but may be purchased separately in some, but not all, locations.

Lease: This is the most common form of retirement village tenure. It is usually long-term (i.e. 99 years) and is registered on the property title which provides both security of tenure and enables the right to use common facilities and areas. You will pay a lump sum for a leasehold. No stamp duty is payable on a leasehold unit.

Licence: While the terms of a licence may be similar to a lease in that it gives a right to occupy a unit and access communal facilities, it is not registered on the property title, which may be less secure for the resident.

Strata title units: Like ordinary strata title units, purchasers of strata units in retirement villages have a right to occupy their unit. They are required to pay quarterly levies which go towards building and garden maintenance and insurance, but their levies can also contribute towards additional services such as social activities, transport and personal services. One issue that can arise with strata title properties is that the operator may put restrictions on how the property will be sold on exit. These can include who will sell the property and the payment of ongoing levies until sale. As an alternative, community title schemes are similar to strata title but may include land for further development in the future. The resident pays stamp duty on the purchase of such units.

Company title/unit trust: In these schemes, the resident buys shares in the company that owns the village and the shares entitle the resident to occupy a particular unit and use the common areas. Again, the resident pays stamp duty on purchase.

Manufactured homes/residential parks: Formerly known as caravan parks, these villages offer transportable homes under a lease or licence agreement which also permits the use of common areas.

Get some advice before signing up

You have decided on your preferred retirement village and now you are having a look at the financial nitty-gritty. Of course, you will ask a professional adviser[19] who is familiar with retirement village contracts for their advice, but here are a few questions you can ask:

1. **What kind of tenure are you purchasing?** Freehold, leasehold, licence, strata, community or company title? Remember that the purchase price or entry payment is likely to be similar, irrespective of the type of tenure but conditions relating to the marketing, re-sale or exiting from the village will differ.

2. **You will need a deposit to secure the unit you want.** Check that this can be refunded during the "cooling off" period. Once you have entered a binding agreement, the deposit forms part of the purchase price.

3. **If you are selling your current home**, have you allowed for the cost of selling, moving and possibly buying new furniture? Are you certain that you will have sufficient funds to purchase your retirement villa/apartment? It may be possible to borrow funds to buy into a retirement village but again, you need a mortgage broker with the right expertise.

4. **Does your contract include a "settling-in" period?** Usually you have 90 calendar days either from signing the contract or from first moving in which to decide whether the village meets your needs. There may be some additional costs payable should you decide to leave in this time.

5. **Do you need to pay stamp duty?** Yes, if you are buying strata, community or company title. Check the contract.

6. **What are the monthly recurring charges** for maintenance (known as a sinking fund), for administration and for a capital replacement fund which might apply when capital items such as stoves or air conditioners need replacement?

7. **What is the charge for personal or additional services?** Are any services, such as cleaning or laundry automatically

included in your recurring charges? Additional services you might need in the future, such as personal care and transport, will incur additional payments.

8. **What is the rate of increase in recurring charges?** Are they aligned with the Consumer Price Index (CPI) or can the operator vary them?

9. **What are your options if you require additional care?** Are you able to access home care packages while still a resident? Is it possible to move into nearby supported accommodation? (That is, into an aged care facility.) If so, can you transfer without losing your current entitlements, or do you have to fully leave one and enter the other accommodation as a new client?

10. **Have you seen the premises condition report** with details of the condition of the fixtures and furnishings, with information on how items will be repaired?

11. **Costs of exiting the village** must be specified in the entry agreement. Sometimes called the "deferred management fee", this fee is calculated at entry and payable on exit. The formula used relies on a percentage of the entry cost multiplied by years of occupancy and may include a proportion of capital appreciation.

12. **How do you end your residence contract?** What are the restrictions on marketing and selling your property? What are the conditions once your property has been re-licensed, or if it is not re-licensed within 90 days? Repayment of a proportion of your refundable premium is dependent on the re-licensing of your property.

13. **Make sure you have visited the village** and met the management staff and some of the residents' committee to get a feel for the village dynamics because you will be living with that for some time to come. You should be provided with a copy of financial statements presented at the last annual meeting of residents and any major changes that have occurred or are intended to occur in the village.

Hidden costs – exit fees

Also known as deferred management fees, exit fees have come under a great deal of criticism because of both their complexity and the lack of transparency as to how they are calculated. Deferred management fees are one way a commercial operator makes a profit and a non-profit operator can provide additional services.

Exit fees may be calculated on an annual basis, or on a capital gains basis and may also require that you refurbish the unit upon leaving. The fee will be calculated as a dollar amount when a valuation is obtained, or you vacate your unit or after a new resident has made an entry payment.

The fee is usually calculated as a percentage per year of either:

- Your ingoing contribution or purchase price
- The new resident's ingoing contribution or purchase price.

These fees are usually calculated up to a specified maximum percentage stated in your contract. Just to give one example, if your exit fees are calculated against the value of your unit at 3% per year, you will lose 15% of the value of the unit if you move out after five years. How exit fees are calculated can certainly have a major impact on the funds that remain on sale of the property.

Typical complaints about exit fees include that it can be financially disastrous if you leave a property within the first five years; that you will have to continue to pay rent until a new tenant is found, or that families had to wait years until the remaining funds were repaid by operators.

Many European and US retirement villages have pay-as-you-go lease contracts which are simpler and make it easier to make cost comparisons between villages.

6

Supported accommodation

"We are all visitors to this time, this place. We are just passing through. Our purpose here is to observe, to learn, to grow, to love ... and then we return home."

Australian Aboriginal saying

Making the decision to live in supported accommodation, otherwise known as an aged care facility, can be complex, whether deciding for yourself or for a parent. Usually it is accompanied by a deluge of emotions ranging from guilt to fear to relief. All of those emotions are very understandable, because the decision is accompanied by the sure knowledge that you (or your family member) are entering a new home to embark on life's final journey. As individuals, we may react with acceptance, resignation, resistance or disbelief to the inevitability of this path.

As a society, there are many conflicting messages about this later stage of our life – to name a few:

- I don't want to be a burden on my family.
- I don't want to go into one of God's waiting rooms.
- It's my duty to care for my parent until the end.
- I'm not leaving. They can carry me out in a box.

There are also many factors that remain unacknowledged until we directly confront them:

- Most adults working full-time cannot afford the time to care for an ageing parent full-time in their own home.

- Ageing people in their later stages can have many complicated health issues/needs such as incontinence, dementia or wound treatment, that can become overwhelming for a single carer to manage over time.

- Often entry into residential care begins unexpectedly after a person experiences an incident such as fall that requires hospital treatment and is unable to return to their home safely.

This section outlines what to expect when going to live in an aged care facility and dealing with the complicated aged care system. I am familiar with issues in part from my own family's experience, as well as working with many clients with parents in aged care. Inevitably, my own experience influences my comments.

It is important to acknowledge conflicting emotions such as grief and guilt that may arise as we observe our loved ones deteriorate. We all want the best outcome for residents in aged care settings.

Fortunately, collective activism by many people to implement legislative standards over the past 50 years has brought a significant improvement in the standard of aged care facilities today. Unfortunately it has not entirely eradicated physical and psychological abuse of elderly residents.

Community awareness and activism has led to higher care standards and staff professionalism of aged care operators, as well as more intense scrutiny of aged care facilities, as demonstrated by the holding of a Royal Commission into Aged Care Quality and Safety.

Recognising the historic inequitable treatment of diverse groups of the ageing population, access to quality, culturally appropriate aged care for Lesbian, Gay, Bisexual, Transgender, Queer, Intersex and Asexual

(LGBTQIA+) people has been initiated by developing LGBTQIA+ inclusive residential care facilities. Similarly, more culturally specific facilities are also being encouraged.

A 2017 survey of 17,195 consumers living in 1,159 residential facilities conducted by the Australian Aged Care Quality Agency[1] found that the vast majority of residents were satisfied with their residential experience, saying that:

- They were treated with respect by staff "most of the time";
- They felt safe with staff "most of the time"; but
- Were less satisfied with the quality of food.

That said, the earlier Productivity Commission Caring for Older Australians report in 2011 found that standards in aged care residential facilities gave variable coverage of consumer needs for a range of pricing structures, with a key factor being the low skill sets and wages of their staff.

These days, most aged care facilities are purpose-built, bright places with diversional programs to engage residents and provide 24 hour care beyond what most families can manage on their own.

Based on my observations, I do not think that it is always better for a person to remain at home rather than move into a residential facility if they need a high level of care.

Often a person living in their own home is socially isolated and living a meagre and confined life, while a well-run residential facility offers a variety of activities, social life, and better food and personal care standards.

However, it is also important that family members and carers should remain engaged with the facility throughout the resident's stay, to ensure that the facility maintains high care standards for their family member.

SOME FACTS AND FIGURES ABOUT RESIDENTIAL AGED CARE:

- In 2013-14, 775,900 people aged over 65 years had accessed Home & Community Care (HACC) (now Home Care Packages). A further 231,500 people had accessed permanent residential care[2] in approximately 2,700 nursing homes at some stage. This figure represents approximately 7% of people aged 65 and over.

- Seventy percent of all aged care facility residents are female, 63% are over 85 years old and their average residency was 2.8 years. Just over half of all residents suffer from dementia. Approximately 30% of people over 85 years have dementia. In 2011 there were 298,000 Australians diagnosed with dementia and that figure is expected to increase to 400,000 by 2020, consistent with an increasingly older population.

- The Health and Community Sector is the second largest employment sector in Australia and employs over one million people, 22% of whom work in aged and community care. In 2012-13 it was estimated there were 2.7 million unpaid carers who provided a total of 1.32 billion hours annually and contributed $40.9 billion to the economy, as well as being in the lowest income brackets.

Assessment for residential aged care

Before being able to enter residential aged care, every potential resident must be assessed by their local Aged Care Assessment Team (ACAT). Usually based in a local hospital or community centre, the ACAT includes different disciplines of aged care professionals such as nurses, social workers and doctors.

They will undertake a holistic assessment of a person's physical and mental capacity and make recommendations for ongoing care either at home or in a residential facility.

An ACAT assessment can be requested either directly through the hospital or community centre by way of a doctor's referral, or it can be done while a person is still in hospital recovering from treatment, through a social worker's request. Typical questions will test for the person's mental functioning, how they are managing daily activities such as dressing or bathing themselves and will take their health needs into account.

Even when you have an ACAT assessment, there is no guarantee that your family member will *willingly* move into residential care. Of course, there are older people who go into residential care knowing that this step into institutional life.

It represents a loss of independence, but they are aware that their families are stressed by caring for them and they decide that they do not want to be a burden to them. Their transition and adaptation to residential care is likely to be far more successful than the transition of an unwilling resident who may, for a long time to come, resent being "dumped" by their family.

In my experience, also supported by research, reluctant residents continue to resent living in residential care. Their families continue to feel guilt and sadness, even while realising there are no viable alternatives. Transitions from hospital into residential care, and from respite care stays in residential facilities to permanent care, can be easier to manage.

From the perspective of the carers supporting the transition (typically a spouse or an adult child) the preparation can be daunting. For those in this situation, you are likely to already have been providing significant support. No doubt you are carrying out the research for the transition, while every day also helping with health professionals' appointments and physical care.

At this stage, I recommend that you obtain an Enduring Guardianship from your family member which gives you the authority to make decisions about their health management before this becomes a crisis. It will also be timely to organise a Power of Attorney to enable you to sign the legal and financial documents on behalf of your family member. Usually this becomes necessary when entering the agreement with the aged care facility and when your family member is no longer able to manage their own affairs. See **Chapter 11 Putting your affairs in order** for more details.

Choosing a residential aged care facility

Once the ACAT assessment recommends a move into residential care, the next task is to find a suitable facility that has a vacancy. Despite the fact that aged care places have increased 1.4 times between 2006 and 2016[3] there is constant pressure in trying to find a bed, particularly in metropolitan areas.

More than half of all incoming residents have a diagnosis of depression or dementia and are described as having "high care" needs. Therefore the preferred facility should offer suitable accommodation to manage those conditions.

Women of non-English speaking backgrounds who predominantly speak another language are also more at risk of needing "high care" in the three major areas of cognition, behaviour and complex health needs.[4]

Around 65% of residential care facilities are run by not-for-profit organisations with the remainder run either by commercial operators or by government in more remote areas.

Broadly, the type of care offered by facilities include:

- Residential care – long term assistance with living;
- Respite care – short-term care up to 3 months;
- Specialised dementia care – secured wings and trained staff, and
- Palliative care – specialised assistance and pain management where recovery is not expected.

Types of actual services offered by a facility are described as:

- "Hotel" services such as room cleaning, laundry, meals and social activities;
- Personal care services such as bathing, eating, assisting with medication;
- Complex care and services such as nursing, mobility items, continence items, wound management and dialysis; and
- Therapy services such as podiatry, speech therapy and recreational activities.

"Hotel" and personal services must be provided by the facility, while complex care and therapy services may be provided but are subject to payment of additional fees.

Checklist for choosing a residential aged care facility

It is worth inspecting a number of residential facilities before making a final decision. By visiting a number of homes, you will start to notice how staff interact with residents and the atmosphere of the place, rather than just the external appearance.

Some questions to ask:

1. **Does this home offer features that suit your family member?** For example, is it language or culturally specific? Will the religious affiliation of the facility matter to your resident? Are there gardens and associated activities if your family member enjoys open spaces?

2. **Does this home offer dementia-specific services?** Does the staff have skills in managing memory-impaired residents with behavioural issues? Is there sufficient security in the facility to ensure such residents will not be able to wander outside?

3. **What activities does the facility offer** for residents, such as music, movement or art? Can you see personal effects of residents around their rooms to reflect their interests and personalities?

6. **Does the facility have adequate mobility aids** such as walkers and wheelchairs available for use by residents?

7. **When you enter the facility**, are you aware of unpleasant odours, piles of washing or grubby floors? Does the facility seem clean and hygienically maintained?

8. **Does the facility have sufficient skilled nursing staff available** to manage complex health issues/needs? How much will these additional services cost?

9. **How are guests and visiting pets treated** by the home? Are they welcomed to come for lunch or to participate in activities?

10. **Do current residents seem to be busy** and happy in the facility?

11. **How convenient is the facility for you** to be able to regularly visit? Are you able to take your family member home for special occasions?

Fees payable for aged care services

From 1 July 2014 the Commonwealth Government changed the fee system for entering into aged care. For a detailed explanation of the fees payable in your circumstances, you should access the calculator on the **My Aged Care** website:

www.myagedcare.gov.au/aged-care-homes/working-out-the-costs

Or call: 1800 200 422

A simplified version of the current fees system that applies in residential aged care:

Low income and low assets (less than $45,000) residents only pay the basic daily care fee, based on 85% of the single person's basic age pension. Their accommodation and additional costs are subsidised by the government. The pension is revised twice per year in September and March and therefore the fees payable also increase. It is also possible to obtain an exemption from payment of the accommodation deposit on the basis of financial hardship.

A person with **higher income and assets** will pay an amount comprised of:

- **A basic daily fee** – the daily fee paid by all people who receive residential care, being approximately $51.21 per day or $716.94 per fortnight and capped at 85% of the age pension. All residents are required to pay this standard fee.

- A **means tested care fee** – an extra contribution paid by residents in addition to the basic fee, depending on individual income and assets capped up to $27,232.33 (as at September 2018) per annum, or a lifetime cap of $65,357.65.

- An **accommodation payment** – also known as a Refundable Accommodation Deposit, is a lump sum payment for accommodation in an aged care home. This fee may be subsidised by the government and will depend on the accommodation fee charged by the facility.

- Fees for **extra or additional services** – where residents choose a higher standard of accommodation or get additional services such as hairdressing, air conditioning or pay TV in rooms. This additional fee may be between $20 - $120 per day depending on the location of the facility and the type of services offered. There can also be a charge for a dementia-specific bed.

Refundable Accommodation Deposits

In practical terms, the most significant change under the current scheme is the introduction of the **Refundable Accommodation Deposit** (RAD) which is the fee charged by a residential facility for occupation of its rooms. Most services charge between $250,000 and $550,000 based on the standard of the accommodation, local property prices, building standards and market demand.

The maximum RAD amount is $550,000 unless the facility has been approved by the Aged Care Pricing Commission to charge a higher rate. The maximum payment must be published on the organisation's website. Usually each facility has a range of rooms with varying prices but they are not always available when needed. It may be possible to negotiate the price of the room but given there are usually extensive waiting lists, you are not likely to receive much of a discount.

The RAD represents a lump sum loan from the resident to the service provider which is refundable on exiting the facility. A provider cannot insist on how you make this payment and there are three methods usually applied when calculating the accommodation fees, depending on a resident's financial situation.

Refundable Accommodation Deposit (RAD) example

Once the Resident Agreement is signed, you are not required to pay the whole amount before entry. There are three options in relation to the payment of the RAD which in this example we will set at $380,000:

- A lump sum payment of $380,000 in full; or
- The RAD is converted to a Daily Accommodation Payment (DAP) which is the amount of the RAD at an agreed interest rate (currently 5.96%) and applied on a daily basis: [$380,000 x 5.96%/365] = $62.04 per day: or
- A partial RAD and partial DAP interest on the unpaid portion: here $200,000 paid as a lump sum RAD and the remainder [$180,000 x 5.96%/365] = $29.39 per day.[5]

For many people, entry into a residential facility requires the sale of their home to make the refundable deposit payment. Usually the service will agree to a delay until the house is sold, although the resident will pay ongoing daily care and accommodation fees until the deposit is paid.

With the help of a financial advisor, you should also consider other options to assist with the accommodation payment, such as renting out the person's home or taking out a reverse mortgage. By using the equity of the family home, a reverse mortgage can provide funds up to 45% of the value of the home to be used as a RAD. When the RAD is refunded or the home is sold, the loan is repaid to the lender. Very few banks will offer a reverse mortgage so you need to do some research.

You should also be aware that selling the family home will likely have financial consequences. In particular, a home-owning person receiving the age pension may no longer be eligible to receive the same amount once they sell their home.

Exiting the aged care facility

Residential aged care facilities are required to refund the whole amount of the RAD less any outstanding amounts within 14 days of a resident leaving the facility. However where a resident dies, the facility must refund the RAD to the estate of the deceased or to a beneficiary if they are satisfied as to their right to receive the monies. While the procedure may vary, most facilities will require the executor to provide a certified order of probate before releasing the deposit to the deceased's estate.

In that period, which begins the day after the death of the resident and ends on the day of the refund, the facility is required to invest the RAD at either a Base Interest Rate (BIR) or at the Maximum Permissible Interest Rate (MPIR). The interest rates vary according to the period in which the resident dies and is determined by legislation. If the facility does not refund the deposit within the 14 days of being shown the probate order (or letters of administration), it will be required to pay interest at the higher MPIR rate.

Making the move into supported care

When someone decides to move into an aged care facility, there are some things you can do to make the transition easier.

- Let their friends and wider family know where they will be living.
- Organise a landline phone with easy-to-read numbers, talking keypad or amplified hearing quality, or a large screen mobile phone to make it easy for your resident to stay in touch.
- Review the clothes they want to take with them. Make sure they are comfortable, don't need ironing, are easy to put

on with buttons and elasticised waists. Have a couple of cardigans for cooler days and some dressier outfits if they want to go out. Some facilities ask that each item be labelled with a name.

- Take some small pieces of furniture such as a favourite chair, bookcase or table and a TV so they are reminded of home.

- Make sure to take any favourite photos, paintings, books, bedspread and other sentimental items to make the resident feel comfortable.

- Regularly arrange to have a family meal with your resident/ family member at the facility without other residents being present.

- Don't keep valuable items in the facility. Even very good facilities can have a high turnover of staff, so that valuable items like jewellery can disappear. Residents with memory issues can be particularly vulnerable. Best to leave these items with a trusted family member.

No matter how well prepared a person may be for the move, it is more than likely they will feel conflicting emotions such as relief, anger, sadness, loss and feelings of anxiety in this new environment.

Key changes requiring adjustment include:

- A resident's personal space now becomes reduced to a single room and they will be subject to a new routine of early breakfasts and early evening meals.

- They will meet many new people – both residents and staff – and they may be confused and anxious until they get to know everyone better.

- It is likely to take at least a month before it begins to feel familiar to a new resident. Some people will never adjust to their new home and will remain angry and confused.

Family members and carers continue to play a very important role both in the initial and ongoing stages of a resident's stay in an aged care home. If you are a carer, you should acquaint yourself with both the general and nursing staff as much as possible so that you can discuss your relative's health and personal issues.

It is a good idea to become aware of the internal rules and conventions of a home, the location of items such as wheelchairs and the usual planned activities so you can attend if you wish. Most facilities these days have security codes to enter and leave the building which you will need to know to ensure residents are secure.

Regular visits by family and friends alert staff to the fact that you are checking on your resident's health and on the standard of care. Unfortunately there have been examples of inappropriate behaviour by staff in residential facilities. By being a regular visitor, you can be aware of what is really occurring on a day-to-day level.

Even amidst the activity of a busy facility, a resident can feel lonely. The most valuable thing you can do is to spend time with your loved one helping them to remember their previous life, their friends and activities through looking at photos or walking in the garden to enable them to talk privately. Bring your family member their special photos, favourite memorabilia and books to remind them of their previous life. Such familiar activities become more significant when the resident experiences confusion and memory-impairment.

Persons with dementia are more likely to be unsettled by a move into residential care. Their carers should provide as much unhurried time as possible to assist them if they are moving into a dementia-specific wing of a residential facility. As a carer, you should consider yourself as working in a partnership with the facility. Communicate your resident's life story to staff and make her/his needs understood, including the foods, clothes and hobbies they liked when they were younger.

Attending resident/family meetings will allow you to meet other families and to share experiences. Being involved in these activities will better prepare you for making decisions about medical interventions if your resident's condition deteriorates.

Making a complaint

If you have any concerns about how your resident is being treated, you should discuss this at first instance with the nursing manager of the facility. In most cases, the manager should be able to make adjustments to make the resident more comfortable. Should the resident incur any injury or incident, the staff should immediately report to the next-of-kin, particularly if medical or hospital treatment is involved.

More serious or systemic issues should be referred to the **Aged Care Quality & Safety Commission,** ph: 1800 951 822. For more general advice, you can contact the National Aged Care Advocacy Line on ph: 1800 700 600.

7

Relationships in retirement

"Lots of people want to ride with you in the limo, but what you want is someone who will take the bus with you when the limo breaks down."

Oprah Winfrey, author, celebrity

If you think about fairy tales, you know they have created a myth: that the perfect person you married when you were young will still be the perfect person when you are older; that you will both live happily ever after. That myth of "happy ever after" haunts us when we choose a partner, however sophisticated we may appear. That myth ignores the reality that change will inevitably continue and people may change unpredictably over time. Then even more daunting: that *we* may not want our perfect person forever, or indeed, they may no longer want us.

If your relationship has weathered the storms of child-rearing, you might think you are safe from separation and divorce. Many couples work hard to stay together for the sake of their children but as they approach retirement, or are in early retirement, the perfect image may begin to crack at a significant cost to everyone involved. The "empty nest" syndrome – where parents feel loss and grief as a result of their children leaving home – may contribute to family breakdowns. Couples who have repressed their various irritations while bringing up children may find they can no longer ignore those issues.

I wonder about those families who have welcomed the return of their "boomerang" children, those adult children who decide to return home to save on their expenses. While I appreciate that, as a social norm, many cultures encourage adult children to live with their parents until they marry, it has not been common in the average Australian family for at least the last 40 years.

Based on my experiences with a variety of cultural backgrounds, my understanding is that if adult children remain at home, they also remain subject to parental (usually paternal) moral and financial controls. Average Aussie "boomerang" young adults are not likely to be very accepting of those kinds of limitations. I will return to this topic later in the chapter.

Relationships can support us in difficult times or they can devastate us when they don't work. In this chapter I consider how relationships change, develop or destruct during retirement and the importance of continuing to create new connections to sustain us into the future.

No doubt, close relationships can be challenging but they also keep us connected and involved in daily life. Relationships play a critical role – as potent as medicine – in preventing mental decline. In his book *Being Mortal* Dr Atul Gawande[1] offers an interesting insight into the role of the family as a means of extending a person's functionality.

Dr Gawande reviews the shortcomings of a purely medical-based model of the treatment of older people. He examines alternative models of residential aged care, particularly in India which give the individual and their family more personal control and less institutionalised care than occurs in industrialised countries.

While first world residents may not have the advantage of the extended family to care for us in our later days, there can be comfort in our friends who remain until the end.

Let's talk about you

> *"Being true to yourself never goes out of style."*
> *Legally Blonde*, the movie

There are so many profound quotes about being yourself: whether it is about finding out who you really are, being that lone rock against a wild ocean, or becoming yourself through others, it can be hard to know how to define yourself. We exist as ever-changing organisms, born with physical and mental characteristics, but moulded by our choices and by circumstance.

Even when we are in our 50s or later, we continue to change and learn – contrary to the stereotype that age sets our patterns in stone. Perhaps you do not want to change but most of us inevitably change our style, our interests and even our friends. Change is not only inevitable but also renews our thoughts and energy, if we can accept and develop our awareness through it.

As a self-aware person, you know that your carefree 20 year old self has gone, both in looks and ideas. Your experience will give you the wisdom to accept new information and adapt it to your situation. And believe me, you will need that in many new situations that you hadn't anticipated in this last third of your life. But I would just like to spend a little time focusing on you, because you're worth it – as some clever advertiser once said.

Making the most of your looks: No doubt you have put on a few kilos, your skin texture and colour is not quite so bright and your hair might be greying and thinning. I do not subscribe to the idea that 60 is the new 50, but you can definitely declutter and replace those tired, sensible 10 year old clothes with some stylish but appropriate new clothes. This is the time to spend money on better quality, rather than quantity to stay attractive and reflect your relevance.

Women continue to be divided on whether to go grey naturally or to colour their hair. Basically you can choose how much time you want to spend at the hairdressers, but even grey hair can be cut and treated well. Like an old car, we need to spend more time and money on maintaining the basics, such as checking our eyesight, teeth and hearing and wearing good quality clothes and stylish but comfortable shoes.

Continuing to learn: There is nothing more potentially ageing than constantly saying, "Back in the day", or "When I was your age". It really can alienate a whole bunch of listeners. Your experience counts, but you need to manage how that knowledge comes across.

For your own satisfaction, I recommend compiling your family history in photographs or doing your own oral history in podcast form for the record. (Unfortunately you will probably have to live to be 101 before anyone will appreciate it, but you will have contributed to history while you can still remember it.)

Keep up with technology: Try to stay current with new technologies such as smartphones, tablets or social media which connects you with information, events and distant friends without leaving the house.

Keep something for yourself: No matter how many joint accounts you have and how much you trust your partner, keep some money aside in an account for yourself. You can treat yourself or your children as you wish without having to explain. This small reserve can be very useful in an emergency.

Commune with nature: It's not just about getting more exercise, which of course is an excellent idea, but also about being in touch with the rhythms of the natural world – near the ocean, in the mountains or sitting by a stream. Gardening can be another alternative, but the peace of wilder places can be a good space to really relax and revive.

Mindfulness: This word often refers to awareness arising from meditation, but I include more general religious and spiritual beliefs that sustain you. Being connected with a larger group who share your beliefs, gives you both social and practical support and can actively extend your lifespan. Having a belief system, however you see it, can give personal strength and reassurance when you confront illness or disability. "Mindfulness" includes being aware of the small details and expressing gratitude for the experience.

Staying together

When I worked in family law, assisting long-time married couples to divorce invariably highlighted their regrets and experience of painful loss. Loss of the family home and the associated emotional and financial stability, loss of trust between the parties, and confusion of adult children who lost their family as they had previously imagined it. That said, the initiating party (usually female) would often recount a long history of unhappiness – they did not take these decisions lightly.

The reasons for separation and divorce are many, but on retirement many people have more time to reflect and reconsider their lives. When one half of a couple (or both of them) retires, their daily routine throws them together far more than they might have expected, fully testing the strengths and weaknesses of their relationship. Come retirement day, everyone suddenly can focus on what is most significant to them.

The common assumption has been that as women usually work part-time or are full-time homemakers, they have better established informal networks. In the traditional view, women manage the transition to retirement more easily because they are more directly involved with maintaining social connections throughout their lives.

However the modern reality frequently contradicts this common view. Most workers, (male or female, working full-time or part-time) who decide to retire, will have no particular external involvements apart from their immediate family. In most families, both parents work either full or part-time, travel to or from work, and spend significant time taking children to or from their after-school activities. Little time remains for either development of personal interests or for involvement in the wider community.

As any number of service clubs, non-profits, religious organisations and hobby groups can attest, memberships of such groups have been steadily falling for many years. They struggle to maintain membership momentum because it has become the social norm to work long hours, with individuals disillusioned about participation in voluntary groups.

So in the classic scenario, the male breadwinner, who has never really spent more than weekends at home, suddenly finds himself at home a lot. The wife (of course!) has her routine – she washes on Monday, cleans on Tuesday, has morning tea with her friend on Wednesday – and so it goes. How does he fit in? With difficulty. For some men, they gradually adjust over time into a new routine while others can enter a period of boredom and depression.

Traditionally, many men try to avoid the problem of self-examination by continuing to work and refusing to consider a retirement date, until ill-health strikes. But for many others, the reality of poor job satisfaction undermines any motivation to continue working for an employer.

In fact, for most of us, if we are motivated and energetic, our retirement offers many more opportunities for self-fulfilment. We can follow our own interests without the limitations imposed by employment. Continuing to work on a part-time or casual basis can be an easier way to gradually transition into retirement.

If we cannot deal with these feelings, we risk falling into depression. But we can create and develop so many other roles, such as:

- Being a better partner,
- Being a community leader,
- Being a loving grandparent.

Negotiating with your partner either before, or in the early period of retirement, should be part of your retirement plan. Some fairly conventional suggestions follow, but I should stress that you need to figure out what works for you.

For example, if you are an aspiring artist, you might want to follow a completely different schedule to suit your creative periods.

WORKING TOGETHER ON YOUR RELATIONSHIP

- Depending on your relationship style – either share or separate the decision-making and the associated responsibilities for daily tasks. But stick with your intention to be fully involved in understanding the financial decisions.

- Allocate regular tasks, e.g. one does dinner every Tuesday, the other does dinner on Wednesday.

- Allocate one night a week for a night out together, say dinner at your local pub.

- Make sure you get out of the house and go outdoors at least once every day. Even if it is just doing the shopping, but it's better to schedule in your own social calendar. Every week pencil in your bridge club, your stretch class and your volunteer morning, for example.

- Visit your local community centre or community college. Sign up for a short course or an ongoing group activity.

- Make regular time to see your children and grandchildren.

- Together – plan ahead for a week-long road trip, or a visit to your relatives. Plan for an overseas holiday that meets both your wish lists.

- Find time to get sexy again. Luckily you don't have to worry about contraception anymore, but lubricants and vaginal oestrogen can improve the mutual experience.

The "sandwich generation"

The term "sandwich generation" refers to the pressures experienced by many retirees/middle-aged people at this stage of their life when they simultaneously provide care to their ageing parents, to their children and even to their grandchildren.

It is a role usually carried out by the daughters in the family, often at the expense of ending their working life in order to be available to both parents and grandchildren.

This case study shows how the "sandwich generation" plays a largely unrecognised and unpaid, but important role, in keeping families working while caring for young children.

CASE STUDY

In this typical example, our not-quite-retirees provide regular assistance to three generations: Eva is a 65 year old accounts assistant who has been working three days per week for the past 10 years. Eva visited her 85 year old mother at least once a week when she lived in her own home, until around five years ago when her mother decided to move into a nursing home. Eva continued to visit her weekly until her mother passed away.

When Eva re-partnered with Eric, his son had just had his first grandchild. Eric was still working so Eva provided regular practical help and babysitting to his daughter-in-law. This couple then had a second child and as they were finding it difficult to cope, both recently-retired Eric and Eva began to provide child-minding assistance to the family twice a week.

Meanwhile, Eva's own daughter had a baby and Eva also provides child-minding one day per week so her daughter can return to work. Eric decided to take on some casual work while he adjusted to retirement, but he still has time to assist his mother with her growing needs.

"Boomerang" children

By retirement time, most of your children will have left the parental home. Although initially some couples might experience a sense of emptiness, eventually this does dissipate. Adult children who continue to live at home will likely provide continuity and increase their support to their parents as they age.

"Boomerang" children who return home from time to time to live because of their own needs, however, can produce more problems through creating conflict with their parents.

A University of Melbourne literature review[2] found an increasing trend for young people to return to live at home for indefinite periods:

- Complex financial, social and emotional factors influence these decisions – for both parents and children.

- Adult children experience benefits in living with parents, but it can affect their sense of independence.

- Parents report financial and emotional negatives when children return to the nest.

- Conflict arises if parents and children do not discuss their expectations about domestic tasks such as cooking and cleaning.

Where adult children returned because of unexpected events such as unemployment or relationship breakdowns (sometimes with their own children), conflict was more likely to occur, with parents reporting loss of their privacy and ability to participate in social events.

Parents reported that the adult children rarely made either a contribution in terms of finances or household chores, which again led to conflict.

However some studies found that where parents gave assistance to adult children, there was more likelihood those adult children would support the parents as they aged.

Grandchildren

The birth of grandchildren usually generates great enjoyment for most grandparents, most of whom willingly take on the responsibilities of regular child care. For parents, having the assistance of grandparents when children are very young enables them to go back to work, knowing that their children will have flexible and consistent care. Grandparent assistance may begin when the children are infants but can continue throughout the school years, including collecting children from school and caring for them during the holidays.

More than 40% of Australian infants and young children have weekly contact with their grandparents.[3] However, many have infrequent contact, limited to symbolic events such as Christmas or birthdays, especially when their parents and grandparents live far apart or have difficult relationships. Australian researchers[4] have identified four types of grandparent caring styles:

- **Avid caregivers** whose lives revolve around their grandchildren.
- **Flexible caregivers** are very supportive to the family but also prioritise their personal time.
- **Selective caregivers** for whom grandchildren are important but do not want to be defined simply as grandparents.
- **Hesitant carers** who did not anticipate caring for grandchildren and who recognise they need to balance multiple roles in their life.

Besides the practical aspect of helping their children, grandparents who care for grandchildren have the opportunity to develop deeper relationships with them. This enables grandparents to pass on their family and cultural history and to enable consistency of values, which stressed parents frequently don't have time to provide. For some grandmothers in particular, caring for grandchildren can become the central core of their lives – but that does not eliminate the possibility of conflict between the parents and grandparents about issues like discipline and "spoiling" the child. In addition, caring for a number of grandchildren for long periods can become very tiring and create too much of a sense of obligation rather than pleasure.

When you consider your own situation, I would suggest that you set a regular schedule of grandchild caring that meets both your own and the parents' needs to avoid resentment and conflict. Ensuring that you maintain your own activities and interests will allow you to maintain support from your own friends. Having refreshed your own needs, you will be more likely to look forward to the time you spend with your family.

Although not frequently mentioned, the parents and courts often overlook the contribution of grandparents when parents divorce, with the courts tending to give little weight to enforcing any ongoing contact if the parents do not agree.

However, if the parents have a major personal or relationship breakdown caused by alcohol or substance abuse, grandparents will often take on a full-time caring role for the children, either informally or formally, as a result of an application to the Children's Court. Such additional responsibilities can have a significant effect on the financial and personal health of grandparents.

Adult children

Many people who re-partner at a later stage have independent adult children from a previous relationship, living elsewhere. Nevertheless the attitude of those children to a new partner can be quite disruptive to a relationship. Never forget that each of you is part of an existing family with its own history and rituals. There is no guarantee that everybody will instantly love and care for each other.

Be respectful towards children and each other. In particular, avoid a situation where your partner must choose between his/her children and you. Adult children will be aware of inheritance issues and this factor can increase hostility towards you.

Discuss these difficult topics openly to address their relevant concerns. Your step-children may not be your favourite people but by being inclusive and interested in them, you will significantly improve the prospects for your new relationship succeeding.

Going it alone

The retirement period can really test the strength of a relationship. Some couples will reconnect in their fundamental commitment to each other and the relationship. This stage can bring a sense of real freedom and potential for them to explore personal interests with the support of their partner, while others will go their own way.

For some people, the initial phase of retirement can be a revelation when they discover they no longer like the person they live with, or that they no longer have anything in common with that person. For others, they may have tolerated years of pain – physical and emotional abuse, alcohol or drug addiction and extramarital relationships that may now come onto centre stage. Some might find that the other person has developed an illness and now requires constant ongoing care and attention for which they are not prepared.

Even in more extreme cases, nobody finds it easy to leave a relationship in which they have invested so much of their life, hopes and dreams. Leaving a significant relationship in your later years also means losing financial security and starting over again, so you need to be strongly committed to the future that you envisage. Any breakup leads down a rocky road at any stage of life, but especially so without the youth and energy to start again in a new direction.

For those who are thinking about starting a new solo life, these are a few suggestions:

- Make a list for yourself about the pros and cons of staying in the relationship. Only you really know what is important for you. Is there some room for compromise by either side, or is it too late? Of course with a violent relationship (or potentially violent), skip this step and head straight for the door.

- Talk to a professional counsellor, not your friends, about how you feel about your current situation.

- Finances: you must be realistic about your partner's response in this critical area. Both sides will be poorer following a split. How will you manage living in a smaller place, without some of the financial support that you probably have now? If you live alone, you will have to pay the rates and the utilities out of one income rather than two sharing the cost.

- Having an acrimonious divorce means you could spend a lot on legal fees, not to mention experiencing the major stress of a court case over several years. Get yourself a lawyer to negotiate consent orders for your property settlement and consider attending a mediation to work out the terms rather than commencing proceedings. Consent orders reflect the agreement that you have made with your former partner. They cost far less to negotiate than a contested settlement and will be approved much faster by the court. Court-approved orders allow you to transfer property between both of you without paying stamp duty on transfer – this can be a significant saving.

- Don't forget your partner's superannuation as an asset that should be included in the property settlement. A larger superannuation entitlement can provide considerable peace of mind when you are no longer working.

- Once you and your partner have decided to separate, you should discuss this with your children and other close family members. Think about how the family will celebrate key holidays, birthdays and anniversaries in the future. You can appreciate that other family members may not be very supportive of your decision, so you need to be firm.

- Act decisively once you make your announcement. Pack up, move out, close any joint accounts or insurance policies and notify utility providers of your new address. Hesitation at this stage can lead to arguments and even violence because of the prevailing emotional atmosphere.

- Divorce is not too difficult these days. You simply need to be separated for 12 months and have no intention of reconciling. You can file your application yourself online, serve a copy on your former partner and do not even have to attend court.[5]

You've taken the big step and gone solo

Congratulations on starting your new life as a solo retiree. And if you have been single for a while, let's be sure that you are living your best life ever. As a single, you are in one of the fastest growing segments of Australia's population. The 2016 Census reported that almost one in four were single person households, representing around two million people, of whom 55% were women.[6] As a segment of the population with a longer life expectancy, women living alone will on average be older than men living alone.

The majority of older women living alone are widows, with a lesser percentage separated or divorced. An even smaller percentage of women have never-married.[7] Culturally, relatively few women of Asian or Middle Eastern background live alone. The largest group living alone are those with an Anglo-Celtic or European background. One of the significant characteristics of older women living alone is that over 60% own their homes outright, unlike younger singletons, while a much lower percentage (less than 30%) are renters.

As discussed in more detail in Chapter 4, home ownership holds the key to financial and emotional security for older women. Interestingly, older women who live alone tend to have a higher education and higher income than men who live alone and generally higher than women with partners.

Ideally then, you are well-educated and financially secure in your own home. But you are not out of the woods just yet. As a person who enjoys your independence and solitude, you also need to be mindful of growing your social contacts and outside activities. Undertaking regular physical exercise and maintaining your health will ensure that you can continue to live in your own home for as long as possible. Studies have shown that people who live alone in the over-75 age group often experience feelings of social isolation, and their physical health may decline because they do not attend to their meals and medication requirements.[8]

Taking some positive steps such as joining an interest group, volunteering with a local organisation, or visiting friends and family on a regular basis, will keep you active and in touch. I would also recommend having internet access on your computer as an easy way to stay aware of news events, social trends and to contact friends who may have moved to different locations.

If you have made the transition from being part of a couple to a solo traveller, it would not be unusual for you to have periods of regret and loss, but these should not become so overwhelming that you feel that you are unable to function properly. Getting some counselling help and possibly anti-depressant medication for a little while will enable you to move on.

You can expect to feel angry, hurt, guilty, unattractive and lonely as part of the range of normal emotions that arise from a breakup. However, try to focus on looking forward to the new lifestyle that you are building for yourself.

Taking time to grieve and discover your own strengths before racing out to find a new relationship will work better for you with less stress. You can be sure that no potential future partner will want to share your reminiscences about your previous relationship, good or bad, until they have become part of your background, rather than the foreground of your life.

You may think it selfish, but if I am meeting a new person, I do not want to share their pain or to counsel them about their situation. Everyone has some emotional baggage, but from my perspective, you need to have dealt with it and reached some balance before you actively search for a new relationship. You should feel ready to be interested in another person and be able to (relatively) dispassionately discuss your personal history without seeking someone's approval about what has occurred. The passage of time and participating in new activities will make you a more attractive and vibrant person to any potential partner.

Online and out there

Having followed the advice to get to know yourself and have some time out, you have now decided that you would like to meet someone new. Perhaps you have tried chatting up the regular guy at your local café or made conversation with that slightly odd chap in your bridge group – without success. You would still rather be in a close relationship than spend Saturday night on the couch, which is quite understandable because there are lots of good things about being in a relationship. But just remember, there are also many compromises to being in a relationship, especially as we get older.

Try a dating site

Online dating sites can be a good way to meet a new person who wants a serious relationship, but you might have to kiss a few frogs along the way. I have heard many stories, both positive and negative, about people's experiences with online dating so success will likely require a combination of persistence and luck.

Going online widens your potential pool of romantic candidates in terms of occupation, social group and location. Generally, the people on a dating site actually want to find a partner – a huge bonus. Usually the dating site will prompt them to nominate what kind of relationship they are looking for. Compare that to your experience in a club, a bar or other venue, where you can waste a lot of time trying to find an available potential match!

In my view, it is worthwhile giving the online scene a try – with just a few warnings.

We live in a world of photo-shopped images and fake news but you must accept yourself as you are, as well as knowing what you want from another person. It's time for a reality check rather than a fairy tale. Constantly remind yourself you that you are worthwhile even if you are not part of a couple. Like musician John Lennon once said: *"You don't need anybody to tell you who you are or what you are. You are what you are!"* And what you are is perfectly okay.

You should be especially wary about entering any relationship which expects you to contribute financially to the other person. In 2013, the ACCC (Australian Competition and Consumer Commission) received 2,770 complaints from people saying they had lost $25.3

million to online dating scammers. The lowest amounts were $10,000 and some people had lost as much as $100,000.[9] *Choice* magazine proposed four signs that you may be dealing with an online scammer:

1. You've never met or seen them: scammers will avoid a face-to-face meeting.

2. They're not who they appear to be: scammers steal photos and profiles from real people. You can run a Google reverse image search on photos and search words in their description to check.

3. You don't know a lot about them: scammers want to know you as much as possible, but are less forthcoming about themselves or are inconsistent.

4. They ask you for money: once the connection's been made – be it as a friend, admirer or business partner – scammers will ask you to transfer money. Don't do it ever!

As a past user of online dating sites, I have some suggestions to make your experience as pain-free as possible. Marketing yourself requires clarity and determination about the product (that is, you) and a certain amount of risk-taking to trial the market. You will not always get an immediate (or suitable) response so you may need to experiment with your approach to improve your response rate.

The first thing I would suggest is writing a list to describe yourself and what it is you want in your ideal person. As a former family law lawyer, let me advise you that you definitely do not want to say that you want a marriage partner. Besides looking very desperate, it leaves you open to being vulnerable and exploited. And in reality – you are looking more for a companion than a marriage partner. Youth and beauty are no longer on your side and you really want shared values and trust that can develop over time.

Love? Love is a bonus. It can grow over time if planted in the warm soil of affection and caring, but it's fairly rare if you are just relying on chemistry and instant attraction.

Describing yourself

You have decided to take the plunge and put your profile out there. Here are a few guidelines:

Disclose only a few relevant things about yourself. *You're divorced, you have adult children, you like pets. Do not include negative things like health issues. Don't include personal information like the name of your pet or your date of birth. If you don't like facial hair on a man, say so.*

Be honest but not too honest. *Your opinion may not be how others see you. Find positive words to describe yourself, e.g. "curvy" rather than "overweight", "petite" rather than "short" and "social" rather than "busy". Once you meet face-to-face, your age and height will be very obvious to the other person so there is no point starting off on the wrong foot. Do not include any actual phone numbers or addresses in your profile.*

What are your best features and key interests? *Mention your love of bushwalking, or baking, or having a social conscience. The idea is to stand out from the crowd, not follow it. Everyone likes travelling and walking on a beach, so use your few words wisely to say what is important to you.*

Choose a flattering photo *– no matter how you look, you will appeal to someone, but make the photo appealing to improve initial inquiries. Some women still think it is necessary to emphasise their physical assets, but you are likely to find that you only attract types who are interested in assets rather than personality.*

Describing your preferred playmate:

1. **Be open to possibilities** – your prospect may not look how you expect and they may be interested in different things to you. You should decide what is important to you in the other person. My experience is that you probably don't even

know what your own priorities are initially. Key questions might be: are they financially secure; are they involved in community activities; do they have outside interests and do they live reasonably close to you? I am sceptical about long-distance romances.

2. **What are your core values?** If you can identify those in the other person, you have a much better chance of having a successful relationship. If a person's religion, politics or major interests are important to you, say so. Education and occupation will be indicators of their similarity to your own experience.

3. **Find out about their personal situation.** As we get older, most of us have some kind of baggage – in the shape of former relationships, children and ongoing responsibilities. What can you live with? What don't you want?

Managing the online dating scene

*   **There are quite a few dating sites,** for example, RSVP, eHarmony, Oasis Active, Plenty of Fish, Zoosk and OkCupid, and the popular app Tinder – but most of these cater to a younger age group. My pick would be RSVP, eHarmony and Oasis as being the most suitable. Most offer a free trial period but check the details before entering into a contract.

*   **Take a chance** – you can contact others as well as receiving contacts from them. Create a separate email address for your online dates to contact you.

*   **When you meet somebody for the first time, choose a public place**, tell a friend where you're going and keep the first meeting brief and inexpensive. If you have further meetings, you can make it a longer event. Pay for yourself initially. Someone who pays for dinner may expect to be repaid in kind.

*   **Be careful** about letting a new person pick you up or drop you at your home.

*   **Don't feel pressured** to become more intimate with someone until you are ready.

You can be lucky and meet someone you immediately like, but realistically, it is more likely to take six months and a number of dates to decide whether the online environment works for you. These days, online dating has established itself as a valid approach to meeting a new partner so don't be embarrassed about it. Two years down the road, your initial meeting will be just a funny story.

Anecdotally, it appears that relationships begun in the online space are just as likely to succeed as more conventionally established relationships. However, initially you might test the other person to verify their family members, their work and domestic situation before you become too serious. Once you have become relatively secure with your new partner, introduce them to friends and family. Listen to what they say about your date, whether you want to hear it or not.

Does your new partner sound genuine when he/she is interacting with your friends or family? Is their story predictable or are there unexplained inconsistencies? You would be justified in being cautious at this initial stage before you get too serious.

CASE STUDY

Miriam and David were a long-time married couple but after their daughter moved out of home, they found they were arguing more and had less in common than previously. One day Miriam noticed that David had been visiting an online dating site on his computer. This led to them separating under the same roof.

Not long after, David began seeing a woman he had met online and he moved out. Reluctantly Miriam also went online. After a few false starts, she also met a divorced man, Nick, and they started going out. Initially Miriam moved into Nick's house but soon they wanted something more suitable. Now that her property settlement was finalised, Miriam was able to buy a half share of a house with Nick with a comfortable remainder to put in her superannuation.

Re-partnering

Re-partnering after separation or divorce brings complications at any age, but specific hazards particularly arise in our later years. Research in this area appears relatively sparse but we can make some generalised statements. As we get older, the pool of available and suitable men reduces compared to the pool of available women, based on such factors as their age, health and financial situation. In short, there are more older women than men who are seeking a partner. Women remain healthier and live longer, while men die younger.

To make a comparison with finding a job in the labour market, it could be said that the marriage market shrinks and everyone's personal capital reduces as we get older. In this situation, women with in-demand characteristics such as physical attractiveness, a high status job or wealth will significantly increase their chances of making a suitable match. Meeting suitable partners becomes less likely as our social networks contract with age, so make sure that you continue to participate in social groups which open up a broader range of similarly-minded people throughout your retirement.

Research seems to suggest that if you have been in a long relationship, even where you have other family support, you are more likely to prioritise finding an intimate relationship which offers commitment and common values. The economic benefits of being in a coupled relationship, whether in marriage or in a de facto relationship, are fairly obvious. With an exchange of skills between parties and an economy of scale, two, can live for nearly the same cost as one.

However according to one study[10], widows have a 2% chance of remarriage while widowers have a 20% chance of remarriage, because men have a much larger pool of women from which to choose. Realistically, women's biology means they can expect to live alone for much of their later life.

Legalities for marriage, Wills and pre-nuptial agreements

One Canadian paper[11] suggested that cohabitation was becoming the preferred option for older couples rather than marriage because individuals can better preserve their pension benefits and control their separate finances. I doubt whether that situation applies equally in Australia, but nevertheless many later-age couples remain cautious about their financial commitments. While many older people are very concerned about preserving the inheritance of their children in a later relationship, Australian law now makes far less distinction between a de facto couple and a married couple.

When two people have cohabited in a domestic situation for two years, family law recognises them as being in a de facto relationship. Should they have a financial dispute, it may be dealt with under the *Family Law Act 1975* in the same way as a dispute between married parties. Unlike a married couple, because there often are a range of living arrangements, de facto couples frequently come to court either seeking to prove or to disprove, that a de facto relationship actually exists.

Under State law, it is also possible to register a shorter relationship in a Relationship Register (the title varies in each State).

It should be said however, that from the Centrelink perspective (i.e. receiving a benefit), a couple are in a de facto relationship from the first day they live together.

Often couples look to pre-nuptial agreements to ensure that there are clear demarcations between his, hers and their property, but such agreements can be challenged in court. In NSW at least, solicitors have been advised by the NSW Law Society to avoid preparing agreements or at least obtain counsel's advice to avoid a claim for professional negligence.

Pre-nuptial agreements are notoriously fraught as they often emerge from a history of financial disparity between the parties, sometimes duress, and over time, as the nature of the property and the relationship itself changes, the parties themselves no longer want to be bound by their previous agreement.

I strongly suggest that couples frankly discuss their financial situation with each other in relation to how they want their property divided after their death. Most parents will want to ensure their own children benefit first rather than the other party, or the other party's children.

Unless a Will is drafted with an intention to marry, marriage automatically nullifies any existing Will. Divorce does not invalidate an existing Will, so if you decide to enter any new relationship, make it a priority to compose a new Will which reflects your new situation.

If one party in a de facto relationship should die without making a Will, it can be more difficult for the other party to prove they were in a spousal situation, unlike parties who are married and are able to simply rely on the production of a certificate. Similarly a de facto couple can be disadvantaged where a member of a superannuation fund dies and the trustee has to decide whether the funds should be distributed to their de facto partner or a former spouse or children. Again, the partner will be required to prove they were in a de facto situation at the time of death to receive the benefits.

It has been said that marriage in later life brings the benefit of resuming a private life for the man and a public life for the woman. A committed relationship at this stage can bring contentment and companionship, and an opportunity to create less of a fairy tale and more of a reality. However, it does take a thoughtful approach to navigate the occasionally more complicated waters of later life.

8

Staying healthy

"To us, health is about so much more than simply not being sick. It's about getting a balance between physical, mental, emotional, cultural and spiritual health. Health and healing are interwoven, which means that one can't be separated from the other."

Dr Tamara Mackean, Senior Research Fellow, George Institute, SA

Like many things, we only appreciate the value of being and staying healthy when we might lose it. Getting older has many compensations for no longer being young – we have acquired patience, acceptance and knowledge. All those qualities are necessary to take us into our final stage of life. But poor health represents one of the biggest threats to a fulfilling retirement because it limits our physical independence and impacts our enjoyment of additional leisure time.

Rather than focusing on the usual diet/exercise routines, this chapter also provides information about the less glamorous aspects of your later years. I'm not trying to frighten you: I want to emphasise that rethinking your lifestyle can reduce your likelihood of suffering lifestyle diseases such as hardening of the arteries and types of cancer. But we all have to die of something.

Consequently, this chapter includes practical information about conditions like dementia to better inform you about caring for yourself and for older people, which can be a daunting prospect.

Being a legal practitioner who has visited clients in the later stages of their life for some years, I have included some of my personal observations of how they have managed their final exit. The experience of visiting residential care facilities, meeting staff and clients continues to be a personal growth curve for me.

Despite all our medical advances, our body starts to become less efficient by middle age (around our 50s). Our metabolism slows, our muscle mass decreases and the liver processes foods and alcohol more slowly.

Fortunately, medical advances have significantly slowed and lessened the impact of our rate of physical and mental decline. This has resulted in a longer and more active lifestyle than a century ago when we would have died off during the first flu epidemic. Some might say medical advances have caused us to live longer, but not necessarily better at the end.

Health in the context of ageing

From a research perspective, the concept of "health" extends beyond the absence or presence of disease. The concept of health reflects genetic, lifestyle and environmental factors, cultural influences, socioeconomic conditions and health care programs and services, including both their availability and quality.

Looking at overall Australian statistics, the leading causes of death for men and women vary to some extent on the age at death. Generally for men and women over the age of 85, dementia-related conditions represent the greatest major cause, followed by coronary heart disease, stroke, chronic obstructive pulmonary disease, cancer and diabetes.[1] These trends reflect Australia's circumstances as a high income country with consequent longer life expectancies.

Australian facts and figures

As mentioned previously, Australia's older people are becoming a larger proportion of our population. People aged over 65 years currently represent 15% of the population (3.7 million), with this proportion expected to rise to 20% by 2046. Of the over-65s more than half are women, particularly in the over-85 age group.[2]

However these basic statistics do not disclose the greater diversity and disadvantage of health statistics of many Australians. One in three older persons was born in a non-English speaking country. Five key groups face far more risk of early health difficulties and disability:

- Aboriginal and Torres Strait Islander persons,
- Lesbian, gay, bisexual, transgender or intersex (LGBTQIA+),
- People in rural or remote areas,
- Defence force veterans, and
- People aged over 55 at risk of homelessness.

The World Health Organisation describes Australia as a high income country with a high quality healthcare system.[3] Nevertheless, socio-economic disadvantage and remoteness from community and health services undoubtedly determines much poorer health outcomes for pockets of Australians, with a striking difference in the causes of death for people in these five groups.

Indigenous Australians born in 2010-12 can still expect to live 10 years less than non-indigenous Australians, with problems including mental and substance use disorders, injuries, cardiovascular diseases, cancer and respiratory diseases. In this context, socio-economic disadvantage adds to high use of tobacco and alcohol, poor dietary factors and greater risk of fatal injuries. In addition, they are likely to enter hospital at 2.5 times the rate of non-indigenous Australians.[4]

Similarly, people living in remote rural areas are 5.4 times more likely to die as a result of a land transport accident. They are more likely to suffer from one or more chronic diseases and more likely to use alcohol and tobacco to excess, compared to a metropolitan resident who has a less risky lifestyle and easy access to good medical treatment.

Defence force veterans also represent a vulnerable group, with the impact of their previous service affecting them throughout their life. They experience a high prevalence of mental health and post-traumatic stress disorders, high alcohol dependency and tobacco use.[5]

Most Australians in the 65-74 age group rated their own health as either good, very good or excellent. However, this perspective diminishes as the group becomes older and experiences more disability and limitation. The most common conditions were diseases of the eye (90%), musculoskeletal conditions (66%); diseases of the circulatory system (57%); osteoarthritis (28%); and respiratory conditions (15%).[6]

Without good health, a longer life span can simply become a burden. That's why researchers use a figure of how many additional disability-free years a person gains as a consequence of living longer. This figure also offers a broad indicator of the national health status of Australia's population.

Using 2009 as a baseline, a 65 year old male could expect to live to 83.7 years and a woman to 86.8 years. Of those years over 65, a woman can expect to have 12.1 years of disability, and of those, she can expect to experience 5.6 years of profound disability. A man over 65 years can expect to live with 10.5 years of disability and to experience 3.5 years of significant disability. Put simply, while we will have a longer life expectancy, approximately 50% of those years will be with some disability and in 18-25% of those years we can expect to experience a significant limitation.[7]

Despite the negative prospect of disability as we age, older people remain demonstrably happier, more satisfied, less depressed, less anxious and with less perceived stress than younger respondents. Research by Dr Laura Carstensen, Director of the Stanford Center of Longevity, found that the differences between the goals of older and younger people disappeared when she removed the factor of age. Dr Carstensen's theory[8] suggests that older people value the "here and now" rather than the perspective of younger people which sees an endless horizon and searches for wider networks of friends and opportunities. Dr Carstensen called this greater satisfaction of older people the "paradox of ageing".[9]

Being healthy and staying healthy

Despite being a topic of world-wide research for about 80 years[10] the effect of retirement on health is inconclusive. This book is not an academic literature review, so I will not dwell on the underlying studies. However, from my perspective, there are some useful findings that illuminate the subjective experience.

First, people who are already experiencing some symptoms of ill-health before retirement will go on to experience a further decline in health. Similarly, people who left their jobs involuntarily without being prepared for the change in lifestyle will also likely experience more ill-health. People who voluntarily retire or continue to work part-time in this new stage are likeliest to have the best long-term health outcome.

Second, most retirees experience some loss in mobility, ill-health and decline in mental health within six years of retirement. Factors that reduce the severity of ill health include being married, having social support, engaging in physical activity and continuing to work part-time.[11]

However there have also been studies which show that for some people, retirement actually leads to an improvement in a person's physical and mental health. They may become far more physically active than in their previous sedentary work life and happier with more interest in their activities.

Maintaining physical and mental health does require a conscious effort. It requires planning, persistence and practice. You ought to be scheduling activities into your weekly timetable which include a physical workout, some social interaction and a spiritual or mental element. No doubt you have seen the many self-help books that can provide more extensive resources for individually making serious lifestyle changes in your life, but I also suggest joining group activities to keep you on track.

The most important aspects of being a healthy retiree could be summarised as making lifestyle choices that encompass and improve mental and physical factors.

Good lifestyle choices

You could write a book exploring any one of these options, but some big picture items that might be on your to-do list include:

Be more active: Take up a recreational sport like croquet, golf, tennis, bowls or swimming. Keep going to the gym, doing yoga or join a seniors' dance class. Walk every day out of the sun, take public transport and leave your car at home. You don't need to run a half marathon but you can work at improving your heart and muscle strength. Regular exercise has long-term benefits like improving your balance and flexibility, while reducing symptoms of depression and arthritis and improving the quality of sleep.

Eat smaller portions: Eat more fresh fruit and veggies, and less meat, salt, sugar and carbohydrates. Being a healthy weight will reduce your cholesterol, your risk of getting diabetes, as well as the pressure on your joints. A brand-name diet might inspire you for a while but consciously making good food choices or trying intermittent fasting are likely to achieve a long-lasting change. Obesity contributes to diseases such as type 2 diabetes and high blood pressure.

Exercise your mind: Join a community college class, read the paper, do the Sudoku puzzle or the crossword, join a book club, learn some new skills such as painting or re-learn an instrument. Rather than "brain-training", experts suggest that as long as you keep your mind engaged in new activities, you can resist cognitive decline. Passive, sedentary activities such as watching television or hours of computer use are detrimental both to the body and the mind.

Get involved: Regularly catch up with your current friends, but also reach out to make new friends. Become part of a local community action group or volunteer to be a visitor at your local hospital. You could even get involved in politics! Being part of a social network increases your overall well-being and can support you when you are feeling low. Living alone can have both physical and psychological impacts as you get older. These problems can include increasing anxiety, vulnerability to emotional isolation and sadness which can lead to premature death.

Foster your intimate relationships: Getting older is not the end of your sexual self. Sexual intimacy provides increased satisfaction in your closest relationship and can continue despite physical and hormonal changes.

Find your happy place: Whether you are a religious person or only slightly interested in spiritual matters, you can make time every day/week to experience self-reflection and peace in the world. Options include doing a yoga class, meditation, walking in the bush or attending church. Caring for your spiritual self reduces anxiety and gives your life meaning, while strengthening your resistance to the trials of daily life.

Minimise tobacco and alcohol use: Excessive alcohol and tobacco consumption significantly increases the risk of cancer. Combined with factors such as high body mass, physical inactivity and high blood pressure, these drugs also contribute to such conditions as cardiovascular disease. Experts recommend that you have no more than two standard alcoholic drinks per day and not more than four drinks on a special occasion to avoid doing any damage. Smoking – it's never too late to stop.

Avoid unsafe environments: "Unsafe" in this context means being careful of unfamiliar situations. Examples could include email fraudsters trying to trick you, online dating scammers, situations such as being offered illicit drugs, having unprotected sex or simply being in any personal situation that you find very stressful.

Have regular check-ups

Even if you prefer alternative medical treatments, using available medical technology can identify symptoms of diseases before they have advanced.

> ### HAVING REGULAR CHECK-UPS CAN LITERALLY SAVE YOUR LIFE.
>
> *Don't forget to include check-ups in your schedule, for example:*
>
> - **Eye and hearing tests:** every year.
> - **Blood pressure and blood tests:** for cholesterol, for blood sugar: every year.
> - **Mammogram:** for early identification of breast cancer: every two years.
> - **Cervical screening:** for changes to the cervix: every five years.
> - **Skin cancer:** detection of melanomas: every year.
> - **Colon/bowel cancer:** for bowel cancer: every two years.
> - **Dental check-ups:** for tooth decay and gum disease: every six months.

On your doctor's advice, some additional tests could be:

- Bone density tests to monitor osteoporosis risk;
- Urine tests for kidney health;
- Sexually transmitted infection tests;
- Mental health check;
- For your family – don't forget prostate cancer checks for the males and everyone over 65 getting a flu vaccination.

Accessing the services of health professionals such as physiotherapists, podiatrists and dietitians can give good advice and effectively reduce symptoms for less serious conditions such as joint and foot pain.

In addition, in NSW, Multicultural Health Workers based in hospital and community health settings provide multicultural language counselling and liaison services for culturally and linguistically diverse consumers, if your family members need additional help.

Alternative therapies

You can find a multitude of medical practices under this heading. Sometimes called complementary medicine or traditional medicine, this type of therapy includes many types of healing modalities, for example:

• Reflexology	• Chiropractic
• Acupuncture	• Traditional/Chinese medicine
• Aromatherapy	• Massage
• Homeopathy	• Bush medicine
• Naturopathy	• Ayurveda
• Osteopathy	• Meditation and relaxation

Although private medical insurers often will cover some types of treatment, such as osteopathy or acupuncture, some medical researchers have criticised the efficacy of various treatments and the truthfulness of claims made. Certainly the mainstream medical profession is more accepting of some treatment than 20 years ago but the scepticism remains. Mainstream medical practitioners continue to prefer evidence-based scientific products and research.

From a legal and scientific perspective, any worthwhile type of treatment should be able to back up its claims with evidence. Practitioners in such areas as chiropractic and osteopathy, which require a university degree in order to gain a qualification, give confidence. However, some notable gaps remain:

• Despite the use of complementary medicines continuing to rise, strong reservations remain from medical researchers as to the validity of their healing claims, the low quality of products and the influence of "spiritual beliefs" in the administration of the products.

- Homeopathy faces intense scientific criticism to the effect that it has very little benefit whatever.

- Claims in relation to alternative cancer cures have been particularly criticised as being unproven.

- Some consumers have become more distrustful of conventional medicine in favour of more "natural" products. Unfortunately some of these products have been found to contain unsafe levels of heavy metals, fungal toxins and pesticides.

Some regulatory changes require practitioners of chiropractic, traditional Chinese medicine and acupuncture to be registered by the Australian Health Practitioner Regulation Agency (AHPRA) to ensure care and quality standards. However, many other practitioners continue to be self-regulated.[12]

Anytime you use an alternative treatment in conjunction with conventional medicine, you need to check that the treatments will coexist well. They can also have unintended interactions, so you should inform your doctor if you are using non-prescription medicines. Typical examples of non-vitamin supplements which claim to have healing properties include fish oil, Omega-3 fatty acid, glucosamine, echinacea, flaxseed oil, and ginseng products.

Managing your older body

> *"Life is like riding a bicycle. To keep your balance, you must keep moving."*
>
> Albert Einstein, scientist

Despite all attempts to keep our youthful looks through healthy living or any other means, our strength, our skin and our hair will inevitably change. Our bodies begin to age from our 30s onwards. Women particularly understand that we have a "biological clock" that begins to tick in our 20s. If we have had children, our bodies bear the marks of pregnancy. By the time we reach our 50s, we are likely to have gone through menopause which marks the end of our fertility.

A hundred years ago, that event in itself marked a woman's transition into old age. Now, however, it represents freedom from childbearing and a new stage of developing physical and mental strength that can extend our active life for another 30 years.

While I don't want to be too negative, in this section I explore both the good and the not-so-good aspects of getting older. There is a lot of information available about our ageing bodies, but I am focusing on those topics that I think have the widest application to a woman who wants to maintain a healthy and active lifestyle for many years to come.

Looking after your health

Menopause

From my observations, the coming of menopause is an intensely personal experience for most women, usually not widely discussed except with close friends, and with symptoms that may be quite challenging for a long period.

The medical definition of menopause is the cessation of menstruation because of hormonal changes which may naturally occur any time from the mid-40s to the mid-50s. The body stops producing eggs and estrogen production declines, which leads to menstruation ceasing. Menopause occurs when menstruation has ceased for 12 months. Accompanying the transition into menopause, women can experience a range of symptoms such as hot flushes, vaginal dryness, insomnia and emotional instability which can vary in intensity for some years.

Loss of estrogen can reduce bone density and lead to osteoporosis (brittle bones). This also brings an increased risk of coronary disease. Both alternative medication and prescription hormone replacement therapy (HRT) can reduce the symptoms. Extended use of HRT in itself may have health risks, so you need your GP's advice.

To reduce the risk of thinning bones, increase your intake of oily fish and calcium-based foods such as yoghurt and cheese. You can minimise any weight gain by increasing your fruit and vegetable consumption, increasing the time between your evening meal and breakfast, and increasing your exercise.

You can begin by doing at least 30 minutes of physical activity every day. This can include incidental activity such as gardening, walking and housework, and progress to moderately active exercise and more weight-bearing activities.

Include more fish, lean meat and vegetables in your diet, and less processed foods such as pies, chips and cured meats.

Hormonal changes

As men and women age, their production of hormones such as insulin, estrogen and testosterone gradually reduce, leading to muscle weakness, loss of muscle mass, decreased sex drive and increased fatigue and weight. Thyroid disorders and other conditions may also cause these symptoms. By the time we are in our 80s, we have lost between 30-40% of our muscle mass, while our skin has thinned and dried as oil glands reduce production.

Coping with cancer

The many types of cancer (over 100 types) are similar in that they begin as cells in the body that mutate and begin to grow uncontrollably rather than dying. As they start to grow they form lumps known as tumours. In leukaemia the cells build up in the blood or bone marrow but do not form solid lumps. Your chance of developing a cancer increases as you get older. Your chances of survival depend to some extent on the type of cancer, how soon tumours are diagnosed and successful intervention treatment.

Cancers are often categorised as localised cancers (stages 1 and 2) or metastatic cancers (stages 3 and 4) which have spread to other parts of the body. Cancer may arise by being born with a genetic predisposition, or by environmental or lifestyle factors such as tobacco smoking, cancer-causing chemicals, radiation, excessive alcohol intake, poor diet, exposure to sun and physical inactivity. In 2018, an estimated 138,321 new diagnoses of cancer have occurred with an estimated 68% of people surviving for at least 5 years. However, cancer-related deaths still represent approximately one in five of all deaths.[13]

Treatment for cancer includes surgery, chemotherapy, radiation therapy and immunotherapy, amongst other therapies. Most treatment has some side effects including fatigue, nausea, bowel and bladder problems and pain. Doctors often recommend changing your diet to adjust for the after-effects of treatment. Most large hospitals have cancer survivor programs to assist patients with their after-treatment care.

You can contact the Cancer Council Helpline on 13 11 20 to get in touch with cancer support groups in your area to talk with others. Pain management and meditation training can improve the experience of living with cancer.

Cardiovascular changes

Our heart, blood vessels and blood itself changes as we get older. The heart stiffens and slows, becomes more irregular and loses effectiveness in pumping blood around the body. The arteries thicken, causing a slight increase in blood pressure. Blood thickens and becomes less capable of resisting infection. Consequently, older people will more likely suffer a range of heart-related conditions such as angina, coronary heart disease, high blood pressure, varicose veins and strokes. In Australia, heart disease rates increase markedly in the over-65 age groups, making it the second highest cause of death in that age group[14].

Research shows that increased physical activity is the best prevention of heart disease particularly for post-menopausal women. Researchers recommend controlling your blood pressure by eating less salt in a healthy diet and doing at least two and a half hours per week of regular exercise. Daily brisk walking which raises your heart rate is an easy way to exercise and has been found to be associated with longevity. Stopping smoking, limiting alcohol intake and reducing stress all help to maintain a healthy heart.[15]

Mental health

Most older people experience good mental health, but 11% can experience high psychological stress. As we age, some of us will suffer from poor mental health (not the same as dementia), but most will not. Causes can include social isolation, physical pain, recent loss of a partner and psychosis.[16]

As the group most commonly diagnosed with anxiety and depression, men over 85 years also represent the most likely age group of all age and gender groups to take their own life. For people diagnosed early in life with mental health and substance abuse problems, anxiety and depression may surface as they age.

Getting help and seeing a health professional starts you on the path of getting specialised psychological assistance and appropriate medication. Most areas have a community-based mental health unit which can refer you to further counselling, or a support network to enable you to meet other people with similar experiences.

Changes to joints and bones

In addition to reducing bone density, ageing affects cartilage and the surrounding tissue making it less flexible, more likely to tear and less likely to heal. Cartilage acts as padding around the joints, reducing the impact on them from daily use. Once the cartilage thins, the surfaces of the joints (particularly the knees and hips) no longer easily slide over each other, causing pain and restricted mobility.

We recognise this condition as osteoarthritis – most people will suffer from this to some extent by the time they are 80. Typically, osteoarthritis appears as pain and swelling around the joints of the fingers, toes, lower back, neck and larger weight-bearing joints. Being overweight exacerbates osteoarthritis of the knees.

Your GP can prescribe either analgesics or anti-inflammatory drugs, but daily strengthening exercises and staying active will increase flexibility and reduce the likelihood of injury. Exercises in a pool give physical benefits while sparing the joints from stress. These days, doctors are reluctant to recommend surgery for knee replacements, although figures for hip, knee and shoulder joint replacements continue to rise each year. New physiotherapy programs such as GLA:D offer education and training to reduce symptoms of osteoarthritis.

According to the Australian Orthopaedic Association National Joint Replacement Registry there were 498,660 hip, 592,577 knee and 32,406 shoulder procedures, which amount to 1,123,643 joint replacement procedures in 2015.[17]

A suggested anti-arthritis diet

A great deal of discussion has occurred around the effect of an "anti-arthritis diet" as a means of reducing the inflammation and pain of arthritis. According to the Harvard Medical School the supporting evidence is debatable, but some suggestions for a healthy diet include:

- Reduce your weight. That improves your cardiovascular fitness and reduces the load on your feet and knees.
- Eating omega-3 rich foods such as salmon, tuna and supplementing your diet with fish oil.
- Increase your vitamin D intake, either by supplements, small doses of sunlight, fish oil and orange juice.
- Follow a "Mediterranean" diet incorporating lots of brightly coloured fruits and vegetables such as pumpkin, capsicum and oranges to reduce inflammation.
- Glucosamine and chondroitin offer a limited beneficial effect on osteoarthritis, but may not be suitable if you are allergic to shellfish.

Staying mentally healthy

For whatever reason – our hormones, our more emotional makeup and inward-looking tendencies, or systematic discrimination – women will likely experience sadness and depression more than men.[18] More than one in three women will experience anxiety in their lives, often resulting in depressive episodes. Women tend to have major transitional episodes in their lives such as pregnancy, birth or menopause which can precipitate these episodes. In my view, retirement belongs on that list.

As a time of transition, retirement often accompanies changes in physical health, in our work structures and in our relationships which can bring feelings of loss. In most cases, these feelings dissipate over time and we recover and move on with our lives. However, depression differs from sadness in that the feelings of misery last for over two weeks accompanied by negative and self-critical behaviour, feelings and thoughts. These experiences may also come with physical symptoms such as headaches, sleeplessness and weight loss.

Symptoms of depression can interfere significantly with every aspect of your life. The most intense form of depression – a psychotic episode – can involve hallucinations and losing touch with reality. Significant depression requires treatment with anti-depressant medication, often in tandem with psychological therapy to deal with troubling thoughts.

Depression in our older years may arise from grief at the loss of a partner or child, or financial stress, pain, illness or social isolation. Left untreated, this depression can manifest in unexplained physical disability, personality changes and a greater propensity to be at risk of self-harm. Professional assistance is usually required in determining whether a person suffers from depression or alternatively the early stages of dementia, because there can be similarities in symptoms.

Importantly, older people who experience conditions such as depression can use effective conventional medication, irrespective of their age. However, serious mental health issues in older people may have more disturbing and ongoing effects.

Having a reasonable standard of housing and financial stability will certainly reduce anxiety attacks or episodes of depression, but will not prevent dementia.

Throughout their lives, women will more likely display psychiatric and psychological distress, especially if they come from poorer families where there is a greater chance of experiencing violence. In their later years, such women also experience more vulnerability to debt and financial exploitation, leading to an increased risk of mental health conditions.

I mention these conditions to make the point that, for most people, their mental health status does not change simply as a result of growing older. Mental health conditions such as phobias, anxiety and panic attacks, personality disorders, schizophrenia and obsessive-compulsive disorders in older people usually begin in their early years. Factors which apparently increase the risk of suicide include declining health, chronic pain, impairment in daily living activities, threats to physical and financial autonomy, social isolation, lack of social support, grief, depression and feelings of hopelessness.

Dementia – that random, relentless thief

What disease cannot be prevented, is difficult to slow down and does not yet have a cure?

Dementia is the simple answer but the term includes an array of diseases and symptoms. Associated with an ageing brain, dementia equally attacks the rich and the poor, the intelligent and the not-so-clever. Dementia-associated deaths probably represent the largest cause of death in the over-85 year old population. That figure increases as our life expectancy increases. But dementia is not the preserve of the very old – it can strike a person in their mid-life when its progress can be most relentless.

Dementia-related diseases primarily affect the functioning of the brain, including the brain's ability to control the movement of other parts of the body. Often the loss of function caused by the progress of dementia may hide the underlying cause of death. For example, dementia-related loss of function affects about 50% of deaths, but these are often identified as respiratory failures (where the patient's body was unable to clear secretions from its airways).

A technical definition of dementia describes it as an "irreversible loss of higher cognitive functions, including memory", manifested in a deteriorated cognitive performance of the activities of daily living. However from a medical perspective, dementia is broadly defined as either a form of primary dementia, that is a disorder of the brain, or a secondary dementia, in that loss of brain function is caused outside the brain, for example by a blockage to the brain's blood supply.

In such memory-impairment diseases as Alzheimer's disease, Lewy body dementia[19] and Huntington's disease, toxins produced by the brain's disturbed metabolism cause damage to brain tissues. These amyloid proteins develop into plaques and result in a loss of brain tissue in areas of the brain's left cerebral hemisphere which controls memory, language and the acquisition of new information. These diseases are forms of primary dementia. Studies of Alzheimer's patients point to such factors as advanced age, family history and a genetic susceptibility (usually female) giving rise to the likelihood of dementia occurring.

Secondary dementias can originate from numerous factors such as damage to the blood supply to the brain, or by toxic substances such as excess alcohol or harmful drugs, environmental pollutants or as a result of a stroke. These dementias are categorised as vascular, metabolic, nutritional, toxic or infectious dementias. Symptoms will often emerge long after the first exposure to the toxic element. New research now also suggests that other factors beginning in childhood may lead to a higher risk of dementia, for example stressful childhood experiences, poor diet or poor parenting.

CASE STUDY

Rachel's mother, Aviva, was beginning to show some difficulty managing her life at home. A fiercely independent woman, Aviva was becoming increasingly forgetful and confused, sometimes leaving pans on the stove until the bottom had burnt out or soiling herself because she was unable to reach the toilet in time. Rachel intended to move into her mother's house to assist her but before she could, Aviva was diagnosed with bowel cancer and underwent major surgery.

After several weeks' recovery in hospital, Aviva's mind appeared to have been affected by the anaesthetic more than expected. After an ACAT assessment, Rachel agreed to have Aviva transferred to an aged care facility. Aviva was not able to comprehend her new living arrangement. Even after several months, she still referred to her home as a "club" and was unable to form any new relationships with other residents. She never accepted the care facility as her home. On a number of occasions Aviva left the facility by walking out with other visitors who apparently thought she also was a visitor.

Rachel did bring Aviva back to her own home at times, but by then Aviva had little recognition of where she had previously lived.

Certainly dementia can be difficult to diagnose in the early stages. A person may have days when their memory and speech may be functioning in a relatively "normal" fashion, but gradually their capacity diminishes. Researchers have suggested that there is a delay of between 10 and 20 years from the inception of Alzheimer's disease to the onset of symptoms.[20]

A family member may take steps to have the person assessed only when the symptoms become unusual or overwhelming. However, while an older person may suffer some loss of memory and functional mobility, this does not necessarily indicate dementia. Professional assistance is required to make a more accurate assessment.

Clinical assessments of a person's capacity usually try to elicit a person's understanding of the following cognitive areas:

- Orientation for time, place and person;
- Registration of new information;
- Verbal memory and immediate and delayed recall;
- Understanding of simple sequential commands;
- Use of language;
- Visuospatial ability.

Diseases such as Alzheimer's (and more often the secondary dementias), can be accompanied by a gradual personality change, which can be very confronting for other family members. Coping with such behaviour can be very stressful for a caregiver and may require the assistance of specialist services or even admission into a specialised dementia unit of a residential aged care facility.

Some symptoms of early memory impairment

The Gerontology Center at the University of South Florida, USA has proposed these warning signs observed in a person's behaviour:

1. Asking the same question over and over again.

2. Repeating the same story, word for word, repeatedly.

3. Forgetting how to cook, make repairs, or play cards – activities that were previously easily done.

4. Losing the ability to pay bills or manage finances.

5. Getting lost in familiar surroundings or misplacing household objects.

6. Neglecting personal hygiene or continuously wearing the same clothes, while insisting they showered or that the clothes were clean.

7. Relying on someone else such as a spouse to make decisions or answer questions that previously they would have done themselves.

If you recognise two or three such warning signs in a person, you should be alert that they may be experiencing some memory loss problems. If you have noticed more than four or five signs, you should consider having that person medically assessed.

CHANGED BEHAVIOUR CAN BE CHALLENGING

Typical changed behaviour that may alarm a family member can include:

- A person's erratic driving of their car and their unconsciousness of near mishaps;

- Repetitive questions or stories from their past;
- Forgetting conversations that occurred a few minutes earlier;
- The person accusing someone of stealing an item from their room with an extreme over-reaction;
- Shouting and abusive language without cause;
- Agitation and restlessness especially in the late afternoon;
- Displaying uninhibited sexual behaviour.

Managing the behaviour of a person who is confused, agitated or distressed requires a calm voice and manner. It includes determining whether the person has any physical pain and removing any triggers that caused the behaviour to arise.

Caring for a person affects both the carer and the extended family. Feelings of guilt, anger and grief are very common, as the carer tries to recover the relationship with the person they used to know.

It is easy to be frustrated, embarrassed and angry with a person's behaviour and then to feel guilty at your own loss of temper and distress about an incident that has occurred.

Unfortunately this situation will not likely improve if the person is moved into care, because they will likely be unhappy and angry at being forced to leave their home. Take a break from the care of the person and talk with other family members to relieve your discomfort. Support groups through such organisations as Dementia Australia (www.dementia.org.au) can also provide help.

Becoming a carer

Being someone's carer is like a job but you will never be paid enough for the things you do. Your most useful attributes will be patience, a sense of humour and endless cheerfulness. Take pleasure in the simple things that restore your resilience and carry you through the painful and sometimes unpleasant tasks associated with caring.

Caring for someone through a long and debilitating condition like Alzheimer's is a major commitment. Should you not be able to maintain that commitment over time, you must remind yourself that whatever your decision, your intention is to provide the best care possible for your loved one.

A CHECKLIST FOR CARERS:

1. **Inform yourself by** meeting **with health professionals** to understand your loved one's medical needs and medication.

2. Assuming your loved one is still relatively well and mentally alert, **make sure you have arranged for them to sign a Power of Attorney and Enduring Guardianship** and that they have an up-to-date Will.

3. **Get some assistance as back-up.** This could include community-based support services or health services such as social workers, physiotherapy and home nursing.

4. **Contact the My Aged Care line on 1800 200 422** to arrange for an assessment for an aged care package for your loved one. Depending on the level of need, you may be eligible to receive paid assistance for such services as showering or house-cleaning, which will reduce your workload to an extent.

5. **Establish a daily routine** for eating, medication, showering, toileting and doing activities which interest your loved one. These may be creative activities such as reading, painting, walking in the garden, or playing with a pet. You need some time as well to continue with your own domestic duties.

6. **Organise visits from other family members** during the day to give yourself a break, to meet friends or to do the shopping.

7. **Join a Caregiver Support group.** Depending on your loved one's particular condition, there are many support groups for carers of people with cancer, memory-impairment and other conditions. Being a carer can be a very isolating experience, so discussing your experiences with others will provide you with an opportunity to better understand your own reactions to the situation.

8. **Sometimes it is not realistically possible** for one person to provide 24 hour/365 days of care to a loved one. Disturbed sleep, increasingly difficult behaviour and greater need for medication can leave a carer very exhausted. If you find you can no longer manage the person staying at home, you have done your best.

If you are the only carer for a loved one, on any day you are likely to experience arguments, conversations, cleaning, feeding and becoming very tired.

When the tiredness becomes too overwhelming for you to remain resilient, it can be far kinder to seek some respite for your loved one. You should take a break – either for a weekend or longer, so that you can give the level of kind and dedicated care that your loved one needs to remain safe at home.

Most aged care facilities offer respite care at a reasonable cost for short periods.

Dying with dignity – palliative care options

We come from a dark abyss,

We end in a dark abyss, and

We call the luminous interval life.

Nikos Kazantzakis, author

While most Australians state they would prefer to die at home , the fact is that 54% of the population die in hospital, 32% die in residential care and only 14% die at home.[21] Most residents of aged care facilities die while resident. However, it is possible to remain in your own home and receive assistance with end-of-life care.

Palliative care offers support for people of any age with a serious, non-curable disease such as end-stage cancer or motor neurone disease. Treatment focuses on making somebody comfortable in the final stage of their life, without necessarily trying to resolve the underlying medical problem. Community-based assistance to a person's family helps enable the person to remain longer at home.

Doctors, nurses and social workers can offer assistance such as:

- Tailored relief of pain;
- Additional equipment needed to aid care at home;
- Links to other services such as home help and financial support;
- Support for cultural needs and traditions;
- Support for emotional, social and spiritual concerns;
- Counselling and grief support;
- Referrals to respite care services.

I strongly recommend that patients in this situation make an "Advance Care Directive" which reflects their own choices as to how they wish to be cared for if they are no longer able to communicate their own decisions to medical staff. An Advance Care Directive is different to an Enduring Guardianship where another person who has been appointed by the patient makes the decisions about the patient's medical care. The Directive has priority over the Guardian's decision as well. A sample Advance Care Directive appears at p 291.

The World Health Organisation defines palliative care as: "Affirms life and regards dying as a normal process; intends neither to hasten nor postpone death; integrates the psychological and spiritual aspects of patient care; offers a support system to help patients live as actively as possible until death."[22]

In Australia, recent palliative care guidelines[23] reinforce this approach to ensure staff in facilities can identify and treat the physical symptoms and meet the cultural, psychological, social and spiritual needs of residents. The comprehensive guidelines include practical guidance to staff about physical care and respecting the patient's right to choose their treatment. Staff already familiar with a resident can be more informal and caring than in a hospital environment during this period.

CASE STUDY

Jean was 74 years old when she was diagnosed with a very aggressive form of stomach cancer. Her ex-husband returned home to care for her and her daughter arranged for palliative care nurses to visit twice a week to drain Jean's abdomen and administer pain-relieving medication. During the next three months, her daughter came every second day and organised friends and family to visit Jean to say their goodbyes. Jean remained mentally alert until the end when she died surrounded by her family.

Australia has a more institutionalised palliative care system than many countries, despite the fact that most people would like to die comfortably at home. Where a person has a chronic condition that is unlikely to be cured, for example, an advanced cancer, it is likely that palliative care will be recommended to manage the pain and side effects of treatment.

Palliative care services can be provided at home, in a residential aged care facility or in a specialist palliative care unit, sometimes called a hospice. Usually there will be a specialist palliative care team who will provide coordinated services including physiotherapy, dietary advice and pharmaceutical advice for the period required. Palliative care is not the same as physician-assisted death. It aims to improve the comfort and quality of a person's life throughout their illness. Euthanasia is not considered part of palliative care practice.

Often families are afraid to have the conversation with their loved one about how they would like to die, even when they know that their loved one has a chronic illness with a foreseeable end. Having that conversation enables your loved one to have a "good death" which gives them dignity, choice and support to address their physical, personal, social and spiritual needs.[24] Being able to plan and prepare for that end of life care in the home gives comfort to both the family and the dying. Going through this process does require courage that you may have not previously realised you had.

9

Leisure and learning

"I'm not someone who thinks about the past. I'm so busy thinking about what I'm going to do today."
Maggie Tabberer, fashion designer, publisher, media personality

One of the great things about retirement is that you can finally catch up and do all those projects that you have been meaning to do for ages. That could be cleaning out the garage, painting the spare room or visiting your aunty in the bush – which should keep you busy for a few weeks. Why not take a long overseas holiday. Okay, done that – so what are you going to do next?

Retirement offers an opportunity to create a life reflecting your own interests and abilities rather than a life built on obligations to an employer or a family.

Planning for your future retirement should be longer than for a few months, but not many of us spend the time considering how this future should look. In this chapter, I suggest some practical and playful alternatives that will help you to create new paths in this, your Third Age.[1]

Finding meaning in the ordinary

Chances are that you are already doing something you really like or are good at. You might play croquet, organise community events or go kayaking on the harbour. If you were retired, you are likely to want to do more of the same. If you choose that option, the prospect of retirement offers far more time and scope to develop that interest.

If you always dreamed of being a writer but somehow never had time to write that novel – well, here is your chance! You can follow up that local writers' group that holds regular writing classes as well as coffee nights. You may never make the best sellers' list but following your own real interests will lead to intellectual stimulation and new friendships that can grow over time.

CASE STUDY

Myra was a social worker by profession but stopped working when her husband took a three-year job opportunity overseas. On their return to Australia they decided to move to a regional city close to other family members while her husband considered retirement.

Despite her age, Myra renewed her social work career and continued to follow her interest in painting which she had as a young woman. Myra's work skills were publicly recognised when her social work team assisted many people through a major flooding incident in the region.

Soon after she retired, with greater freedom to concentrate on her painting, Myra printed her own business card which stated her occupation as "artist". She continued to paint and exhibit locally, often selling her work until her death some 15 years later.

While I can suggest activities that you may have not tried, or groups that you may not know about, I cannot guarantee that participating will make you happy or will give new meaning to your life. That is something you must do yourself. Some people find meaning through their religious practice, through the music they play or growing their plants.

In my view, a meaningful life focuses on creating and caring for things that you value outside yourself. Putting in time and effort, and being rewarded by having made a difference. Formulate your own priorities, then follow through to make it real. Sometimes your path may be less travelled, but it is more fulfilling because it is unique to you

When thinking about life as a retiree, women have had relatively few role models. In previous times, women who retired from the workforce apparently left silently, almost invisibly. Our perception of older women builds on our childhood memories of our grandmothers – motherly housewives who baked cakes and carried Band-Aids for our cuts. This stereotype carries no more nor less truth than that of a kindly, bowls-playing grandfather with many valid exceptions to both.

Older women don't have to be motherly, they don't have to play tennis or volunteer for the church morning tea. Let's go beyond these stereotypes to write our own scripts: women can follow their own dreams and be as militant or agreeable as they choose.[2] The Knitting Nannas Against Gas and Greed, or the Grandmothers Against Detention of Refugee Children are just two groups who take pride in their age and their militancy!

Women retiring from the workforce bring new perspectives into the post-work world. They bring knowledge of the corporate world, of business, of politics and the arts. That experience will change how women see themselves in their future roles. Women who have been leaders and policy makers in their working life will have the skills, time and knowhow to effect change in their later years. Life does not end at 65!

Previously, women's restricted access to financial resources and housing limited their options. Now many women own their own home, earn a decent income and have adequate super benefits without relying on a male partner to support them. As long as a woman has a basic level of financial security, she can thrive as a single person, have a socially vibrant life and contribute to society.

Women who have children or grandchildren are likely to spend more time with them, if not actually becoming an essential factor in enabling the parents to return to work. Spending more time with a partner might not be the whole answer in retirement. Statistics say that women tend to outlive their male partner. For at least some of their retirement, many women are likely to be carers for their partner, their parents and their grandchildren.

When all those obligations have been met, most women will find themselves living alone. If you have been working on your networks throughout your retirement however, you will still have your own interests and supportive friends to meet for coffee. So keep working on your retirement plans and maintain your personal networks throughout your Third Age.

How do you spend your time?

No doubt you have heard about groups of very old people who live on islands, like Okinawa, part of Japan, or Sardinia in the Mediterranean. While their particular diet contributes to their long and healthy life, I notice that these elders lived an agrarian lifestyle relatively isolated from the stresses of large cities. Most of us will have good reason to continue our suburban life with all our current commitments. However, some key points for us to note from their cultures include:

- Follow a diet that is mostly plant and fish-based, with limited portion size.
- Stay active, gardening and walking every day.
- Stay connected with a group that supports you.
- Laugh about the good and bad things that happen.
- Express gratitude for things that make you happy.
- Recognise goodness in others and respect their talent.
- Live simply, get enough sleep and spend time in nature to avoid stress.
- Give back to the community.

In complete contrast to the Okinawa example, Merrill Lynch, now part of the Bank of America Corporation[3], conducted a very interesting US study of attitudes to retirement and leisure. That study found a workaholic culture exists in the USA, demonstrated by its average of 11 vacation days per year, one of the lowest figures amongst any industrialised country.[4] Their work focus and the short vacations of American society substantially limit their culture of leisure.

But the cohort of new 65+ aged retirees – at least those who are physically active with financial flexibility and time-affluent – experienced much greater freedom, with their options continuing to evolve. Describing retirement as being "transformed and transformative"[5] this study reports on new retirees whose happiness suddenly soared because they escaped from the pressure of work. The study found that they enjoyed many more leisure hours in their day, based on their financial stability.

The lifestyles of the Okinawa people and American retirees could not be more contrasting. Yet there are many similarities between the lives of happy retirees and the lives of Okinawans. Having retired from their workaholic lifestyle, successful (and this certainly does not include everyone) US retirees began to change their values:

- They lost the routine of work, the regular payday and the shared activities with their colleagues, but they looked to establish new social relationships. They valued leisure time shared with friends. They feared that relocating could jeopardise their connection with friends or family.

- They valued their families, enjoying life with a partner and with their grandchildren. The reward was greater after always working and not spending enough time with their children.

- They might have a wish list of places they wanted to visit, but not necessarily the budget. Consequently they valued the experiences they could enjoy rather than the locations.

- They expected to be healthy and active until 75 years, with the loss of physical independence representing the greatest threat to their happy retirement. That threat to happiness included the prospect of additional medical costs incurred to stay healthy.

- Many retirees wanted to continue to work in some capacity and wanted to "give back" to the community.

Interestingly, in this comparison of their radically different lifestyles, both the long-lived Okinawans and the US retirees found happiness in interacting with their friends and family, in both giving and receiving support. Sharing a mindset that simplified their lives, both groups wanted to retain their physical independence and efficacy for as long as possible. I find it inspiring that the US retirees no longer focused on the hours spent on an activity, but immersed themselves in their lived experience.

Retirement leisure planning

As a suggestion to pre-retirees and retirees, the study suggests making a "retirement leisure game plan"[6] which supports many of the suggestions that I make in this book.

HOW DO YOU WANT TO SPEND YOUR LEISURE TIME?

- What special interests or hobbies do you already follow?

- What new hobbies or skills would you like to acquire?

- If you want to travel, where would you go if you could afford it?

- What especially important peak experience would you like to pursue?

- Who would you like to share your experiences with?

Reality check – do your habits support your good intentions?

The US Bureau of Labor Statistics offers a reality check to balance those aspirational goals. They found that on average, retirees aged 65 - 74 watched 3.92 hours TV on a weekday and those aged over 75 years watched 4.15 hours. The main activities for over 75 year old retirees were housework, cooking, vehicle maintenance, pet care, garden maintenance, volunteering, sleeping and personal care.[7]

Making conscious choices

So what will you choose? An ocean of daytime TV to wash away any self-doubt? Or active ageing when you reconsider your own values and beliefs to transform your life? Your Third Age offers the opportunity for ongoing participation and contribution in the social and cultural life of your community.

Retirement also provides the opportunity to re-evaluate your spiritual or religious life, however you define it. For many people, exploring their beliefs can better prepare themselves for the last stage of their life. The question arises: what do you really stand for, and what will be your contribution? How will you use the precious remaining time that you have?

Go ahead and set some priorities about what you will do with the remainder of your life. Knowing that our life has a beginning and an end means we have less to lose; the greatest loss would be to waste the opportunity that we have. Acknowledging our frailty and our own eventual death makes us less fearful and more accepting of that process. For me, it jolts me into a more mindful and meaningful perception of the remaining life I have.

Key elements for your retirement plan

Knowing yourself in terms of your real interests, likes and dislikes and your willingness to develop new interests, will help you set (or reset) your priorities. If you already know exactly what you want to do, the following suggestions might give you some additional ideas to add to your weekly schedule.

Remember, you need regular activities in each of these areas: **physical exercise, intellectual activity** and **social networking**. If you organise an activity in each area, plus other tasks like minding the grandchildren or volunteering, you will be busier and more satisfied than you can imagine.

In my view, it is never too late to expand your knowledge. Is there a subject you have always wanted to learn? Perhaps another language or a higher degree to finish off your education? I have heard of retirees beginning their undergraduate degree on retirement and starting their second career as a lecturer in their 70s. These stories can be an inspiration to you in setting up your own goals.

Exercise

We all agree that more physical activity keeps us healthier. But some research suggests that exercise may also be a factor that keeps major diseases like cancer, type 2 diabetes and high blood pressure at bay. For this to work we need to incorporate exercise into our life in a way that it becomes an established habit. We need a routine that makes physical activity as integral to our daily life as going out to lunch.

To establish a routine, the activity should be:

- Easily accessible from your home;

- Affordable;

- Interesting to you, either in that it allows you to set personal goals, or you are part of a group that will support you to reach your own goals;

- Something you can do three times per week, or alternate with another activity to alleviate boredom.

SOME SUGGESTED ACTIVITIES:

- *Studios*: Pilates; yoga – Hatha, Iyengar, Bikram; barre body, Zumba, tango, salsa dancing. Look these up and see what appeals to you. Different localities offer varied options, so don't expect them all to be exactly as you expect!

- *Swimming pool*: swimming, aqua aerobics, noodle classes, shallow and deep water fitness.

- *The gym*: exercise routine, cycle classes, group fitness classes, cardio blast, boxing, body pump, circuit training.

- *In nature*: bushwalking, mountain bike riding, rock climbing, bird-watching, rock-hunting, canoeing/kayaking, fishing, scuba diving, marathon running, skydiving. (Caution required: not all of these are for everyone!)

- *Sporting clubs*: golf, tennis, croquet, lawn bowls, barefoot bowls, netball, basketball, volleyball, squash, cricket, badminton. (Some of these put more demands on an ageing body than others!)

Even if initially you are not the fittest person, you can improve your level of health and fitness in an enjoyable way. We often read about people who took up marathon running to overcome other health difficulties – you can do your own version of that. Taking part in shorter fun runs or regular jogging enables you meet new people, supports good charities and also keeps you fit.

Take the example of a semi-retired friend who loved to watch the hang-gliders drift by, close to his holiday house. One day he decided to give it a try himself. Now as a regular member of a local group, he gets to hang out above one of Australia's best coastlines.

Here is a case study which demonstrates that you can write your own story while still remaining connected with your family during retirement.

CASE STUDY

Arriving in Australia after World War II, Vesna followed her interest in cutting and polishing semi-precious stones to set into silver jewellery for some years. Finally she took the plunge with her savings to start her own business, selling silver and stones to craftspeople who also wanted to make their own pieces. On reaching pension age, Vesna sold her business and made her first visit to Europe since migrating to Australia.

After her return, she and a friend bought a small campervan and they toured around Australia for a few months at a time, camping out and searching for rocks and fossils in remote locations. They came back with boxes of rough agates, petrified wood, even sapphires. Vesna resumed cutting stones and making jewellery. She exhibited her work and occasionally got commissions to create new pieces.

Vesna continued this lifestyle until well into her 80s, but also made sure she was available to care for her grandchildren when needed. Those grandchildren grew up knowing the names of all the stones Vesna had found and used.

Arts and culture

There are so many creative activities to do and groups that you can join, that you never need be at home if you don't want to be. In most cases, you don't need to be "creative" (however you define that expression) because there are classes for all ability levels and exhibitions happening all around your neighbourhood.

Many small groups run out of your local community centre, council building or library, while others are associated with established locations, for example art galleries or museums. Looking online will enable you to find groups that are close to your area. However, personal recommendations can still be the best source of contacts.

Learn new skills: painting, drawing, knitting, sculpting, cooking, ceramics, crochet, sewing, landscape photography, woodcarving, quilting, podcasting, short film-making, story writing, or playing an instrument. Now is the time to take up those unexplored avenues.

Join a group: an embroidery group, historical society, bush care group, book club, a choir or a band, the hospital auxiliary, or a bonsai society. For instance, joining a choir benefits your health because it improves your lung capacity, your posture and your muscle strength. Singing in a group enhances your positive feelings, while building trust and communication with others. The benefits far outweigh the mere time spent singing. Research shows that belonging to more groups improves your well-being and can lengthen your life expectancy.

Join formal arts-related organisations like: art gallery societies, museum societies, writers' groups, theatre groups, ballet and dance societies or music societies. You can meet like-minded people, learn about new trends and attend a variety of social events.

Go to festivals, fairs, exhibitions, conferences, talks and events that grow your networks: Again this will depend on your interests. For example, if you are developing your artistic skills, volunteering will connect you to loads of artists and their work. Going to talks by recognised experts will improve your knowledge as well as meeting others.

Case Study

In some respects, Laurie should have been a full-time artist but she never had the confidence to rely solely on an artist's income. At the beginning of her career she taught art and then moved into a series of casual jobs. Laurie's personal relationships had always been rather unpredictable. After moving to the Blue Mountains, west of Sydney, she became more of a hermit, focusing her energy on repainting and repairing her home while creating new artworks.

Finally Laurie managed to get a part-time retail job. One day, a customer struck up a conversation with her and invited her to go out for coffee. After a while, her new friend suggested that she come with him to his regular tango class, to which she agreed. After a year she found that she really enjoyed learning this complex dance and meeting new people. Her local network has since grown.

Laurie is still painting prolifically and now with her friend's support she is finally preparing to mount her own art exhibition.

Become a community leader

Perhaps you have never thought of yourself as being an influencer in your community. Perhaps you never had the time because you were working. However, now you actually have the time and the experience to make a difference.

Assuming you have lived in your area for a while, you already know the issues that concern other residents. You may decide to join a local residents' group and attend a few meetings. You can start by writing letters to the editor of your local newspaper, or maybe take it up a notch and write to your local Member of Parliament.

You can hold a public meeting and may even speak at a protest rally. You think that retirees don't make this happen? It certainly happened in my area when a new road and tunnel was proposed.

Another friend moved into a large residential strata complex, only to find herself taking up the cause of not only her own owner's corporation, but the state-based association as well. Her previous experience in government policy work has equipped her very well for taking on a new advocacy role.

Don't forget that joining a political party can be an effective way to influence your community and to meet like-minded people. On any polling day, you can be sure that many retirees are staffing polling booths for parties of every stripe.

Being retired does not mean retiring from life. On the contrary, it means getting more involved in those issues that you never had time to follow when you were busy with work and family.

Finally you are no longer restricted by other peoples' opinions and you will find many people who share your views. You may care about saving local open spaces or you may want to raise funds for better equipment in your local hospital – your time and effort can make a real difference to the issues you care about.

Join up!

In the section on arts and culture I encouraged you to join a group. Again, I suggest that you look at organisations that you could join, from the perspective of contributing to the community. (In many cases, you can do both from a single organisation.) Community organisations include many social clubs and groups, some aimed specifically at older people and others that encourage membership related to special interests and volunteering.

With a plethora of clubs and groups in our communities, it can be confusing trying to identify where you can contribute and where you will fit in. You probably already have a group of friends, but perhaps they are too busy with their own affairs or your interests have changed and you are looking for something new. My suggestion is to follow your immediate curiosity, check out a group website and contact them for an initial discussion.

Most groups will welcome you with open arms because all groups want new members to contribute their energy, ideas and time. Go along for a few meetings before deciding whether you actually want to join, even if that may be a little scary at first. You probably want to see if you have ideas in common with the group, whether you like their vision and if you feel comfortable with the other members.

I certainly recommend that everyone should stretch themselves a little in their early retirement (or even pre-retirement) to make some new friends through meaningful activities. I include my own small case study as a classic example:

Case Study

In the early years of my legal practice, at times I felt overwhelmed by lawyers, clients and legal issues. So when I saw an advertisement in the local paper for a new club that was starting up for business and professional women, I was immediately interested. I knew I had to have more balance in my life by meeting other women and being able to talk about something besides my work.

I joined and met a group of dynamic women running their own businesses. Over the years, we organised speakers each month for our regular dinners. One evening, the branch manager of a local community bank attended and announced that their board was looking for women directors. That idea had never previously occurred to me but it sounded interesting, so I met the chairman and joined as a volunteer director.

Some years later, I am still a director on the board and it has been a challenging learning experience. I have met new people, am refreshing my legal skills and knowledge, am involved in running a business, but also am able to influence grants to community groups which is personally satisfying.

Moral of the story: networks can lead you to new opportunities for learning and growth, far beyond your expectations.

General interest clubs

I would describe most clubs for older people as being community minded, service-focused, and open to both men and women. Most such clubs maintain an active social agenda but also are involved in projects to raise funds for disadvantaged groups, for example, children's cancer research or providing equipment for children with diabetes.

To name a few:

Australian Rotary – You are likely to have seen their volunteers of all ages making the best sausage sandwiches at every fete you visit, but every club has its own local or international project which invites the practical assistance of their members. They usually meet every week.

Lions Australia Clubs – Similar to Rotary, have younger members too and meet monthly.

Probus Clubs – Describe themselves as offering friendship, fellowship and fun in retirement. They offer speakers and social activities for retired and semi-retired people.

VIEW Clubs – VIEW stands for the Voice, Interests and Education of Women. VIEW is a women's national volunteer organisation that meets regularly and aims to help disadvantaged Australian children.

RSL Clubs – Most of us will be familiar with RSL (Returned Services League) Clubs which provide a range of facilities for all ages, as well as being eating and gaming venues. These clubs originally formed to support returning WW2 veterans. Veterans will know the RSL as an organisation available as a source of support and networking.

CWA (Country Women's Association) – Formed in 1922 to support country women, the CWA stands as one of the largest women's associations in Australia, with a focus on lobbying and advancing women in regional areas.

Interest-specific groups

Being lonely whilst surrounded by thousands of people is not an isolated experience in any large city. When everyone is busy with work and family, it can be difficult to develop your own friends who share your interests and attitudes. If you have specific interests such as the opera or netball, being involved in those activities will bring you into contact with similarly interested people.

If you don't care for trivia nights in the pub, the internet can be a good source for finding new social groups. For example, the website *Meetup* offers a huge range of interest-specific meetings, including regular age-specific (over-50s) events. Other listing directories such as *events4singles* advertise a range of clubs such as the Grads Social Club, the New Pioneers Social Club and the After Work Social Club.

Find out more here:

www.meetup.com/en-AU/cities/au

www.events4singles.com/social_clubs_syd.htm

Other more informal interest-based groups such as the LOVE (Living Older Visibly and Engaged) Project is an umbrella organisation for LGBTQIA+ people to join social and sporting clubs.

Online and out there

Being digitally literate is now one of the most important skills anybody can have. It is important for many reasons – contacting friends, banking, staying current, informing yourself and contacting government entities that increasingly do much of their business online.

Staying connected online

Despite computers being part of most workplaces for at least the last 30 years, around 700,000 older Australians have never used the internet. Reasons given include the cost of being online, not having a computer and being "not interested" in having access.

Nevertheless Australians have been leading adopters of smartphones with 88% of the population now owning one, along with tablets and smartwatches.[8] While older people have been driving that growth, they still do not use their phones in the same way as younger users who remain the biggest users of data downloads for video and TV online streaming.

A 2016 study by ACMA (the Australian Communications & Media Authority) looked at how and when over-65 year olds accessed their digital media. Around 79% of older Australians have accessed the internet even though they are less frequent users (both in daily use and in number of hours per day) than the general population.[9] The most frequently used social media sites were:

- **Facebook**: 88%. A global network of around 1.7 billion users which can be used for connecting with friends, exploring special interests or sharing videos.
- **Google**: 16%. The most-used world-wide search engine that encourages the use of its Play Store, email and marketed products.
- **LinkedIn**: 12%. A business and professional website that enables you to connect with others to develop your professional network and increase job opportunities.
- **Pinterest**: 8%. A visual discovery engine based on finding and sharing visual images of products.

- **Twitter**: 4%. A social media network based on sharing opinions of people/personalities that you "follow". It can be a very immediate news source as events happen.

- **Instagram**: 2%. Mostly used as a means of sharing phone photos between friends, but has developed a strong marketing presence mainly amongst younger users.

In general terms[10] older users use the internet for similar activities as younger users, namely, sending emails, doing banking transactions, paying bills and buying or selling items. Unlike younger users, older users will be less likely to use the internet as an entertainment source. They retain a strong preference for traditional media such as free-to-air TV, listening to the radio and reading the newspaper. When accessing health or government information, younger users will more likely access the internet. Only 15% of older users obtain their health information online, despite the fact that most government departments focus on conveying their message online rather than in print media.

Adventure before dementia

If there is one thing that characterises the moderately financial retiree, it is the desire to travel in the early post-work stage of life. For many of us, the most significant indicator of freedom from our working life is that we can choose to travel when and where we wish. We are all too aware of not wasting this short period when we have the money, the time and our health to do what we have always wanted to do – hence the title for this section.

Retirees are keen to fulfil their "bucket list" – that list of places they must visit before they die. It's a hackneyed expression you will frequently hear in the travel space. Whether we want to go to Patagonia or to travel around the country for three months in a caravan, there is a sense of reckless abandon. We must have this worthwhile experience before we are too old!

Of course, as inveterate travellers at any age, Australians will likely go overseas many times, as well as travel around the country until forced by failing endurance to stay at home. "Baby boomers" have been called one of "the greatest marketing movements that we have ever seen in this country [the USA]".[11] The Australian experience is no different. Baby boomers comprise one of the largest cohorts in our population and can be characterised as one of the best educated, most affluent, healthiest and least conforming groups, having lived through the 1970s era. They are also adventurous and seek memorable and innovative experiences when they travel.

According to the Australian Bureau of Statistics, overseas travellers in the 65-74 age group have increased by 80% over the past five years[12]. These baby boomers choose to travel to more exotic locations in greater numbers, perhaps carrying on the backpacking tradition from their younger days. However their desire for greater convenience and comfort has led to the rise of more escorted tours and cruises.

In addition, you can find an increasing range of tours to meet specialised markets, such as cycling, embroidery or cooking tours. Another trend has been the development of operators who specialise in volunteer tourism – arranging travel to countries to enable travellers to assist in orphanages or wildlife reserves for three months at a time, for example.

Before you travel

Even travelling with a tour group requires some preparation. Here are some suggestions, particularly if you are a woman travelling solo:

1. **Read the travel warnings** and advice on smartraveller. gov.au for countries you will be visiting. Every country is different, but women can be quite vulnerable if they arrive without a companion. Planning ahead can reduce any risky situations. Registering with **Smartraveller** is a good idea if you are going to a more isolated region.

2. **Download an application like Google Translate** on your phone before leaving home so that you can read the signs in the country where you are travelling.

3. **Make sure you have the right travel insurance** for medical treatment and personal items. Compare what different insurers actually cover. Some will cover the loss of cash or baggage, or costs when missing flights, and others will

not. The difference in the premium will be insignificant compared to any cost you may incur if you have to pay the loss yourself. Make sure your insurance is valid if you are going into a region which has a travel warning.

4. **Health** – If you are going to India, Africa or South America, make sure you are appropriately vaccinated some weeks before your departure date. Sometimes several injections are required and sometimes an injection can make you feel quite ill, so you need to recover before leaving. Take enough medication for the whole time you will be away so that you stay well particularly if you are going into a malaria zone. If you are travelling in summer, take Australian insect repellent with a high DEET rating designed for tropical conditions. Sunscreen is always recommended.

5. **Take your own handbag 'travelling kit'.** Mine includes a hand sanitiser, tea tree oil, a small pack of tissues and a good quality hand moisturiser which can double as a face moisturiser.

6. **Make sure your passport is current** with at least six months left. Check if you need a visa to enter the country and any restrictions on the length of stay. Always have a photocopy of your visa and passport in case either get lost or stolen Write your passport number somewhere convenient or take a photo of your passport and email to yourself, just in case. Have a couple of spare passport photos if you need to get a permit or licence while there.

7. **Organise your mobile phone** arrangements before you leave Australia. Most of the big telcos have special overseas rates and you should call to notify them when you will be overseas. Alternatively, there are companies that have overseas sim cards that you can use at lower rates. If you take your own phone, be sure to switch off data roaming on your phone settings so you won't be charged astronomical rates for data downloads. If you are overseas and want to make calls or send texts, use a free app like WhatsApp, or access emails using the free wi-fi available in your hotel or public locations.

8. **Be aware** that some countries like China will block your access to the internet and familiar applications like Google.

9. **Money** – It may seem trivial but you should familiarise yourself with the currency of the country/ies you are going to and the exchange rate. Personally I like to take some notes with me to pay for taxis and tips, but it isn't always possible. These days most people take a debit card from one of the big banks with them which can be used in most overseas ATMs.

10. Make sure you **advise your bank** before you leave that you are going overseas so they do not call you about suspected fraudulent use. Be aware that not all bank cards can be used overseas. My preference is for a reloadable travel debit card that has lower exchange fees on transactions but I also take a credit card as well, for those more expensive purchases.

11. Because European countries (including the UK) are relatively expensive compared to the Australian dollar, I usually **calculate double** the daily spending allowance compared to Asian or Indian sub-continent countries.

12. **Schedule all your regular payments** to be paid online while you are away, for example, the rates, mobile and landline phone bills, so there are no nasty surprises when you return.

13. **Your itinerary** – Having travelled both on organised tours and independently, I have found that preparing an itinerary is an invaluable aid to having a stress-less holiday. Since printed tickets no longer exist, I always print out a copy of the ticket/booking itself to take with me. I then draw up an itinerary so that on one page I can see the date, flight number, departure/arrival time, terminal number and the hotel address, etc. By working out my travel in advance, it avoids that unexpected realisation that I have lost or gained a day somewhere when crossing time zones, or that I am going to be arriving at midnight rather than midday, as I had thought.

14. Of course, **using the services of a travel agent** makes your travel so much simpler! Give a copy of your itinerary to a family member so they know where you are supposed to be on any given day.

15. **Suitcases** – It may be obvious, but I am including this comment because I still see friends and relatives trying to squeeze the kitchen sink into their suitcase. Leave some space in your case for additional purchases. Even where you have a larger luggage allowance, take a suitcase that you can lift by yourself up and down the stairs. Damsels in distress cannot always rely on finding a prince charming to carry their gear.

My preference is for a brightly coloured, lightweight spin suitcase with an obvious name tag so that I can find it on the luggage carousel. I also take either a big tote bag or a not-precious shoulder bag that can withstand spilled water and other substances. Without naming brands, there are some functional, woven nylon bags that have varied sizes and shapes that I prefer.

16. **Don't bring back items made of wood**, shell, animal skin or plant material, unless you are prepared to have them confiscated at customs no matter how authentic they may be. Our quarantine restrictions are tough compared to most other countries.

17. **Arrange your affairs at home** – We do not know our future. Have an up-to-date Will and if you are going to be away for a longer time, give a trusted family member a Power of Attorney to take care of your bills and personal matters.

18. **Plan ahead** – Have your accommodation organised for the first few days at least. These days, short term letting and even hotels are likely to be cheaper if you book in advance. Often you can get cheaper tourist train and bus passes by buying in advance. Book your travel early if you are visiting in peak tourist times. Read about the history of the countries you will be visiting before you get on the plane to really understand their culture and people. Develop some depth of knowledge in one area of interest, for example, art, theatre or food, to be more than a tourist. Bring appropriate, modest clothes to avoid being harassed on the street or refused entry when visiting religious buildings.

Solo travel that works for you

It would be easy to write a whole book about travel options. If you are part of a couple, you have a world of choice when you do your own research. However not everyone travels as part of a couple, so this is a singles-oriented section. Solo travellers get a pretty poor deal when travelling. They usually have to pay the single supplement which is about the same as for a couple, or share with a stranger which can be rather intrusive. Of course you can organise your own travel, but I have some alternate suggestions as well.

There are tour companies who will charge you the single supplement and there other companies who will offer you a share room with another woman when you travel so that you only pay the couple rate. In my experience, Australian companies tend to offer the shared room option, while European companies value your privacy and do not offer sharing a room with a stranger.[14]

Group travel

No doubt some readers would never want to be part of a tour group, but on the whole, my experience has been fairly positive. There are some distinct advantages for the group traveller:

- You don't have to research the hotels or their locations, and the bulk pricing of a tour will usually include reasonable standard hotels for less than an individual would pay.
- You have comfortable, more efficient transport between attractions, enabling you to see major attractions in a relatively short time rather than trying to meet schedules for public transport.
- Your guide will generally give you informed local knowledge and more in-depth commentary than your guidebook.
- As part of a group, you feel relatively safe and you are likely to meet people with similar interests.

To meet the changing market however, some tour companies now offer solo traveller tours, with some companies catering exclusively for independent female travellers. Most of these tour companies cater for small groups and specialise in cycling/adventure/walking tours, cruises or mixed cruise/land tours. For example:

- Adventurous Women (wider age group) (www. adventurouswomen.com.au)
- Travelling Divas (boutique travel) (www.travellingdivas. com)
- Women's Own Adventure (womensownadventure.com.au)
- Encounter Travel (over-50 and age specific solo travellers) (www.encountertravel.com.au/about-us/singles-holidays-over-50s)
- G Adventures (a younger crowd) (www.gadventures.com. au/about-us/why-travel-with-gadventures/solo-travel)
- The Individual Traveller (45+ age group) (individualtraveller.com.au)
- The 50+ Travel Club (50plustravelclub.com.au)
- Explore! Singles over 50 (www.exploreworldwide.com.au/experiences/holidays-for-solo-travellers/solo-holidays-over-50)

Cruises

From 2003 to 2016, the Australian cruise industry doubled its passenger numbers, numbers of ports visited and numbers of visiting ships, with passenger expenditure rising 12-fold.[15] The highly competitive cruise industry has built 100 new ships since 2000, with ever-more luxurious on-board facilities at affordable prices. But again for singles – the single supplement can be a significant additional cost, so enterprising cruise lines have developed two innovations – singles' cruises and specialty cruises. It will pay for you to shop around to get a good deal as a solo traveller. Cruising specialists can offer you choices of cruises that are age specific, or open-age with special deals for solo travellers.

As a mode of travelling, cruising has well known benefits: not having to constantly pack and unpack; better for travellers with health or mobility issues; plus a consistent level of good quality accommodation and food on-board. Reported disadvantages include the possibility that passengers can experience gastric infections, and occasionally some groups of passengers can be quite disruptive.

Types of cruises on offer include:

- Adventure cruises – visit Antarctica, cruise around Thai and Indonesian islands, do a polar expedition and visit Spitsbergen or cruise around Spain, Portugal and Morocco.
- River cruises – in Europe, Russia, South America or Asia.
- Land and cruise packages – which can include locations like the Caribbean, around Japan or a smaller trip around New Zealand.
- Theme cruises – for example, needlework/ quilting/ patchwork cruise and tour; wellness and fitness cruise; Cruise 'n Groove cruise (Elvis Presley theme); polar photography; Melbourne Cup cruises.
- Single-specific cruises can also offer themed options at a reasonable price.

Some alternative options

Voluntourism: volunteering holidays used to mean a relatively long-term commitment by volunteers with very specific skills in a developing country. These days you can spend just two weeks looking after orphan animals in any number of countries and you have made a 'meaningful and sustainable contribution'. Of course, there are longer and more demanding roles available aimed at younger age groups but frankly, the contribution seems to benefit the volunteer more than the disadvantaged community.

However, if you are interested in a longer term role in a project it is still worth following up with such organisations as Global Volunteer Network and Australian Volunteers Abroad. Another option is to volunteer with WWOOF – World Wide Opportunities on Organic Farms. In Australia (and overseas as well) there are host farms where you can work 4-6 hours and you are fed and housed in return.

House exchange: this scheme is ideal if you are intending to go overseas for a longer period of time. There are a number of companies such as HomeExchange, House Swap Holidays and Love Home Swap, which have websites that allow you to directly organise a home swap in another country for an agreed period. Most reports suggest that these can work very well, especially in cities like New York where short-term accommodation is very expensive.

Retreats: It would be very remiss not to mention the growth of the retreat as a form of spiritual or health holiday. Defined as a 'withdrawal from the world', many religions emphasise the retreat as a means of spiritual reflection. The modern retreat usually includes a spiritual aspect, but not always with mainstream religious thought. Frequently the retreat offers an equal emphasis on providing healthy food and luxury accommodation. Certainly austerity does not figure highly.

Most "wellness" retreats offer a combination of meditation and yoga practice, and some services like massage and facials, in a natural and peaceful environment. Nurturing the body and mind is the key objective of these retreats, either locally or abroad. Other retreats run weekend getaways/workshops with a specific focus, such as dealing with anxiety or learning Vipassana meditation (which can be of great benefit to a weary soul and is free of charge).

Learning in the Third Age

"The more you know, the less you need."
Australian Aboriginal saying

This section reflects my view that learning should be as integral to a person's life as their spiritual beliefs. Lifelong learning improves an individual's knowledge of the world and their personal capacity for satisfaction in their life's activities. I describe lifelong learning as the ongoing learning that we undertake voluntarily. Governments have adopted the concept into policy in many countries, for example the European Commission[16] and the UK. The European Commission emphasises lifelong learning as essential for social inclusion, active citizenship and personal development.

LEARNING AS A LIFE-ENHANCING PERSPECTIVE

In a UK study, Learning in Later Life: Motivation and Impact, researchers found some learners were more motivated to learn after giving up work, although participation in learning generally declined after retirement. Their findings included:

- Eighty per cent of learners reported a positive impact of learning on at least one of the following areas: their enjoyment of life; their self-confidence; how they felt about themselves; satisfaction with other areas of life; and their ability to cope.

- Forty-two per cent reported an improvement in their ability to stand up and be heard and/or their willingness to take responsibility.

- Twenty-eight per cent reported an increased involvement in social, community and/or voluntary activities as a result of learning.

- Disability or poor health can block participation in learning. However, higher proportions of learners with a disability or health problem reported various positive benefits of learning, compared to those in good health.

- The most important reasons for learning were intellectual, for example wanting to keep the brain active, enjoying the challenge of learning new things and wanting to learn about things in which they were interested. These learners were greatly influenced by teachers from their early life and family members who imparted a love of learning, a theme which continued throughout their retirement.

- The most common reasons for not learning were a lack of time and a lack of interest in

> learning. A quarter said they had done enough learning in their life while 22 per cent felt too old to learn. Family responsibilities were important to non-learners who reported they were more likely to spend time with grandchildren.

As a concept, lifelong learning includes both formal and informal means of learning and the development of flexible structures that meet learners' needs. In Australia, Adult Learning Australia nominated 2018 as the Year of Lifelong Learning, and called on the Australian government to adopt "a formal policy on lifelong learning as an essential feature of a healthy, active democracy".[17]

If we reflect on changes to our working lives over at least the past 20 years, virtually every profession insists that we engage in continuous learning every year to ensure that we stay current in our jobs. Likewise, in the work environment we must adopt and become proficient with new technology and programs as part of our ordinary duties (obviously, this varies according to our work).

Yet when we retire, many people seem to have an attitude that we don't have to learn any more – daytime TV will fill the gaps in our ongoing knowledge, or we can always call the kids to figure out how to use our mobile phones…

Lifelong learning does not mean we have to study to get a qualification for a job. We can now learn things that really interest us, whether theoretical or practical, or both. Opportunities for adult learning can come in the shape of day courses, weekend courses or more formal studies.

The UK study[18] found that women, people with a disability and people over 60 were less likely to be involved in any form of learning than the general population. Significantly, this study and others referred to the lack of technological acceptance and use amongst older learners.

Certainly older adults appeared to have more difficulty in becoming proficient users of computers, which may also reflect on the techniques used to teach the subject. This does affect older people (and society in general) when governments, businesses and others distribute their important information via the internet, social media, computers and email. The very people for whom the information is intended may in fact, not be able to access it. In particular, many courses rely on an ability to research and respond online so consequently such learning will be avoided by the less technologically capable.

There is some evidence that older learners (over 60 years) may learn differently due to a gradual slowing down in their learning capacity and other physical changes However, there is also no doubt that with continued learning, older learners can make a reflective and considered contribution to the growth of knowledge in an area.[19]

European Commission policy on learning stresses the intergenerational nature of the exchange of information; that older people can provide traditional knowledge, skills and competencies to younger people who can provide insight into contemporary social issues to older learners. In this exchange, both groups of learners can benefit from the other.

Being a life-long learner

1. **Decide what your real interests are**: Think about topics you never had time to learn about when you were working – now you can follow them up with more depth.

2. **What is your learning style**? Are you a hands-on person, or do you prefer lectures? You might prefer learning as part of an informal group or would rather just go online. Maybe just a one-day class will be enough to get you interested before you become more serious about that subject.

3. **Time**: How much time are you willing to put into your learning? You should be able to schedule regular time to attend classes and do assignments if necessary.

4. **Do your research**: Find the right teaching environment for you in a suitable location, and work out the costs of the course and the materials.

5. **Get involved with others** who are also interested in your interests, through Meetup groups for example, or setting up a learning circle.

6. **Perhaps you have skills you can share**: Join up with a voluntary organisation or a community college that has a course that you can teach. You could even design your own course.

7. **Understand what kind of training you may need**: how serious are you about your interests? Do you just want to do your own projects or do you want to enter local, national or international competitions?

Learning options

Adult learners have two options for their ongoing learning:

- Formal – Structured learning with a curriculum in an educational or training institute;
- Non-formal – Learning without formal credentials provided by educational institutions or groups, sometimes related to on-the-job training.

Universities, TAFE Colleges and community colleges offer formal courses, while educational associations such as the WEA (Workers Education Association) provide informal, interest-based courses. The lines between the two types of courses are more blurred these days as many universities offer short courses as part of their continuing education program. Many short courses use the same lecturers as their mainstream courses as well as providing introductory courses for those wanting to enter formal courses. In addition, many private institutes offer combinations of face-to-face and online courses aimed at obtaining formal qualifications.

Warning: online study can be difficult because you have to undertake your whole study program by yourself. Unlike traditional university studies where you attend lectures and tutorials with other students, you basically do the entire degree by yourself all the way through. Yes, there are online discussion forums and these can be useful. However they do not replace direct personal contact between students. You could sign up with a friend to make it easier.

Online study also requires reasonable computing skills, so be prepared to expand your abilities where needed. Course organisers usually provide help to assist students with technical issues.

The Australian Qualifications Framework (AQF) sets out the educational aims that encompass universities, colleges, vocational education, training and schools in Australia, with the intention that it is possible to achieve any of the 10 levels of post-school education between types of institutions.

Your study in a Commonwealth-supported place (at a university) can be funded through the HECS-HELP system, effectively as a loan to you for undertaking the course. The loan becomes a repayable debt when you have an income of at least $55,874. The cost of undertaking TAFE and community college courses can be supplemented by taking up a VET Student Loan.

For those willing to study online, you will find a huge variety of great options online, both in Australia and overseas – including many free of charge. Often promoted under the banner of a "Massive Online Course" or MOOC, many have solid university connections, but not all offer degrees. For more, start with:

www.gooduniversitiesguide.com.au/study-information/free-online-courses-moocs

University of the Third Age (U3A)

U3A offers an alternative option for learners over 50 years through a yearly membership of $35. It enables learners to attend any of their 100 courses with no exams or homework. U3A has seven regions across metropolitan Sydney. Other states and regions may have similar opportunities. The wide range of courses includes topics such as cake decorating, astronomy, painting, history, law and computing.

CASE STUDY

Theresa had worked in hotels all her life and at 65 decided to retire. In her youth, after completing the Leaving Certificate, she had started a university degree. However as she was an orphan and had no financial support, she dropped out after a year. It was the greatest regret of Theresa's life that she did not finish university. After retirement, she decided to take an adult education class in Latin through a university.

The teacher of the class encouraged her to enrol in a degree, which she did. When Theresa successfully finished her undergraduate studies, she was offered a job as a teacher of the same adult education class that launched her studies. She then studied for a Masters in Ancient History, just for the fun of it. Her second retirement came 20 years later when, at the age of 85, she decided to stop teaching.

Teaching truly gave Theresa a second lease of life. She became happier and more fulfilled than she had ever been.

Lifelong learners can also be teachers

Of course, one of the best ways to continue learning is to become a teacher. Many community colleges, educational groups and even TAFE colleges require the services of experienced and knowledgeable teachers. Should you go down this path, you will find that your depth of subject knowledge and your mentoring skills will grow as you interact with the next generation.

10

Accessing support services

*"When men reach their sixties and retire, they go to pieces.
Women go right on cooking."*

Gail Sheehy, author *Passages*

This chapter is focused on providing information and links about the financial benefits and practical services available through government agencies to assist you to meet later-life needs.

Three-quarters of all people over 65 years receive some government support, either through Centrelink or the Department of Veterans Affairs. More than half of the population over 65 relies on government assistance as their sole means of financial support. In addition older people are the highest receivers of government-assisted domestic, home and garden assistance as well as being the most frequent users of hospital, pharmaceutical and allied health services.

Some facts and figures about the older population

Like most first world countries, the proportion of Australia's older residents continues to grow compared to the whole population as advances in living standards and health care enable them to live longer and better. While politicians complain about this expanding drain on economic resources, there is no doubt that the aged care sector contributes strongly to the economy as an employer. Not only that, retirees contribute as unpaid and largely unrecognised volunteer labour force for the greater part of their lifespan following retirement.[1]

The extent of an increasing older population can be seen in these broad demographic changes. In 1901, only 4% of the population was aged over 65 years. In 2014, 15% of the population was aged over 65 years, with this figure expected to rise to 25% by 2101. Currently about 3.46 million Australians are over 65 years.[2]

As might be expected, the number of recipients of home assistance has increased rapidly as well. Over the last decade, there has been a 31% increase (around 249,000) in people receiving residential care, home care or transition care services in Australia[3].

Government funded aged care services into the home have increased substantially with women most likely to be the recipients. As women live longer, their need for higher levels of care increases as they age. Women also outnumber men as residents of aged care facilities. Of all people over 85 years, 63% women and 43% men are likely to live in permanent residential aged care.

Reflecting their shorter life expectancy, Aboriginal and Torres Strait Islanders receive more services provided to their home and will likely enter residential care at a younger age than the general population.

What is the cost to the Australian economy? Aligned with the ageing population, the cost of providing aged care is likely to double in real terms per person over the next 40 years.[4] Commonwealth spending is steadily increasing for aged care, home support, home care and residential care.

At the same time, *consumer* spending on aged care (not including accommodation deposits) represents nearly a quarter of federal funding. By 2020 federal funding is expected to reach $20.8 billion per annum.

In turn, the aged care sector generates revenue of about $21.5 billion per year, contributing approximately 1% to the gross domestic product. Continuing consumer demand for residential and home care packages has led to a high level of growth with an expected greater need for chronic health services.

Government policy emphasises that consumers with financial capacity must make substantial contributions for residential aged-care expenses to reduce government expenditure. Daily care fees, the means-tested fee and the accommodation fee based on an individual's assets and income can cost over $50,000 per year for an average resident. That fee derives from a resident's pension and their own financial assets – substantially funded (for most people) from the sale of the family home.

No wonder that most people find themselves confused when they discover the complexities of entering residential aged care. In a CoreData survey in October 2015, respondents (aged 45+) reported that they had experience dealing with aged care issues for a family member or that they expected to within 5 years. Of those who had experience, over 50% found it difficult to find suitable care and manage the associated financial and emotional issues.

In reality, 64% of all retirees will need the age pension to supplement their superannuation savings.[5] Other important non-government sources of retirement funds include cash savings (30%), selling your home "downsizing" (18%) and selling an investment property (16%). All these assets and possible income sources become significant when you decide to apply for an age pension or any other Centrelink benefit.

Applying for the age pension

As part of the Australian Department of Human Services, Centrelink delivers social security payments such as aged pensions, disability and carers pensions, and aged care packages through its **My Aged Care** portal. The Centrelink website offers online application forms and information to obtain the age pension and other social security benefits. The **My Aged Care** website is useful in locating both government and non-government providers of social and health supports.

Find out more:

- **Centrelink:**
  www.humanservices.gov.au/individuals/subjects/
  payments-older-australians
- **My Aged Care:**
  www.myagedcare.gov.au/service-finders

In this complex area, the options obviously vary according to your individual situation. I have only outlined the key points below to consider when applying for a pension[6]. To find out more, it might be useful for you to attend one of Centrelink's Financial Information Service (FIS) seminars, which you can book by calling 132 300.

The age pension provides income and concessions for older people, provided you meet the income and assets test. Assistance is also available in terms of rental assistance, energy assistance, health concession cards and hearing services programs.

Many of the conditions that apply in claiming the age pension also apply to other pensions, namely:

- Age Pension
- Wife Pension (not available since 1995 to new retirees)
- Bereavement Allowance
- Carer Payment
- Disability Support Pension
- Widow B Pension

To be eligible to receive the age pension, you must have:

- Reached age pension age (this is gradually being increased);
- Be an Australian resident, normally for at least 10 years, and
- Be under the income and assets test limits.

Age pension eligibility

Your birthdate	Eligibility for age pension
1 July 1952 to 31 December 1953	65 years and 6 months
1 January 1954 to 30 June 1955	66 years
1 July 1955 to 31 December 1956	66 years and 6 months
From 1 January 1957	67 years

Residency requirements

Having reached the age for pension eligibility, you must have been an Australian resident for at least 10 years, with no break in residency for at least 5 years. There are some exceptions to this rule if you are transferring from another allowance.

This may include a widow's pension or a partner's allowance, if you are a refugee, or if you have lived and worked in another country which has a social security agreement with Australia (such as Canada, Cyprus or India).

Your pension rate may change if you travel outside Australia. If you remain overseas for less than 12 months, there will be no change. However if you are overseas longer than 5 years you may have to reapply for Medicare and other benefits with proof of residency when you return.

You are obliged to advise Centrelink when you travel overseas. If you have been a resident for a shorter period, there may be a proportionate reduction in your rate of payment.

If you leave Australia to live permanently in another country, your pension rate is likely to be reduced. This may also be influenced by any existing social security agreement with your new destination.[6]

Income test limits

Income is calculated to include monies received from any sources such as superannuation, shares, loans, gifts and term deposits. Centrelink applies a "deeming" rate to all income, irrespective of actual interest received.

The deeming rate is interest which the government assumes you will earn on your investments. By setting a fixed rate for all earnings, the government does not have to accept any possible understatement of earnings. The deeming rate is varied by the responsible Minister and does not necessarily reflect the cash rate set by the Reserve Bank which determines the actual interest paid by financial institutions on deposits.

Where the deeming rate is set artificially high, it reduces the individual's pension entitlement because it assumes that recipients are earning more from their investments than is the reality.

Pension limits – as at 20 March 2019[7]

Single person income – You can earn up to $172 per fortnight and retain a full pension. Income earned above that amount of the pension reduces by 50 cents in every dollar. The pension cuts off when you earn $2,004.60 per fortnight or more.

Couple living together income – Your combined income can be up to $304 per fortnight and retain a full pension. Income earned above that amount of the pension reduces by 50 cents of every dollar. The pension cuts off above a combined income of $3,066.80 per fortnight.

Work bonus – If you have reached pension age but are still working, you may qualify for a part, or full age pension depending on your income. Under the Work Bonus scheme, the first $250 of fortnightly income derived from employment is exempted under the income test. If your work is casual, you can accumulate any unused Work Bonus up to $6500 in those weeks when your income is lower than $250 per fortnight.

Assets test limits

Calculation of your pension entitlement involves a combination of your assets and your income. Many types of assets are included:

- Real estate (solely or jointly owned) including granny flats,
- Life interest in property,
- Retirement village contribution,
- Financial investments,
- Superannuation investments,
- Business interests,
- Household contents, and
- Cyber currency.

The asset test includes assets owned within a private company or private trust, a testamentary trust over which you can exert control or from which you receive income.

Your family home is exempt from being included in the assets test, but special rules apply to primary producers and rural home owners where a rural property may be exempted even where it is still operating. If you are a non-homeowner, your asset levels are higher than for a homeowner.

Centrelink may "deem" assets which are gifted or transferred for less than market value to family members. This could be cash, a car any other kind of asset. When Centrelink applies the "deeming" principle to a gift, it means they treat the asset as if it was still yours. Either singly or as part of a couple, you are permitted to gift $10,000 in one year, or $30,000 within a five year period. Centrelink requires you to make a compulsory disclosure when you make a gift.

Retirement village payments

If you retain your family home while living in a retirement village, Centrelink counts the home as one of your assets unless your partner/dependant is still living there. In addition, any rent you receive counts towards your income. In general terms however, any payment of an accommodation bond counts as if you have become a homeowner, and then that amount is not counted as an asset. It is possible to receive rent assistance if you have paid less than $203,000 to enter a retirement village or if you are living in a caravan park or mobile home park.

Full pension threshold

If your assets are below these limits, you will be eligible for a full pension under the 2018 assets test. The limits are adjusted every year.

Full pension	Current (2019) asset limits
Non-homeowner (single)	$473,750
Non-homeowner (couple)	$605,000
Homeowner (single)	$263,250
Homeowner (couple)	$394,500
Homeowner (couple, 1 partner eligible) combined	$394,500
Non-homeowner (couple, 1 partner eligible) combined	$605,000

Part-pension thresholds

If you have assets above these limits, a part-pension will no longer be payable.

Part pension	Current (2019) asset limits
Non-homeowner (single)	$782,500
Non-homeowner (couple)	$1,070,500
Homeowner (single)	$572,000
Homeowner (couple)	$860,000

Full age pension rate

From 2 March 2019, fortnightly pension payment rates that apply:

Amount payable	Single	Couple (each)	Couple (combined)	Couple (separated)
Maximum basic rate	$843.60	$635.90	$1,271.80	$843.60
Maximum pension Supplement	$68.50	$51.60	$103.20	$68.50
Energy supplement	$14.10	$10.60	$21.20	$14.10
Total	**$926.20**	**$698.10**	**$1396.20**	**$926.20**

Concession cards

In addition to receiving the age pension or other income support, you will also become eligible to receive various concession cards that will reduce the cost of buying medication or receiving medical services. They may also allow you to apply for concessional rates of public transport. Types of cards available:

Commonwealth Seniors Health Card – You may be eligible for this card if you have reached age pension eligibility, are an Australian resident, do not receive an age pension/DVA pension and receive a lower income than the current income test. The income test levels (2018) are $54,929 a year for singles; $87,884 a year for couples; and $109,858 a year for couples separated by illness, respite care or prison, and includes both adjusted taxable income and deemed amounts from income streams. This card does not have an assets test.

Benefits of this card includes: Reduced cost of pharmaceuticals, bulk-billed medical services, and a bigger refund for medical costs when you reach the Medicare Safety Net. In addition, depending on the state or territory in which you live, you may also receive reduced property and water rates; reduced electricity and gas bills; reduced public transport fares and reduced health care costs such as ambulance, dental and eye care.

Pensioner Concession Card – You may be eligible for this card if you receive an age pension, a carer's payment, a disability support pension or a bereavement allowance or still have partial capacity for work. You may also receive a non-pensioners concession card if you lost eligibility for the age pension (following changes to eligibility age requirements in October 2017). This card is valid for two years and entitles you to receive reductions in pharmaceutical and medical costs, hearing tests as well as discounts for property and water rates, and public transport costs depending where you live.

State/territory Seniors Card – The benefits available vary in each state. In NSW, for example, the Seniors Card offers discounted public transport intrastate which can also entitle you to Australia-wide discounted travel costs and discounted business services. In NSW anyone who is over 60 years, retired and not working over 20 hours per week is eligible for the Seniors Card. There is no income test eligibility requirement. NSW has also introduced a Senior Savers Card which offers discounted business services, but not reduced-cost transport services.

Pension supplement – A combined payment of pharmaceutical allowance, utilities allowance, GST supplement and telephone allowance. This amount is payable in addition to the age pension and other carer's allowances.

Pension Loan Scheme – This scheme is intended to financially assist homeowners of pensionable age. They may or may not receive the maximum rate of the pension by providing a loan at a (current) rate of 5.25% up to 150% of the maximum annual pension amount.

For example, a single age pensioner who receives the maximum pension of about $24,000 p.a. will be able to draw up to $12,000 each year as a loan. This loan becomes a debt due to the Commonwealth and is administered by the Department of Human Services and must be secured against the property owned by the pensioner. The interest accumulates against the property until it is repaid, which can be when the property is sold or from the borrower's estate when they die.

While this new proposal can assist borrowers to have a greater cash flow in their later years, it can also affect the remaining value of the property for beneficiaries. It is similar to the commercial reverse mortgage equity scheme which has had limited success.

Financial support in the event of a death

If you are responsible for organising a person's affairs following their death, your first task will be to obtain a death certificate from a doctor showing the cause of death before funeral preparations can begin. Where the deceased person has been receiving Centrelink benefits, you should use an Advice of Death form to notify Centrelink, who will share that information with Medicare. It is also advisable to contact any relevant insurance companies and superannuation funds to similarly advise them.

You may be eligible for short-term financial assistance as well as counselling support through Centrelink. Available payments include:

- **Bereavement Allowance** – A short term income support payment for recently widowed people to help them adjust after their partner has died.

- **Bereavement Payment** – Helps ease your adjustment to changed financial circumstances after the death of a person for whom you were caring, your partner or child.

- **Double Orphan Pension** – Provides help with the costs of caring for children who are orphans or who are unable to be cared for by their parents in certain circumstances.

- **Pension Bonus Bereavement Payment** – A payment to the surviving partner of a member. The application must be made within 12 months of the person's death and is only payable if the deceased was a member of the Pension Bonus Scheme who did not claim the bonus before their death.

- **Widow Allowance** – Enables women to have an adequate income if they have become widowed, divorced or separated later in life, were born before 1 July 1955 and have no recent workforce experience.

You may be eligible for bereavement payments if you and your partner were receiving the age pension, or you were receiving the carer payment/allowance. You should make further inquiries to see if you are eligible in other circumstances. It is also possible to receive advance lump sum payments in a crisis situation.

At this point, it is worth reminding you that you should also notify the deceased's superannuation fund if you are likely to be a beneficiary.

Accessing care at home

Government policy encourages people to continue living in their own home if they become ill or disabled, by providing financial and practical assistance to both the carer and the care recipient.

It has been estimated that there are 2.7 million carers in Australia caring for others who have a disability, long-term health conditions, mental illness, or are frail or aged. Research also shows that 80 per cent of carers may not be aware of the support available.[7]

If you are the carer, you can be eligible to receive a Carer's Payment[8] and a Carer's Allowance with these conditions:

- The person for whom you are caring must be either ill, have a disability, or be frail, aged and that the condition has existed for at least six months.
- You are both Australian residents and you must care for the person on a daily basis.
- The person receiving care must be eligible under the income and asset limits.

The person receiving care must have been assessed on the ADAT (Adult Disability Assessment Determination) or (DCLAD which relates to a child) tests as having high care needs. The ADAT questionnaires are used to determine how much assistance the care recipient requires to undertake daily living activities such as mobility, communication, hygiene, eating and management in both cognitive and behavioural areas.

The carer completes the first questionnaire and a treating health professional completes the second one. The combined scores will determine the level of care required. An assessment is valid for two years.

Types of carer payments

Carer payments: Income support if you are unable to work because you provide care for someone with a severe disability, medical condition, or who is frail and elderly. There is an income and asset test similar to receiving an age pension and the amount received is similar. The income test applies to your information, the carer recipient's information and any partner's information.

Carer Allowance: A fortnightly income supplement for carers providing additional daily care for someone with a disability or medical condition, or a frail older person, even if you work or study. There is no assets test, but a couple's combined income cannot exceed $250,000 p.a.

Carer Supplement: An annual lump sum to assist with the cost of caring for a person, payable if you receive a Carer Allowance or Carer Payment.

A carer may retain the Carer Payment but still undertake up to 25 hours a week away from caring to do paid work, volunteer work, study or training. Any additional income will likely reduce the Carer Payment. As a carer you may also travel overseas for up to 6 weeks and retain your payments either alone or with the person receiving care. You may also be eligible for a Pensioner Concession Card.

In addition to the Carer Payment, a carer may be eligible for a Carer Allowance which is an additional fortnightly payment where the care receiver has a condition that will last over 12 months. The Carer Allowance is not income or assets tested or taxable and can be paid in addition to any other support payments received. You can also apply for a Carer Supplement, which is an annual lump sum payment of $600 to assist with the costs of caring as well as rent assistance.

Carer payments are similar to age pension payments in amount, but there are extra conditions that must be met by the. Carer payments are not age-restricted and apply to anyone who cares for another person, including a child.

Therefore, income reviews and medical reviews are regularly conducted to ensure that the qualifying criteria are met. Income earned will affect the Carer Payment amount you are eligible to receive.

For example, if you are single and you earn more than $1,868.60 per fortnight, you will not be eligible for any payment. If you are part of a couple and your fortnightly income exceeds $2,860.00 you will not be eligible to receive a payment.

More detailed information is available from the Carer Gateway:

www.carergateway.gov.au/carers-payments-explained

In this situation, the person receiving care must also meet guidelines for payments. If they are under age pension age, they can be eligible for a disability support pension. After that age, they must meet the usual age pension requirements.

Some additional limited payments are available to assist persons requiring care, namely:

- The Continence Aids Payment Scheme helps people to buy continence aid products.
- The Essential Medical Equipment Payment assists with the additional costs of medical equipment requiring heating and cooling.
- The External Breast Prostheses Reimbursement Program helps with the cost of new or replacement external breast prostheses.
- People over 65 are not eligible for the National Disability Insurance Scheme at present.

Carer supports in the home

Caring for someone may occur in your own home, their home or in a residential care facility. It can be for an hour each day or for many hours each day and night. Caring can be rewarding but more often it is also emotionally challenging and physically draining over long periods of time.

There are some programs available to assist you to reduce your stress and to manage the level of care that is required. Being able to share the load with other family members or friends at times will greatly improve your own capacity to continue to care. You need to communicate your own needs and ask family or friends for assistance, even where they may be reluctant to become involved. Suggesting specific tasks for family and friends to assist, such as cooking meals in advance and freezing them, can reduce your load and allow them to contribute as well.

You can also contact *Gather My Crew* who may be able to provide practical support:

www.cancer.org.au/news/blog/support/introducing-gather-my-crew,-the-online-tool-to-help-those-in-a-health-crisis.html

Contacting agencies such as Carers NSW[8] on free call 1800 242 636 can assist you and put you in touch with support groups and information to manage your role better.

Respite care

Respite care can be both informal and formal. You can arrange to pay for a carer to come in-home for a few hours while you take a break. Some local areas have community-based respite care services, where the person receiving care can go to a community centre for day respite or even stay overnight in a cottage-style respite centre. The client will still need to have an assessment carried out by the Regional Assessment Service to determine their suitability under the Commonwealth Home Support Programme. But once approved, they will work with the client to find suitable services.

Most often, however, respite care occurs in a residential aged care facility where a person is able to stay for a period up to 63 days in any financial year. The person must have an ACAT (Aged Care Assessment Team) assessment to be eligible for respite care. The facility can only charge basic costs for respite care, namely a booking fee of not more than a full week's basic daily fee charges, or 25% of the charges for the whole stay, plus a basic daily fee. That fee is set at 85% of the single rate of the basic age pension, which currently is $51.21 per day. This figure is reviewed twice a year in March and September. The facility may not charge an accommodation bond or a means-tested fee.

Emergency respite care is also available by calling a Commonwealth Respite and Carelink Centre on 1800 052 222 during business hours and 1800 059 059 outside business hours.

Arranging an assessment

Other support services can assist a person remaining at home. An initial assessment will be required firstly to determine the level of care that is required. You can find information about the subsidised home care packages through the online website, **My Aged Care**: www. myagedcare.gov.au/home-start-here

However you need to take the first step by **calling 1800 200 422** to arrange for an initial assessment. The Helpline officer will designate your case as either requiring a basic assessment, or a comprehensive assessment in the case of more complicated health conditions.

The Commonwealth Home Support Programme (CSHP) enables you to receive services to help you stay at home. From July 2015, the CSHP consolidated the Commonwealth Home and Community Care (HACC) program and a number of other existing respite and care programs into one package. Consequently **My Aged Care** acts as a centralised point when a potential client calls requesting home assistance. The **My Aged Care** officer organises the initial assessment. Once the client is approved, the assessor assists the client to find a service provider who can provide the level and types of services required by the support plan.

Commonwealth Home Support Programmes (CSHP)

These are entry level forms of assistance to enable people to live independently and remain in their own home.

Eligibility: To receive a home care package you must experience difficulty doing everyday activities without help and need support to live independently. The minimum age limits are:

- 65 years or older (50 years and identify as Aboriginal or Torres Strait Islander), or
- 50 years or older (45 years and identify as Aboriginal or Torres Strait Islander) and be on a low income, homeless or at risk of homelessness.

Assessment: The assessor will visit the person's home and consider relevant information such as referrals from a doctor or other health professionals, the extent of support a person currently receives and their safety in the home. An income assessment also determines the client's capacity to contribute towards the cost of services.

An assessor from the Regional Assessment Service (RAS) handles basic assessments which can approve entry level support. Once approved, a support plan is drawn up for the client. The client can then contact a service provider in the area to determine whether they are able to provide the required service. Service providers are either not-for-profit or commercial organisations such as aged care facilities or multi-service organisations. The government directly funds the provision of either home care packages, transition care or residential aged care services. For a list of service providers in your area, access the Ageing and Aged Care website:

www.agedcare.health.gov.au/programs/home-care/researching-home-care-providers-considerations-and-checklist

An entry level Home Care Package is not means-tested and service providers will provide basic services such as meals, cleaning and transport assistance. Costs for services are not fixed but negotiated between the client and the provider. The consumer will pay a fixed hourly rate with the addition of a government subsidy which is taken out of the client's budget.

Anecdotally, reports have been that waiting times to receive anything other than an entry level package can be very long, from 6 to 18 months, so it is advisable to apply for a package well in advance of when it might be needed.

Home Support Packages are a combination of government subsidies and client contributions:

Service level	Support level	Govt subsidy
1	Basic care needs	$8,250
2	Low-level care needs	$15,000
3	Intermediate care needs	$33,000
4	High-level care needs	$50,250

Client contributions are calculated against an income assessment and comprise a daily care fee and income-tested care fee. Note that service providers are entitled to charge a management fee which can range between 30-50% for providing the service as well as an exit fee, which should be published on the provider's website.

From evidence given at the Aged Care Royal Commission, management fees charged by a service provider can be quite onerous and can greatly limit the funds available to the client to receive services. The service provider and the client will sign a Home Care Agreement before services can begin to be provided to the client, often with quite a long delay.

Services provided: Under a home support package, services provided include:

- Domestic assistance, such as household cleaning and laundry;
- Personal care;
- Home maintenance;
- Home modification including aids and equipment;
- Nursing care, allied health professional support;

- Transportation; and
- Meals and food services.

Short-term care services are available in the home or in residential care settings for situations such as restorative care (return to independence), transition from hospital or recovery from an accident or illness.

Home Care Packages

For more complex health situations, an Aged Care Assessment Team (ACAT) carries out a comprehensive assessment that will recommend either a high level Home Care Package, residential care in an aged care facility, residential respite care or short-term restorative or transition care.

If ACAT assesses a new applicant as needing a higher level of care, they can be approved to receive one of four levels of home care packages, as follows:

- **Level 1: Basic care**, approximately 2 hours care per week,
- **Level 2: Low-level care**, approximately 3-4 hours care per week,
- **Level 3: Intermediate care**, approximately 7-9 hours care per week, and
- **Level 4: High-level care** needs, approximately 10-13 hours care per week.

Once a person has been approved for a package, they will choose a service provider and sign a Home Care Agreement with them. This outlines the services to be provided and the fee that the client will be paying. Service providers are funded by government subsidies to provide specific services required by the client. However these packages are means-tested and the client must also contribute depending on their financial capacity and the level of care required, up to a maximum of $29.63 per day. You may be able to negotiate the type of services being provided by asking for an itemised costing, for example, for assistance with washing, ironing or personal care.

Typical subsidies for each level of care are set out below:

Home care package:	Per annum	Weekly rate
Level 1	$8,158	$156.88
Level 2	$14,837	$285.33
Level 3	$32,620	$627.31
Level 4	$49,593	$953.70

Theoretically, a client receiving a Level 2 package has $14,837 available to spend on the provision of services to her home. However, as the service is entitled to charge for the cost of a case manager, which might be as much as $4,000 p.a., the client actually has less than $11,000 p.a. available.

The agreement should be reviewed every 12 months and should include such matters as how to request a change of care worker, the notice period to terminate the agreement and outline their complaints process. A family member can attend such meetings to give the client further support.

In addition, end of life care packages are available if you are caring for someone at home and need extra assistance with nursing, personal or other care during that time.

Cost of CSHP services

You may be required to pay three types of fees for these home-delivered services:

- **A basic daily fee** – This is based on a rate of 17.5% of the single person pension. From 20 March 2019, the basic daily fee is $10.54 per day, or $147.56 per fortnight.

- **An income-tested care fee** – If you have a means-tested pension such as an age pension, a disability pension or service pension, you do not have to lodge a form. For any other retiree who is self-funded or who has a non-means tested pension (such as a Blind Pension) you should lodge an income test application form or pay the maximum fee.

- **Extra care fees** – For additional services.

There are daily contribution caps (limits) on the amount payable by a consumer (the care receiver) based on whether they are under or over the income threshold:	
Where the consumer's income does not exceed the income threshold	$15.12 per day
The annual cap where the consumer's income does not exceed the income threshold	$5,506.48 p.a.
Where the consumer's income exceeds the income threshold	$30.25 per day
The annual cap where the consumer's income exceeds the income threshold	$11,012.99 pa

Estimating an average total weekly cost for home services provided to a consumer can be difficult. Most service providers are reluctant to publicise their rates on their websites, and prefer to negotiate their fees on an individual basis.

Recently some seniors' advocacy groups[9] have been critical of the disclosure practices of service providers. Some providers have been less than transparent advising consumers of administration fees, case management fees, advisory fees and exit fees which can represent a significant portion of the funds allocated for their assistance.

Mobility aids and modifications

In general terms, the CSHP packages provide services rather than equipment. If you require specific equipment or modifications to better manage a disability, you should contact your state health department.

In NSW, EnableNSW[10], a division of NSW Health, provides equipment, services and travel assistance to people with chronic health conditions or disabilities. They assist patients with mobility, communication and self-care, and to access specialist medical treatment which is not available locally. Their available equipment includes prosthetic limbs, speech generating equipment and home respiratory equipment.

Community services

Every local council will offer some types of community services and activities, but the range can vary greatly depending on the council area and its financial viability. The main advantage of council or community-based services is that they are run by local staff and will reflect the local residents' range of interests.

Most local councils offer activities for seniors such as exercise and movement classes, music and art classes, and excursions and cultural activities. Some councils offer specific classes in areas such as computers, using the internet, creative writing and drama, which encourage ongoing learning. Most councils offer access to local community groups such as choirs and bush care groups. Your local library can be a community hub for such information.

Traditionally, local councils were the original providers of low-cost home support to seniors. They supported services such as Meals on Wheels, home library service and transport services. To some extent, this role has been overtaken by the Commonwealth Home Care Packages, but larger metropolitan councils still retain community development officers who will have links with police, hospitals and welfare agencies.

Maintaining quality standards

The Australian Aged Care Quality Agency (AACQA) sets standards of care in residential aged care facilities and home care packages. Currently, accreditation standards exist for residential care facilities and for home care service providers. As part of a general reform of aged care standards, the Australian Government is developing a draft framework to integrate all types of services, in conjunction with a public consultation.

The proposed single framework includes policy about: maintaining consumer dignity and choice; ongoing assessment and planning with consumers; personal care and clinical care; services and supports for daily living; and the organisation's service environment.

AACQA assessors regularly audit residential care providers and prepare publicly available reports. Providers must adhere to agreed quality standards and report any notifiable events (such as an alleged assault of a resident or an unexplained absence of a resident) to police and the department. Part of the accreditation process now includes unannounced audit visits (to more realistically determine adherence to standards of staffing and management), resident personal care, health, lifestyle, physical environment and safety.

Relationships and expectations between aged care providers and consumers are set out in the provider's Client Service Charter and include that the service provider will refund 95% of the accommodation deposit within 14 days of making the refund declaration.

Despite the accreditation process, incidents of elder abuse have been found to occur within residential facilities. Elder abuse can include many forms of violence to an older person such as psychological, social, physical, sexual, and financial as well as neglect. As part of the 5th National Elder Abuse Conference, a final report, *Abuse of Older People: A Community Response* is now available at: www.seniorsrightsservice. org.au/community-response

A report by the NSW Nurses and Midwives Association[11] surveyed their members working in aged care facilities. It commented that approximately half of residents suffered from dementia of varying types, with some of these residents exhibiting cognitive deficits and challenging behaviours. This report identified physical or verbal abuse occurring either resident to resident, resident to staff, and between visitors or relatives and residents.

Definitive figures for these incidents remain difficult to confirm. However, the report suggested that insufficient staff to resident ratios were at least partly to blame for these incidents arising. Ninety percent of their responders stated they had been abused by residents in the past three years, but most had not reported the incidents that had occurred.

The Royal Commission into Aged Care Quality and Safety has commenced its inquiry and will provide a final report and recommendations by 30 April 2020. Submissions and evidence have been received from all across Australia and can be expected to initiate far greater accountability by aged care providers.

Making a complaint

All complaints should initially be addressed to the manager of the residential services. If the complaint remains unresolved, the next step should be to contact the Complaints Scheme/Commissioner on 1800 550 552 or by writing to:

The Aged Care Complaints Scheme/Commissioner
Australian Department of Social Services
GPO Box 9820
In your capital city, state or territory, postcode
Website: www.agedcarecomplaints.gov.au

You could also consider contacting an advocacy services for older people, such as:

The Seniors Rights Service
Level 4, 418a Elizabeth Street
Surry Hills NSW 2010
Ph: (02) 9281 3600 or 1800 424 079 (toll free)
Website: www.seniorsrightsservice.org.au
Email: info@seniorsrightsservice.org.au

11

Putting your affairs in order

"Ask not – we cannot know – what end the gods have set for you, for me."

Horace, The Odes

Much of this chapter applies to a person of any age. Being prepared for the inevitable or the unexpected is not age-related, but is a sensible precaution for every adult. By taking some simple steps in advance, you can direct your legacy after your death to your family, friends or favourite charity.

Taking no action merely results in expense, uncertainty or disagreements for those you leave behind. Your indecision may even result in your legacy going to parties whom you definitely did not want to benefit.

Your future will be different to the present

Right now, you may not own any real property – land, house or apartment – but you may in the future, either as a result of your own or a combined effort, or as a result of an inheritance or litigation. You may not have a large bank balance at the moment, but you may accumulate funds in the future. Ditto – you may not own shares right now – but for any of the previous reasons stated above, you may acquire shares, a car, artwork, or win second prize in the lottery. You may think that what you own is not worth much, but it can make a huge difference to your prospective beneficiary.

For your own future peace of mind, and for family and friends you care about, your affairs should be organised for a time when you do not have the mental or physical capacity to make an informed decision yourself. If you have not yet done so, this chapter should assist you in deciding on your next steps.

Additionally, there may be occasions when you may not be able to manage your own affairs temporarily, whether that results from an accident or a health condition. Fortunately we cannot know our own future, so being over-prepared is the only way to ensure that your interests are best protected, particularly if you live in complicated circumstances, such as in a blended family.

For older readers, this advice applies even more pertinently. You should consider reviewing documents that were prepared 10 years earlier to ensure they reflect your current situation. You might realise that the executor of your Will has passed away, or that your best friend beneficiary moved overseas five years ago, so your grandchildren would appreciate that gift instead.

Getting your basics organised

From my experience in family law for many years, women frequently have little involvement in family finances even where they may actually do most of the shopping and pay the bills. The male breadwinner often makes the big decisions because there is some perceived competency, or because many women believe the details of loans, investments and payments to be too boring or difficult to understand.

Whatever the reason, dear reader, this situation should not apply to you. On retirement you must develop a serious understanding of your own and your partner's financial and legal position in order to be able to make important decisions in an informed manner. For example, your partner may pass away unexpectedly but you may still need to file their final tax return. You will still be responsible for paying the mortgage and the bills, of which you may not even have been aware.

CASE STUDY

Andrea seemed to have a perfect life. A beautiful home on Sydney's northern beaches, an investment unit, two great children and a hard-working husband who often did not come home from work till late. Until one year, two days after Christmas, her husband died of a heart attack. Imagine Andrea's shock when she discovered that their investment unit that she thought was nearly paid off, was actually mortgaged to the hilt.

For the past five years, her husband had been steadily increasing the investment loan to support his gambling addiction. Rather than working late, he had been playing the machines at his local club. Andrea was forced to sell the unit at a rock-bottom price to fend off the bank selling it first.

Here are some practical steps to take control of your affairs:

1. **Organise financial records**: Create a list of all assets such as bank accounts, investments and insurance policies to keep with any original documents. Review and locate your credit cards and bank accounts and ensure that all statements are filed in order for easy reference. Reduce the number of credit cards you have and close any unused bank accounts.

2. **Bank accounts and assets in joint names:** Make sure that the main account and any terms deposits are in joint names. Having accounts in joint names ensures that you have access to funds if your partner is suddenly not around.

3. **Eliminate your most expensive debts:** Pay out any hire purchase loans and any credit card debt as soon as possible. The most expensive debt means that loans with the highest interest rates should be paid out first.

4. **Review your housing loan**: If you do not own your home outright, consider whether you are able to pay out the balance using your superannuation benefit. Reducing your liabilities as soon as possible will give you long-term security. Ensure the bank has discharged the mortgage if you have paid out the loan.

5. **Property title deed:** If you own your home, locate the Certificate of Title for the property. Check that the solicitor who did the conveyance still holds the title. Make sure that you are named as a joint owner of your home. If not, seek legal advice about having your name added to the title.

6. **Check your Will**: Locate any Wills (you need the original), Powers of Attorney or other legal documents that you or your partner may have previously prepared. Consider whether they still apply to your current situation or need to be updated.

7. **Record all passwords**: Keep a record of all your own and your partner's passwords and PIN numbers needed to access computer equipment, ATMs and secure sites such as online banking. Also record any codes for phones and home safes.

8. **Check your insurance policies**: Locate any life insurance policies and study the terms of their operation. Find out whether your health insurer will reduce your premiums now that you have retired.

9. **Review your superannuation accounts**: Locate any smaller super funds and consolidate your funds to reduce administration costs. Ensure you have made an up-to-date binding nomination specifying your intended beneficiaries.

10. **Review your financial affairs with experts:** Talk to your accountant about how best to structure your financial affairs to reduce your tax payable, and receive other concessions available to retirees. Consider obtaining further legal advice to use your Will as an effective planning tool in distributing property.

11. **Seniors card**: Apply for your Seniors Card and your transport concession card (e.g. Opal in NSW) to reduce transport costs. Also apply for the pensioner concession card if you are eligible.

12. Reduce the clutter: Start de-cluttering by going through old bills and papers and only keeping documents that are less than 7 years old. Everything else will no longer be needed for tax purposes. Keep all original certificates and documents in a labelled folder and label all your rearranged accounts so they will be easy to find for a family member. Redistribute those unread books, unworn clothes and unused family heirlooms.

CASE STUDY

Mary-Anne and her husband Geoff had just returned home from a celebratory lunch to mark their 45th wedding anniversary with one of their best friends, retired lawyer Emily.

Earlier that day, Geoff had been to his doctor and got the all-clear to renew his driving licence. Shortly after getting home Geoff suddenly collapsed. An ambulance was called but later that evening Geoff passed away, having suffered a severe stroke.

Mary-Anne was devastated of course and her retirement plans suddenly evaporated. Worse than that, she did not know the PIN for their joint ATM debit and credit cards, nor Geoff's computer password. Geoff had always managed all of their financial matters including giving her any weekly cash that she needed.

Mary-Anne had never used an ATM machine or accessed online banking. It was only with Emily's knowledge of computers and online banking that Mary-Anne was able to retrieve the respective PINs and passwords, and have access to financial support until probate was obtained.

Some handy legal phrases

Here is a quick guide to phrases that are likely to arise when preparing your documents:

Executor – Either a person, a solicitor or an organisation such as The Public Trustee & Guardian whose role is to administer the estate according to the terms of the Will.

Beneficiary – Either a named person, or a class of person (such as "all my children") who has been given a gift under a Will.

Bequest – Any gift to a person or a charitable body and includes money or property.

The Public Trustee & Guardian – A statutory body that specialises in assisting people to make their Will, their Power of Attorney and to administer deceased estates. The Public Trustee will charge for the work that it carries out, including the management of ongoing trusts and conveyancing and litigation. It can also take on a guardianship role for persons with a disability including administering a legacy over a longer period.

Testator – The maker of the Will.

Testamentary capacity – An essential requirement for any person making a Will or Power of Attorney. A person must understand the effect of making a Will and must be able to identify the assets that they possess and whom they intend to benefit. Sometimes this has been referred to as a person having "sound mind". Occasionally medical advice might be required to determine whether a person is able to make a rational decision and is not affected by mental illness.

Fiduciary – The responsibility of a person who has a duty to act in the best interests of the beneficiary. Typically, this term refers to the role of the executor who may also act as trustee of property left to beneficiaries. A person in a fiduciary role may not profit from their position and must account for any monies spent or obtained.

Grant of probate – An order made by the Supreme Court to confirm the Will and permit the executor to administer the estate according to the terms of the Will.

Intestacy – Where a person dies without having made a Will. In such a case, the court will grant Letters of Administration to an Administrator to deal with the estate according to the statutory order for distribution of property.

CASE STUDY

Brendan filled in a "do-it –yourself" Will form – intending to leave the whole estate to his wife, Dayna. He inserted Dayna's name in the section of the form appointing her the executrix but forgot to insert her name in the section for nominating a beneficiary – in effect, he left his whole estate to nobody.

Getting legal advice when preparing your Will is not very expensive, compared to having to go to court to determine what was really intended.

Not to be morbid, but dying costs

Some people absolutely refuse to discuss their future funeral arrangements, while others have written their obituary years in advance.

As we get older however, having a plan for our own and our partner's funeral arrangements can save a lot of aggravation at an emotional time. It is not being morbid to think about an arrangement that satisfies competing family demands and our own religious preferences, well in advance of when it might be needed.

Relatives should also be aware of any specific directions by the deceased as to the donation of their organs or their body after death. Organs (other than the cornea) must be donated shortly after death, so there must be communication with the hospital at the time, but generally this should not affect the usual burial process.

Prepaid funeral plans:

There are three types of prepaid options – funeral plans, funeral bonds and funeral insurance.

- A funeral bond is effectively a managed investment on which interest is paid on the initial investment. It must be assigned to a funeral director to be used to pay for funeral costs, to avoid being considered to be an assessable asset by Centrelink.

- Funeral insurance is a scheme whereby monthly premiums are paid for a fixed amount of cover, payable on death.

- A funeral plan is a contract between a funeral director and an individual for a certain level of service and coffin, etc.

There are disadvantages and advantages to each option. You should do further research before making a final choice.

Warning: watch out for scams. Check what you get for the actual costs. While some products offer good value, others simply rip you off. Sometimes it is cheaper to put money in the bank instead of using one of these plans. Check any product on Google to see what others' experience has been.

Prepaid site, either for burial or cremation:

In Sydney at least, given the pressure on available cemetery land, the option of having a pre-paid burial site is becoming increasingly popular. Decide whether you prefer to be buried or cremated and choose a cemetery with available space. Some cemetery trusts will allow payment by instalments, and payment secures a spot for the next 25 years.

Note that a burial plot (either for burial or cremation) is exempt from inclusion as an asset for the purposes of the age pension. This means that, when you pay in advance for a burial plot, your assets will actually be less as far as Centrelink is concerned, which might help you qualify for the pension. It will also reduce stress on your family when it comes time for them to organise your burial or cremation.

Planning for a burial site in advance enables you to choose the location to some extent, for example, being close to where other family members are buried. Family historians will thank you for your thoughtfulness.

Funeral costs:

Costs of a funeral can be divided into three categories, with significant variations as to the total cost:

Funeral director fees – This includes professional fees, coffin, transfer of the deceased, the hearse and obtaining the death certificate, newspaper notices and flowers. Average cost is around $6,500.

Headstone costs – From a simple marker for around $1,000, to double headstones at $14,000. Obviously, you won't be around to admire it.

Cemetery fees – Burial plot, interment costs.

The cost of the site can vary greatly, depending on the cemetery location and the actual site, whether a burial plot, a garden niche, a wall niche or a crypt. In the Sydney metropolitan area, the cost of a burial plot has more than doubled in the past 5 years and can range from $5,720 – $14,300 depending on the location.[1]

The plot is only part of the cost and some people choose to scatter the ashes of their loved one at sea or in a favourite park. The cost of cremation is considerably cheaper.

A coffin or casket can range from a simple shroud or eco-friendly cardboard coffin, to an elaborate casket. A cremation capsule will cost around $300, a basic coffin around $1,000, while a top of the line coffin with plated handles, velvet interior and elaborate carvings will be more than $10,000.

According to one article, the average cost of a funeral in Australia, including funeral director's fees, burial site and headstone, totals $19,000.[2] Planning ahead can significantly reduce the financial strain on your loved ones if they have to meet such costs unexpectedly.

CASE STUDY

Brian was an energetic businessman in his early 70s, but larger than life to his friends and family. He happened to be visiting one of his mates who lived up the coast when he noticed some worrying physical symptoms. Within days he was hospitalised. Three weeks later he returned home and was again hospitalised. Two weeks later he passed away from a rare condition, leaving behind a bewildered family.

Over a week went by and there were no newspaper notices in relation to a funeral service. This was because his children could not agree on where the funeral should be held or where he should be buried. Some family members wanted the funeral to be held in their local church, while others wanted the service in Brian's own church.

To resolve the disagreement, they asked a long-time family adviser to read the Will and decide on the funeral and the burial location, with everyone present. Two weeks later, a funeral service was held in Brian's local church where he had been an active member. Each child and friend was able to contribute to a memorable event.

Paying for the funeral:

While the Department of Social Security and Department of Veterans' Affairs may pay small amounts to assist pensioners in arranging a funeral, it is more common to approach the relevant bank to ask for a release of funds. Alternatively, the bank may agree to a small loan to pay for the funeral.

Where there is a Will, you can have your way

A Will is a legal document that sets out how you would like your assets divided after your death. If you have no Will, the statutory rules of intestacy apply and family members in a specified order of priority will receive a share of the estate.

If there is no appropriate relative, your property will go to the state. In other words, if you don't make your wishes clear, the government may impose theirs.

Retirement is an ideal time to review any bequests under an existing Will. Over your lifetime, it is likely that you will have bought and sold assets, and it could result in some beneficiaries not receiving what you had intended. A very typical situation these days is that people enter de facto relationships, often with existing children. Great clarity is required to ensure that the wording of a Will reflects what you really want, particularly in a larger estate where a family provision claim is more likely.

Blended families are probably the largest growing family type in Australia. Preparing a Will that involves a blended family should focus on giving an equitable result to all the children, to reduce any possible dispute between them when the inheritance crystallises. One method is to include a testamentary trust within the Will of each parent. This preserves each child's share of the property, while ensuring that the surviving parent can remain in the family home. You will need expert legal help in drafting a Will in such a case.

As an example, you may be in a long-term de facto relationship, but wish to exclude your partner's children from inheriting your property. Obviously you need good legal advice to assist in the drafting of the terms of the Will.

However, you should also consider the effect on those children when they realise that you have deliberately excluded them from receiving any gift. Sometimes long-term dissatisfaction arises not just from the size of the gift, but also the fact of being excluded from the affections of the deceased.

Remarriage revokes any previous Will in existence, but not a gift to the person to whom they were married. It is worth noting that with the 2017 changes to the *Marriage Act* 1961 (Cth), same-sex couples should also reconsider the terms of any existing Will.

Most lawyers charge relatively low fees to draft a Will. Using a do-it-yourself Will Kit is an alternative only for the simplest bequests. If you want to make any specific gifts, it would be better to approach The Public Trustee & Guardian that has very reasonable drafting fees, but does charge a commission on the administration of the estate.

For a Will to be valid, these criteria must be met:

- The testator must be over 18 years, unless if younger and married.
- The document must be in writing, whether handwritten, typed, or even by digital text message. (See the case study following, but texts are not recommended.)
- Any alteration in the document must be initialled by all parties and witnesses.
- The document must be signed on each page by the testator and two independent witnesses. On the last page, there should appear an attestation clause, that is, a clause stating that the Will was signed by the testator in the presence of both witnesses. (The independent witnesses must not be beneficiaries or the spouse of a beneficiary.)
- The testator must have testamentary capacity. That is, they must understand the nature of the document they are signing, to reduce any possibility that their Will could be challenged in court.

The testator may suffer from a disability such as blindness, or inability to write, or they may not be fluent in English. In such cases, the solicitor will need to amend the attestation clause to ensure that the document fully represents the intention of the testator. A court may also interpret an informal document as representing a person's testamentary intentions, as in the case study following:

CASE STUDY

MN made and saved a text message on his mobile phone shortly before taking his own life. A friend, searching the contacts list to determine those to be informed of the death, found the text and took a screen shot. The court decided that the text message was a document.

Its contents – the message referred to 'My Will', identified property to be kept, and nominated the placement of ashes – satisfied the requirement that the text purported to state testamentary intentions. The Court held that the message was made at a time when MN was contemplating death. The fact that the phone was found with the body, the contents and detail in the message and the absence of contrary wishes – satisfied the Court of the further requirement that the deceased intended the unsent message to operate as his Will.

Re Nichol; Nichol v Nichol *[2017] QSC 220*

Legally, the *original* Will is required after death – a copy of the Will is not sufficient. The original Will should be kept in a safe place by the testator, but copies can be given to family members or to the executor for their records.

The role of the executor

This role carries a lot of responsibility and it is usual to appoint a younger person who is also likely to take the largest share of the estate. The executor can appoint a solicitor to actually carry out the work in more complex cases. The executor is usually responsible for making the funeral arrangements, including locating the death certificate and deciding how the body will be disposed. Where there is no suitable next of kin to carry out this role, often the Public Trustee & Guardian[3] is appointed as executor and will be entitled to charge a commission related to the value of the estate.

Changing a Will

Some events automatically affect a Will: marriage automatically revokes a Will, unless the Will was made in anticipation of marriage. However if you divorce after making a Will, only gifts made specifically to your spouse will be revoked. It will not affect your spouse's appointment as executor, trustee or guardian. *It is strongly advisable to draft a new Will on divorce to reflect the new situation.* Smaller changes to an existing Will can be made by adding a codicil which must still meet the formal requirements of signing a Will.

Challenging the Will

There are numerous circumstances which may lead to an application to the Supreme Court disputing the terms of a Will, regardless of how competent the drafting might be. Often a child who may have been excluded by the testator will be the most likely challenger to a Will.

Other grounds can include that the testator lacked the mental capacity to make a Will; that the testator was unduly influenced in the making of it; or that it was not the last Will made. Whatever the reason, such applications are expensive, extremely disruptive to the family and settlement can be difficult to achieve.

Obtaining a grant of probate

Having collected evidence of all the real property, bank accounts and debts owed, the executor will make an application to the NSW Supreme Court for a grant of probate, which will confirm the executor and the beneficiaries. The court charges a filing fee on the application based on the value of the estate.

Once the grant is given by the court, the executor will sell the assets, pay any debts owed and ensure that the funds or property is distributed to the beneficiaries. Good accounting records are essential in this process.

CASE STUDY

Mr K died in July 2013, having been diagnosed with a chronic paranoid schizophrenic disorder in the 1970s. As there was no other family and apparently no Will, a number of his first cousins applied to have the property distributed to them under the rules of intestacy. However before the distribution could be made, a Will dated October 1995 drafted by a solicitor and signed by the testator was found. Under the Will, the testator gave his entire estate to the "Socialist Party of Australia" and appointed the then General Secretary of the Party as his executor. One year later that organisation changed its name to "The Communist Party of Australia".

The cousins challenged the validity of the Will on the basis of Mr K's testamentary incapacity. Based on the evidence of the solicitor, the fact that the General Secretary had been a visitor and friend to Mr K over a number of years, and a letter written by Mr K himself at the time rejecting his family and referring to his instructions to his solicitor, the court held that Mr K did have capacity to make the Will.

In part Mr K's letter to the solicitor stated, "Having an interest in Communism, which in retrospect is not such a bad system after all and far preferable to that which obtains today in Australia ... I prefer to leave my entire estate to the Socialist Party of Australia as specified above for the reasons specified above."

The effect of the paranoid schizophrenia on Mr K's mind was considered but found to be only a partial impairment. It was more relevant that he had a continuing connection with the Party, was aligned with their beliefs and intended his gift should further their cause rather than members of his extended family with whom he had no contact throughout his life.

Briton v Kipritidis *[2015] NSWSC (14 Oct 2015)*

Managing your affairs when you no longer can

Right now, you are healthy in mind and body, but you should also consider that there may be a time when you will not be able to manage your own financial and legal affairs. Either as a result of increasing cognitive impairment, a serious accident or a medical emergency, you may be unable to make informed decisions either on a temporary or long-term basis.

With our longer lifespans and healthier living conditions, more people will suffer from dementia. This includes 30% of people over 85 years and 52% of all aged care facility residents.

Dementia is the term used to describe the symptoms of a large group of illnesses which cause a progressive decline in a person's functioning, including a loss of memory, intellect, social skills and physical functioning. In 2016, dementia, including Alzheimer's disease, was the second highest cause of death, with 13,126 deaths Australia-wide. It represented 8.3% of all deaths that year, increased from 5.3% of all deaths in 2007.[4]

It is essential to be prepared for such a time well in advance of any diagnosis of your symptoms. Most importantly, you will be relying on a trusted family member or friend to manage your affairs for your benefit, so you should make this decision when you are able to resist family pressure. Early "elder abuse" research[5] indicates that there is an increasing financial abuse of older people, through the abuse of the Power of Attorney, by family members wanting to access their inheritance early. It is important to appoint a trusted person as your attorney when you are still capable of making an informed choice.

There are two types of documents known as Powers of Attorney – a General Power of Attorney and an Enduring Power of Attorney. For our purposes, we will deal with the Enduring Power which is intended to take effect where the person (usually known as the principal in relation to the drafting of a Power) no longer has capacity to make their own decisions.

The General Power is usually used in limited circumstances for example, if a person is overseas when a critical document is required to be signed.

Aspects of an Enduring Power of Attorney

When you (the principal) appoint an attorney (sole or jointly), you are effectively authorising them to make any legal and financial decisions for you. This includes accessing your bank accounts, selling your property and entering contracts on your behalf. The attorney takes on this role in a fiduciary capacity. That is, they may not personally benefit from the appointment and must act in the principal's best interests.

The principal must have the mental capacity to make a Power of Attorney. The usual standard of mental capacity is similar to that required in the making of a Will[5] and requires the capacity to understand the nature of the transaction and its broad operation.

The Power may also permit the attorney to recompense themselves for their reasonable expenses, as well as give themselves or a third party a gift. In any case, the attorney must keep their own monies separate from the principal's, as well as keeping adequate records of any monies expended either for themselves or for the principal. They must be able to account for monies spent if they are ever challenged by an interested party, usually a beneficiary under a Will once the principal has passed away.

In NSW, a new statutory form of Power of Attorney was introduced in 2004. More detailed than previously, it confers a wide authority on the attorney, unless specifically limited. Both the principal and the attorney must sign before a prescribed witness (usually a lawyer, but can also include a licensed conveyancer and others). A Power cannot commence until the appointment is accepted.

A Power of Attorney is of no effect in respect of a conveyance of land, unless the instrument is registered by the Registrar-General, NSW Land Registry Services. Registration is relatively low-cost and easy to do. Once registered, the Power of Attorney acquires a registration number which will be cited in any future conveyance of property.

Limitations on an Enduring Power of Attorney

The principal can put conditions on the exercise of the Power, for example:

- The commencement of the Power;
- Restrictions on selling property;
- Restrictions on accessing funds without permission of the principal.

Commencement of the Power of Attorney: The prescribed form anticipates that the Power commences either immediately, when the attorney accepts the appointment, on a specific date, or when the attorney 'considers that I need assistance managing my affairs'. Obviously the latter situation can lead to some uncertainty and in such a case, it would be advisable to obtain a supporting letter from a treating medical practitioner before exercising the Power.

Continues even when the principal loses mental capacity: It is the intention of this document that the appointment of the attorney is irrevocable and will continue when the principal is no longer able to make decisions for themselves. Any challenge to the attorney's appointment is to the New South Wales Civil and Administrative Tribunal (NCAT) or the Supreme Court.

Extent of the exercise of the Power of Attorney: The attorney cannot do acts which are personal to the principal, such as making a Will, make decisions about health care or enter personal contracts (such as marriage) on their behalf. It is assumed that the attorney can access the funds of the principal, can deal with real property (that is land, a house or unit) and manage their business unless specifically limited in the document.

In general terms, a Power of Attorney does not permit the attorney to give benefits to either themselves or another person unless specified. Where permitted, it is expected that the gift will be to a relative or close friend of the principal or the kind of gift that the principal might make as a result of their special relationship with another.

The attorney can be specifically authorised to have their "reasonable living and medical expenses" met such as housing, transport or medication. Any such gift or reimbursement should not be so excessive that the attorney receives recompense at the expense of a beneficiary losing their gift.

In the common situation where a large deposit is required for a residential accommodation deposit before the principal can enter residential care, it is advisable that the attorney consults with the beneficiary/s to obtain their consent before selling the principal's main house. Selling the family home which is often the principal's largest asset, can be a much contested issue between possible beneficiaries under the Will.

Review of Power of Attorney

A Power of Attorney can be reviewed either by the NSW Civil and Administrative Tribunal Guardianship division (NCAT) (previously known as the Guardianship Tribunal) or the NSW Supreme Court. The review can be sought by an "interested person" who may be the attorney, the principal, or a guardian acting on behalf of the principal. In general, only applications which raise complex or "novel legal issues" would be initially referred to the court. Typical matters for consideration by the Tribunal would include: whether the principal had mental capacity, or was unduly influenced at the time of making the instrument; whether the instrument is invalid either wholly or in part, or if the attorney had complied with the Act.

Where the tribunal decides to make no order in respect of an application for a review, it may decide to treat it as an application for a financial management order, which in effect is a suspension of the Power of Attorney. In this manner, the NCAT enlivens its alternate role under the *NSW Trustee and Guardian Act* 2009 to make orders in respect of property and its protective role of minors and incapable persons, which forms a significant part of its ongoing functions.

Directing your future treatment

Appointing an attorney under a Power of Attorney ensures that your legal and financial matters are administered by a competent person in the future. However, the attorney has no role in making decisions about your health care. Until very recently, a hospital or aged care facility would be content to accept the directions of the person nominated as next of kin. Now, most institutions require an incoming resident to nominate a person as their enduring guardian.

In NSW a separate document is required to appoint an enduring guardian to manage future decisions about a person's lifestyle and medical treatment. This document should be distinguished from an Advance Care Directive (see an example at the end of the book). The role of the enduring guardian, as set out in the *Guardianship Act* 1987, can be summarised as follows. The enduring guardian may:

- Decide the place in which the appointor is to live (such as a specific nursing home, or the appointor's own home).
- Decide the health care that the appointor is to receive.
- Decide the other kinds of personal services that the appointor is to receive,.
- Give consent to the carrying out of medical or dental treatment on the appointor.
- Perform any other function relating to the appointor's person that is specified in the instrument of appointment.

The enduring guardian's authority may be specifically limited by the instrument of appointment.

The Act also emphasises that the welfare and interests of the appointor (that is, the person appointing the enduring guardian) is of paramount importance and they should be encouraged to live as normal a life in the community as possible.

Typically, appointing an enduring guardian often occurs at the same time as appointing an attorney. Often a person will appoint their child or children to make decisions about their future medical treatment and accommodation, particularly if they are considering entering supported care. When preparing any document, the principal must have the mental capacity at the time to understand the purpose and effect of the instrument they are creating. In this case, they are enabling another person/s to make decisions about where they will live and what medical treatment they will receive.

For a concerned relative, an enduring guardianship is an important document because it enables them to be informed about the medical treatment that the principal has received. In these days of privacy restrictions, access to information about medical treatment can be refused without an enduring guardianship in existence.

It is not uncommon for older people to be forgetful about treatment they have received or to refuse to have treatment which could improve the quality of their life. That said, a principal can put restrictions on the scope of treatment that they may receive but this is more of an indication to the enduring guardian as to how their treatment should proceed. Usually a person will appoint either an enduring guardian or rely solely on their Advance Care Directive.

CASE STUDY

Andrea, 75, was recently diagnosed with terminal cancer and was aware that by the end of her illness she might not be capable of making her own decisions.

There was division in Andrea's family based on religious beliefs. Andrea was concerned that if she lost capacity, her wishes as to her future care might not be carried out.

Andrea contacted her solicitor who prepared her enduring guardianship document. Andrea appointed her friend Marina, who held similar beliefs, as her enduring guardian. Andrea believed that Marina would ensure her wishes would be carried out in respect of her future treatment, especially in regard to not being kept alive on a life support system. Andrea also advised her family members that she had appointed Marina to make these decisions.

Relevant aspects when appointing an Enduring Guardian

The appointor must be over 18 years of age and must have *capacity* to understand the effect of appointing another person to make their medical decisions.

Having a slight intellectual disability or being in the early stages of dementia may not in itself be sufficient to invalidate such an appointment and if there is any doubt, medical advice should be sought. NSW Justice has developed a booklet and form for use when appointing an enduring guardian. Most solicitors will also have a template.

Certain people are excluded from being appointed as an enduring guardian, namely any person who is paid to provide a service to the appointor, such as a community nurse. However, a person receiving a Carer's Allowance to care for the appointor is permitted to take on this role. An enduring guardian must be over 18 years, should live relatively close to the appointor and should be prepared to make potentially difficult decisions about the appointor's condition.

The appointor's signature must be observed by an eligible witness, such as a solicitor. While it is preferable that the enduring guardian/s accepts and signs the form at the same time as the appointor, the document can be signed separately. If the appointor is not able to sign the document personally, another person can sign on their behalf – provided they are not the intended enduring guardian. Enduring guardians can be appointed jointly, that is they must both agree when making a decision, either jointly and severally (that is, one person or both people), or as a substitute enduring guardian to ensure that there will always be a decision-maker available.

The guardianship takes effect either immediately or when the appointor has lost capacity and is no longer able to make decisions about their own medical treatment. Determining when that point has been reached can be difficult, as individual capacity can vary in cases of mental illness or early stages of dementia. A medical certificate may not be conclusive, in which case an application may need to be made to the Guardianship Division of NCAT.

Typically the enduring guardian will be able to decide on the appropriate dental and medical treatment for the appointor, and can give their consent to the treatment being carried out. Their consent is not required in cases of urgent treatment which may save a person's life. They can also decide on the most appropriate accommodation for the appointor if they believe they can no longer manage in their own home.

Revoking the appointment

Provided the appointor has capacity, an enduring guardianship can be revoked at any time in writing and witnessed by an eligible witness. Similarly, the enduring guardian can resign in writing at any time.

Advance Care Directive

An Advance Care Directive (sometimes known as a "living will") is a specific direction to medical staff as to what treatment a person wishes to receive when they are unable to communicate or do not have capacity to decide. It is a valid direction and must be followed. The Directive may include nominating a person who you wish to be responsible for making any decisions on your behalf. In NSW there is no specified form for setting out your wishes, although NSW Health does provide a useful template which outlines such factors as personal values, and values about dying, which should be considered. A sample Directive can be found in **Chapter 13 References and resources.**

There can be difficulties in how an Advance Care Directive is interpreted. For example, medical staff might decide that your particular situation differs from the situation anticipated in the Directive and therefore the Directive does not apply. Anecdotally, an Advance Care Directive is of most value in the situation of an ongoing chronic health situation where a person is aware of how their illness will proceed. In such a case a person may wish to limit the extent of medical interventions which may prolong life but not necessarily the quality of life.

In NSW it is not possible to include euthanasia in an Advanced Care Directive as assisted dying is illegal in this state. Directives made in other states are recognised in NSW.

12

The Retirement Quiz

The Retirement Quiz[1] consists of 35 questions based on the Retirement Resources Inventory (RRI). Retirement resources, as assessed by the quiz questions, helped predict retirement adjustment and satisfaction. Originally developed as a psychometric testing tool, the quiz was developed to identify physical, financial and psychological factors which assist retirees to adjust and experience a more rewarding retirement.

The Leung & Earl study created 'subscales' that measured different types of resources. The groupings were identified as:

- RT1 (Resource Type 1) – Health and Finances
- RT2 (Resource Type 2) – Social Resources
- RT3 (Resource Type 3) – Emotional, Cognitive and Motivational Resources.

As you answer each question, add up your score for each section. Once completed, you should add up your scores for all three sections of the quiz. Then refer to comments at the end to find out how you are travelling. There are no right or wrong answers – this quiz is a self-assessment tool for you to identify areas that could use some improvement.

Resource Type 1 – Health and Finances

Question 1: I would consider my general health condition to be
_____

1. Extremely poor
2. Fairly poor
3. Average
4. Good
5. Extremely good

Question 2: I am _____ affected by one or more major physical illnesses (e.g. heart disease, diabetes, foot problems, arthritis, hypertension).

1. Severely
2. More than moderately
3. Moderately
4. Mildly
5. Not

Question 3: I am _____ affected by one or more mental disorders (e.g. memory-impairment, depression, anxiety disorder, panic disorder).

1. Severely
2. More than moderately
3. Moderately
4. Mildly
5. Not

Question 4: I have _____ energy to carry out daily activities or activities that I am interested in.

1. Very little/no
2. Limited/inadequate
3. A moderate amount of
4. A substantial amount of
5. Excess

Question 5: I possess _____ income to support my/my family living expenses.
1. Very little/no
2. Limited/inadequate
3. A moderate amount of
4. A substantial amount of
5. Excess

Question 6: I have _____ financial support from my personal savings.
1. Very little/no
2. Limited/inadequate
3. A moderate amount of
4. A substantial amount of
5. Excess

Question 7: I have _____ financial support from my investments.
1. Very little/no
2. Limited/inadequate
3. A moderate amount of
4. A substantial amount of
5. Excess

Question 8: I have_____ financial support from my superannuation fund.
1. Very little/no
2. Limited/inadequate
3. A moderate amount of
4. A substantial amount of
5. Excess

Resource Type 1 (RT1) Total Score _____

Resource Type 2 – Social Resources

Question 9: I have _____ friends whom I can interact with regularly.

1. Very few/no
2. Few
3. A moderate number of
4. A substantial number of
5. Many

Question 10: I have _____ family members whom I can interact with regularly.

1. Very few/no
2. Few
3. A moderate number of
4. A substantial number of
5. Many

Question 11: I know_____ people from various sources (e.g. religious groups, leisure groups, sporting teams, volunteer groups, part-time employment).

1. Very few/no
2. Few
3. A moderate number of
4. A substantial number of
5. Many

Question 12: I would consider interactions with friends (in general) to be _____ supportive.

1. Not at all
2. Fairly
3. Moderately
4. Quite
5. Very

Question 13: I would consider interactions with family members (in general) to be _____ supportive.

1. Not at all
2. Fairly
3. Moderately
4. Quite
5. Very

Question 14: I would consider interactions with acquaintances from various sources (e.g. religious groups, leisure groups, sporting teams, volunteer groups, part-time employment) to be _____ supportive.

1. Not at all
2. Fairly
3. Moderately
4. Quite
5. Very

Question 15: I _____ receive informational support from others. (Informational support refers to receiving information or advice from someone on handling difficult circumstances, rectifying a situation, following through with a solution, following-up on a difficult event, and receiving constructive criticism.)

1. Never
2. Rarely
3. Sometimes
4. Often
5. Very often

Question 16: I _____ receive emotional support from others. (Emotional support means someone was available to listen, to acknowledge my feelings, to support me in stressful situations, to act as a confidant, and to express interest in my well-being.)

1. Never
2. Rarely
3. Sometimes
4. Often
5. Very often

Question 17: I _____ **receive tangible support from others.**
(Tangible support refers to receiving help with meal preparation,
temporary housing, household chores, shopping, respite, financial
needs, transportation, care of the house when away, and the loan of
something I needed.)

1. Never
2. Rarely
3. Sometimes
4. Often
5. Very often

Resource Type 2 (RT2) Total Score _____

Resource Type 3 – Emotional, Cognitive and Motivational Resources

Question 18: I experience _____ positive emotions (i.e. interested, excited, strong, enthusiastic, proud, determined, alert, inspired, attentive, active).
1. Very little/no
2. Limited/inadequate
3. A moderate number of
4. A substantial number of
5. Excess

Question 19: I have _____ability to perceive my/others' emotions accurately.
1. Very little/no
2. Limited/inadequate
3. A moderate
4. An extensive
5. Excess

Question 20: I possess _____ knowledge about how emotions vary or influence behaviour.
1. Very little/no
2. Limited/inadequate
3. Moderate
4. Substantial
5. Excess

Question 21: In general, I feel that I have _____ ability to use emotions to facilitate my thoughts and communication.
1. Very little/no
2. Limited/inadequate
3. A moderate
4. An extensive
5. Excess

Question 22: I have little control over the things that happen to me.

1. Strongly agree
2. Agree
3. Neutral
4. Disagree
5. Strongly disagree

Question 23: I feel that I am a person of worth, at least on an equal plane with others.

1. Strongly disagree
2. Disagree
3. Neutral
4. Agree
5. Strongly agree

Question 24: I _____ forget things in the immediate past or where I have placed things.

1. Very often
2. Often
3. Sometimes
4. Rarely
5. Never

Question 25: I have _____ ability to recall events that happened a while ago.

1. Very little/no
2. Limited/inadequate
3. A moderate
4. An extensive
5. Excess

Question 26: I have _____ ability to recall meanings and spellings of different words/concepts.

1. Very little/no
2. Limited/inadequate
3. A moderate
4. A significant
5. Excess

Question 27: I have _____ ability to acquire new knowledge or skills.
1. Very little/no
2. Limited/inadequate
3. A moderate
4. A significant
5. Excess

Question 28: I would consider my speed of processing information (e.g. numbers, texts) to be generally _____.
1. Very slow
2. Slow
3. Moderate
4. Fast
5. Very fast

Question 29: I have _____ ability to understand and solve problems.
1. Very little/no
2. Limited/inadequate
3. A moderate
4. A significant
5. Excess

Question 30: I have _____ ability to perform good decision making (i.e. selecting the most appropriate choice from the available options).
1. Very little/no
2. Limited/inadequate
3. A moderate
4. A significant
5. Excess

Question 31: When faced with difficulty, I usually increase my efforts.
1. Strongly disagree
2. Disagree
3. Neutral
4. Agree
5. Strongly agree

Question 32: Even when things seem hopeless, I keep fighting to reach my goals.

1. Strongly disagree
2. Disagree
3. Neutral
4. Agree
5. Strongly agree

Question 33: I can easily adapt to changes in goals, plans or circumstances.

1. Strongly disagree
2. Disagree
3. Neutral
4. Agree
5. Strongly agree

Question 34: When I get stuck on something, it's hard for me to find a new approach.

1. Strongly agree
2. Agree
3. Neutral
4. Disagree
5. Strongly disagree

Question 35: I create many problems for myself because I set unrealistic goals.

1. Strongly agree
2. Agree
3. Neutral
4. Disagree
5. Strongly disagree

Resource Type 3 (RT3) Total Score _____

Understanding your results

Remember that some resources are better predictors of retirement satisfaction and adjustment. The order of importance is:

- Health and Finances – tangible resources including physical and financial resources.

- Social resources – including sources and quality of social interaction and social support.

- Emotional, Cognitive and Motivational Resources – personal psychological resources.

Scoring

Low scores	Medium scores	High scores
RT1 Less than 21.94	21.94 – 32.23	More than 32.23
RT2 Less than 22.25	22.25 – 34.53	More than 34.53
RT3 Less than 59.85	59.85 - 76.11	More than 76.11

If your scores are in the medium to high range in most cases, there is no cause for concern. You might like to review the individual items scored lowest and set goals to improve. Some things are obviously easier to change than others, so start with the easier ones first, working gradually to the more difficult.

What if your scores are in the low range? It is possible that this process might evoke concerns about your own lifestyle and health. If this is the case, you can start by contacting support services for additional support and advice. The key to making improvements is to work at changing the low scoring items, but also to acknowledge the items you scored highly on. Just as suggested to the medium and high scorers, start with the easier items first and then work with the more difficult.

For example, if you are highly motivated (measured by RT3 items 31-35) but lack financial income resources (RT1 items 5-8) right now, you still have the necessary energy to investigate other ways of generating income even if there is no immediate solution. If you have a major physical illness that affects your daily living, then the key might be more about trying new treatments, better management or optimising your health in other ways to compensate.

Productive ageing

If you are planning to retire, doing the quiz can help you organise your resources for a successful retirement. If you are already retired, the quiz can kick-start a conversation about setting new goals, trying new approaches or seeking help in particular areas that may have been overlooked.

Retirement is one of the most important life transitions in later adult life. While some people enjoy retirement, approximately one third of retirees find the transition to retirement stressful or show a decline in well-being. While physical and financial resources are important, you also need social and emotional resources such as optimism and resilience to meet the demands of the retirement phase.

Realistically, retirement requires adapting to a new role and establishing new goals to replace those previous roles of worker and community leader. Retirement can be a time of exploration and self-realisation, which must be weighed against the inevitable losses of declining health and strength. Hopefully you will find gaining wisdom and a life well-lived sufficient reward..

13

References and resources

Chapter 1: What does retirement mean to you?

Resources

ASFA Research & Resource Centre, *Superannuation balances by age and gender*, December 2015, Ross Clare, Director of Research, The Association of Superannuation Funds of Australia.

Australian Institute of Health & Welfare, *Changes in life expectancy and disability in Australia 1998 to 2009*, Bulletin 111, November 2012, <www.aihw.gov.au/reports/life-expectancy-death/deaths-in-australia/contents/life-expectancy>.

Butler M, *Advanced Australia: The Politics of Ageing*, MUP, Vic, Australia, 2015.

Grattan Institute, *The implications of ageing for economics and politics*, IBR Post Retirement Conference, 10 October 2017.

Nelson A E, *Retire Well, Retire Happy*, Global Publishing Group, Victoria, Aust, 2014.

NSW Treasury, *NSW Inter-generational Report 2016*, <www.treasury.nsw.gov.au/sites/default/files/2017-01/Budget_Paper_5_-_Intergenerational_Report_2016_-_full_report.pdf>.

Pascale R, Louis H Primavera LH, Roach R, *The Retirement Maze: What You Should Know Before and After You Retire*, Rowman & Littlefield Publishers Inc, UK, 2012.

Strauss W & Howe N, *Generations: The History of America's Future 1584 to 2069*, William Morrow & Co, NY, USA, 1992.

Weiss RS, Buss SA, *Challenges of the Third Age: Meaning and Purpose in Later Life*, Oxford University Press, NY, 2002.

Chapter 2: Preparing for retirement

References

[1] Workplace Gender Equality Agency, *Gender workplace statistics at a glance 2017-18,* Fact sheet, Feb 2019, www.wgea.gov.au/data/fact-sheets/gender-workplace-statistics-at-a-glance-2017-18. See also Treasury, *2015 Intergenerational Report to 2055*, March 2015, p 17. treasury.gov.au/sites/default/files/2019-03/04_Chapter_1.pdf

[2] Treasury, *2015 Intergenerational Report to 2055*, March 2015, p 18, treasury.gov.au/publication/2015-igr

[3] Association of Superannuation Funds of Australia, *Superannuation balances by age and gender*, December 2015, Ross Clare, Director of Research, ASFA Research & Resource Centre.

[4] Australian Institute of Health & Welfare, *Life expectancy & deaths, Deaths in Australia*, 18 July 2018, overview. <www.aihw.gov.au/reports/life-expectancy-death/deaths-in-australia/contents/life-expectancy>.

[5] Treasury, *2015 Intergenerational Report to 2055*, March 2015, p 17, <treasury.gov.au/publication/2015-igr>.

[6] Rowe, JW, MD, Robert L. Kahn, RL, PhD, *Successful Ageing*, The Gerontologist, Volume 37, Issue 4,1 August 1997, pp. 433-440, <doi.org/10.1093/geront/37.4.433>.

[7] Friedman, HA, and Martin, LR, *The Longevity Project: Surprising Discoveries for Health and Long Life from the Landmark Eight-Decade Study*, Hudson Street Press, 2011.

[8] Merrill Lynch, *Beyond the Bucket List*, p. 18, <agewave.com/wp-content/uploads/2016/05/2016-Leisure-in-Retirement_Beyond-the-Bucket-List.pdf>.

Resources

Donaldson, T., Earl, J. K., & Muratore, A. M. (2010). *Extending the integrated model of retirement adjustment: Incorporating mastery and retirement planning.* Journal of Vocational Behavior, 77(2), pp. 279-289.

Chapter 3: Leaving work

References

[1] These suggestions based on an article by Stephanie Sarkis PhD, *Psychology Today*, 19/1/2017, <www.psychologytoday.com/blog/here-there-and-everywhere/201701/10-ways-cope-big-changes>.

[2] UN, Population Division, *World Population Ageing*: 1950-2050.

[3] Australian Bureau of Statistics (ABS) 2013. *Population projections, Australia, 2017* (base) to 2066. ABS cat. no. 3222.0. Canberra: ABS, <www.abs.gov.au/AUSSTATS/abs@.nsf/mf/3222.0>.

[4] Australia Bureau of Statistics (ABS), *Retirement and Retirement Intentions, Australia, July 2016-June 2017*, released 20/12/2017, <www.abs.gov.au/ausstats/abs@.nsf/mf/6238.0>.

[5] As above

[6] *Superannuation Guarantee (Administration) Act 1992*

[7] Key findings from the Workplace Gender Equality Agency (WGEA) using data from the Australian Bureau of Statistics (ABS), November 2017, <www.wgea.gov.au/sites/default/files/2016-17-gender-equality-scorecard.pdf>.

[8] Reported in The Guardian, 17/10/2017, <www.theguardian.com/australia-news/datablog/2017/oct/18/australia-gender-pay-gap-why-do-women-still-earn-less-than-men>.

[9] Senate Economics Reference Committee, *A husband is not a retirement plan: Achieving economic security for women in retirement*, 29/4/2016, Commonwealth of Australia, <www.aph.gov.au/Parliamentary_Business/Committees/Senate/Economics/Economic_security_for_women_in_retirement/Report>.

[10] Australian Human Rights Commission, *National prevalence survey of age discrimination in the workplace report 2015*, <www.humanrights.gov.au/our-work/age-discrimination/publications/national-prevalence-survey-age-discrimination-workplace>.

[11] Brotherhood of St Laurence, *Rusty, invisible and threatening: ageing, capital and employability*, Australia, 7 June 2016.

[12] Australian Centre for Financial Studies, *Involuntary retirement: Characteristics and implications*, authors: Deborah Ralston, Martin Jenkinson, March 2014, <australiancentre.com.au/publication/involuntary-retirement-characteristics-and-implications/>.

[13] Preservation is a restriction that prevents a member from accessing superannuation benefits until retirement or satisfying a condition of release. You can access your super benefits once you have reached your preservation age and retired. You are not required to automatically access your super benefits when you reach your preservation age. See **Chapter 4 Financing your retirement** for more on this.

[14] A formal volunteer is a person who assists an organisation as part of its usual programs while an informal volunteer is someone who assists another person not living in their home.

[15] These figures are taken from Volunteering Australia, *Key facts and figures about volunteering in Australia*, 16/4/2015 and are based on a voluntary Work Survey conducted by the Australian Bureau of Statistics in 2011.

[16] See also Giving Australia 2016, *Individual Volunteering* fact sheet, <www.volunteeringaustralia.org/wpcontent/uploads/giving_australia_2016_fact_sheet_-individual_volunteering_accessible.pdf>.

[17] O'Dwyer, L, Flinders University, *The Real Value of Volunteering*, Australian Population & Migration Research Centre, Policy Brief, Vol 1, No 11, November 2013, <www.volunteeringaustralia.org/wp-content/uploads/VA-Key-sources-of-info-about-Australian-volunteering-16-Apr-15.pdf>.

Resources

Australian Bureau of Statistics (ABS) 2013. *Population projections, Australia*, 2017 (base) to 2066. ABS cat. no. 3222.0. Canberra: ABS, <www.abs.gov.au/AUSSTATS/abs@.nsf/mf/3222.0>.

Australia Bureau of Statistics, *Retirement and Retirement Intentions, Australia*, July 2016-June 2017, released 20/12/2017, <www.abs.gov.au/ausstats/abs@.nsf/mf/6238.0>.

Australian Human Rights Commission, *National prevalence survey of age discrimination in the workplace report 2015*, <www.humanrights.gov.au/our-work/age-discrimination/publications/national-prevalence-survey-age-discrimination-workplace>.

Australian Taxation Office: <www.ato.gov.au>

Giving Australia 2016, *Individual Volunteering* fact sheet, <www.volunteeringaustralia.org/wpcontent/uploads/giving_australia_2016_fact sheet_-_individual_volunteering_accessible.pdf>.

O'Dwyer, L, *Flinders University, The Real Value of Volunteering*, Australian Population & Migration Research Centre, Policy Brief, Vol 1, No 11, November 2013, <www.volunteeringaustralia.org/wp-content/uploads/VA-Key-sources-of-info-about-Australian-volunteering-16-Apr-15.pdf>.

PWC, *Understanding the unpaid economy*, Economics & Policy, March 2017, <www.pwc.com.au/australia-in-transition/publications/understanding-the-unpaid-economy-mar17.pdf>.

UN, Population Division, *World Population Ageing: 1950-2050*, 2002, <www.un.org/esa/population/publications/worldageing19502050/>.

Workplace Gender Equality Agency, *Australia's gender equality scorecard*, November 2017, <www.wgea.gov.au/sites/default/files/2016-17-gender-equality-scorecard.pdf>.

Chapter 4: Financing your retirement

References

[1] If this phrase confuses you, it has often been used by Australian politicians to accuse people saving for a house of squandering their money on smashed avocado breakfasts in trendy cafes. I offer it as a humorous reference to the widely experienced difficulty in making ends meet.

[2] Pape S, *The Barefoot Investor*, John Wiley & Sons Australia, 2017, pp. 61-73

[3] Each year Australians buy an average of 27 kg of new textiles and discard about 23 kg into landfill. Two-thirds of those discards are synthetic/plastic fibres that may never breakdown. Sustainability consultant, Jane Milburn, 18/01 2016, <textilebeat.com/aussies-send-85-of-textiles-to-landfill/>.

[4] Olivia Mellan, *Money Harmony, 2015*, <www.moneyharmony.com/moneyharmony-quiz/show-all-types>. There are many similar categories identified by other writers which list these key characteristics.

[5] <finder.com.au>, RBA.

[6] CANSTAR database, 5 October 2016, <www.canstar.com.au/credit-cards/aussies-pay-24-billion-average-interest-over-four-years/>.

[7] <Finder.com.au>, RBA, 18 December 2017.

[8] *APRA Private Health Insurance Statistics, Dec 2017*, p.5, www.apra.gov.au/PHI/Publications/Documents/1802-QPHIS-20171231.pdf>.

[9] Australian Institute of Health and Welfare 2017. *Health expenditure Australia 2015–16.* Health and welfare expenditure series no. 58. Cat. no. HWE 68. Canberra: AIHW. Cited in an article by Georgina Dent, Sydney Morning Herald, 8/4/2018, quoting Dr Hugo Sachs, president of the Australian Dental Association.

[10] AIHW report, *Admitted patient care 2014-15: Australian hospital statistics, Summary,* <www.aihw.gov.au/reports/hospitals/ahs-2014-15-admitted-patient-care/contents/summary>.

[11] Consumers Health Forum of Australia, Media release, *Out-of-pocket pain*: $10,000, 5 April 2018. <chf.org.au/media-releases/out-pocket-pain-10000-issue-0>. Cited in an article by Georgina Dent, Sydney Morning Herald, 8/4/2018, quoting Dr Hugo Sachs, president of the Australian Dental Association.

[12] UBank, *Know Your Number Index data* conducted and compiled by Galaxy Research of 1,015 Australians., 18 February 2018, <www.ubank.com.au/newsfeed/articles/2018/02/86-per-cent-of-australians-dont-know-their-monthly-expenses>.

[13] *ASX Investor Study 2017*, prepared by Deloitte Access Economics, <www.asx.com.au/education/2017-asx-investor-study.htm>.

[14] As above.

[15] A Ponzi scheme is defined as "a form of fraud in which belief in the success of a non-existent enterprise is fostered by the payment of quick returns to the first investors from money invested by later investors."

[16] ASFA superannuation statistics, December 2017, <www.superannuation.asn.au/resources/superannuation-statistics>

[17] ACOSS, *Poverty in Australia 2016*, Social Policy Research Centre, p.33, <www.acoss.org.au/wp-content/uploads/2016/10/Poverty-in-Australia-2016.pdf>

[18] Australian Bureau of Statistics, *2016 Census QuickStats*, <www.censusdata.abs.gov.au/census_services/getproduct/census/2016/quickstat/036>. This figure is not to be confused with the average weekly income of $1,597.90 (Nov 17).

[19] ACOSS, *Poverty in Australia 2016*, Social Policy Research Centre, p.32, <www.acoss.org.au/wp-content/uploads/2016/10/Poverty-in-Australia-2016.pdf>.

[20] <www.canstar.com.au/superannuation>

[21] SuperGuide, <www.superguide.com.au/smsfs/smsfs-lead-the-super-pack-again>.

[22] "Non-preserved" benefits usually applies to contributions made prior to 1 July 1999 and can be released on demand to the member without meeting other conditions.

[23] Association of Superannuation Funds of Australia, *ASFA Retirement Standard*, <www.superannuation.asn.au/ArticleDocuments/238/ASFA-RetirementStandard-Summary.pdf.aspx?Embed=Y>, p.4.

[24] Association of Superannuation Funds of Australia, *ASFA Superannuation account balances by age and gender*, October 2017, p.5, <www.superannuation.asn.au/ArticleDocuments/359/1710_Superannuation_account_balances_by_age_and_gender.pdf.aspx?Embed=Y>

[25] Australian Institute of Superannuation Trustees, *No place like home, the impact of declining home ownership on retirement*, Saul Eslake, March 2017.

[26] The *Treasury Laws Amendment (Reducing Pressure on Housing Affordability Measures No. 1) Act 2017* applies to properties sold after 1 July 2018 and permits the contribution of up to $300,000 to an individual's superannuation.

Resources

ACOSS, *Poverty in Australia 2016*, Social Policy Research Centre, <www.acoss.org.au/wp-content/uploads/2016/10/Poverty-in-Australia-2016.pdf>.

AIHW report, *Admitted patient care 2014-15: Australian hospital statistics*, Summary, <www.aihw.gov.au/reports/hospitals/ahs-2014-15-admitted-patient-care/contents/summary>.

APHA figures, 2016, <www.apha.org.au/wp-content/uploads/2016/06/Private-hospital-service-provision-June-2016.pdf>.

APRA *Private Health Insurance Statistics, Dec 2017*, <www.apra.gov.au/PHI/Publications/Documents/1802-QPHIS-20171231.pdf>.

Association of Superannuation Funds of Australia, *ASFA Retirement Standard*, <www.superannuation.asn.au/ArticleDocuments/238/ASFA-RetirementStandard-Summary.pdf.aspx?Embed=Y>.

Association of Superannuation Funds of Australia, *ASFA Superannuation account balances by age and gender*, October 2017, p.5, <www.superannuation.asn.au/ArticleDocuments/359/1710_Superannuation_account_balances_by_age_and_gender.pdf.aspx?Embed=Y>.

Australian Bureau of Statistics, *2016 Census QuickStats*, <www.censusdata.abs.gov.au/census_services/getproduct/census/2016/quickstat/036>.

Australian Institute of Health and Welfare 2017. *Health expenditure Australia 2015*–16. Health and welfare expenditure series no. 58. Cat. no. HWE 68. Canberra: AIHW.

Australian Institute of Superannuation Trustees, *No place like home, the impact of declining home ownership on retirement,* Saul Eslake, March 2017.

CANSTAR database, 5 October 2016, <www.canstar.com.au/credit-cards/aussies-pay-24-billion-average-interest-over-four-years/>.

Consumers Health Forum of Australia, Media release, *Out-of-pocket pain: $10,000,* 5 April 2018, <chf.org.au/media-releases/out-pocket-pain-10000-issue-0>.

Deloitte Access Economics, *ASX Investor Study 2017,* <www.asx.com.au/education/2017-asx-investor-study.htm>.

<Finder.com.au>, RBA, 18 December 2017.

Krueger D, Mann JD, *The Secret Language of Money*, McGraw-Hill Education –Europe, US, 2009.

Mellan O, *Money Harmony*, 2015, <www.moneyharmony.com/moneyharmony-quiz/show-all-types>.

Milburn J, *Textilebeat*, 18/01 2016, <textilebeat.com/aussies-send-85-of-textiles-to-landfill/>

Newnham M, *Funding Your Retirement, A Survival Guide,* Wrightbooks, 2011, 42 McDougall St Milton Qld 4064.

Pape S, *The Barefoot Investor,* John Wiley & Sons Australia, 2017, pp. 61-73.

Sampson A, *The new retirement/how to afford the good life,* John Fairfax Publications P/L, Sydney, 2007.

SuperGuide, <www.superguide.com.au/smsfs/smsfs-lead-the-super-pack-again>.

Treasury Laws Amendment (Reducing Pressure on Housing Affordability Measures No. 1) Act 2017.

Chapter 5: Housing options

References

[1] The concept of the "fourth pillar" was coined by economist Saul Eslake in a report he prepared for the Australian Institute of Superannuation Trustees (AIST), *No place like home, The impact of declining home ownership on retirement,* March 2017. In that report Mr Eslake discusses that projections by superannuation funds on the adequacy of retirement income is based on the assumption that a person will own their home outright at the time of retirement. With increasing house prices, larger mortgages, and more people privately renting, that assumption is becoming less valid, with a continuing reliance on the age pension as a basic means of support. <www.aist.asn.au/media/20734/ AIST_Housing%20affordability%20and%20retirement%20incomes_ FINAL%2021032017.pdf>.

[2] Many studies refer to factors which impact on the social exclusion of older people. These comments are based a number of UK studies such as that by Barnes M, Blom A, Cox K, Lessof C (2006) *The Social Exclusion of Older People: Evidence from the First Wave of the English Longitudinal Study of Ageing* (ELSA) Office of the Deputy Prime Minister, London, UK.

[3] Morris, Alan, *The Australian Dream, Housing experiences of older Australians,* CSIRO Publishing, 2016, Victoria, p.7.

[4] Source: ABS, *Housing Occupancy and Costs,* cat. no. 4130.0, 1995–96, p. 19, Table 6. Also ABS, *Housing Occupancy and Costs,* cat. no. 4130.0, 2013–14, Table 10, All households, Selected household characteristics by age of household reference person.

[5] Based on ABS, *Survey of Income and Housing 2015-16,* 13/10/2017.

[6] These generalised comments are taken from the publication by the Productivity Commission, *An Ageing Australia: Preparing for the Future,* 2015, Canberra, p.5.

[7] Nearly half of indigenous Australians over 55 are renters although they are more likely to live in social housing.

[8] The Australian Council of Social Service in 2016 defined poverty level as being 50% of the median wage, being $426.30 for a single person and for a couple with 2 children $895.22 including housing costs. There are various figures used depending on whether housing is included or not in the calculation. ACOSS, *Poverty in Australia 2016.* 36.1% of all social security recipients were living below the poverty line.

[9] Productivity Commission, *An Ageing Australia: Preparing for the Future*, 2015, Canberra, p.5.

[10] Crystal Waters at Conondale, Qld is such an example. The Ridge is a commune in northern NSW which has operated for over 40 years. There are a number of others throughout Australia which offer an "alternative" lifestyle. Typically new communal village struggle with getting local planning approval to get established.

[11] <www.myagedcare.gov.au/caring-someone/becoming-carer>

[12] To find out more about eligibility and conditions for receipt of the allowance, refer to <www.humanservices.gov.au/individuals/services/centrelink/carer-allowance>.

[13] Weston, R., & Qu, L. (2016). *Attitudes towards intergenerational support* (Australian Family Trends No. 11). Melbourne: Australian Institute of Family Studies. This study was used to support comments in relation to intergenerational support in this section.

[14] <www.humanservices.gov.au/individuals/enablers/granny-flat-interest>.

[15] 3101.0 – Australian Demographic Statistics, Mar 2016, Australian Bureau of Statistics, 2049.0 – *Census of Population and Housing: Estimating homelessness, 2006*.

[16] NSW *Parliament Aged Care Industry Facts*, May 2015, <www.parliament.nsw.gov.au/committees/DBAssets/InquiryOther/Transcript/9768/Aged%20care%20industry%20facts.pdf>.

[17] <www.propertycouncil.com.au/Web/Advocacy/Retirement/Web/Advocacy/SectorBasedAdvocacy/Retirement_Living.aspx>

[18] In making these points, I acknowledge an article by Richard McCullagh, *Retirement Villages: a reality check*, appearing in the NSW Law Society Journal, February 2018 at p.88.

[19] Such an adviser could be a lawyer, but often financial planners and specialist aged care consultancies will also be able to assist you.

Resources

Australian Bureau of Statistics, *Housing Occupancy and Costs*, cat. no. 4130.0, 1995–96, p. 19, Table 6. Also ABS, *Housing Occupancy and Costs*, cat. no. 4130.0, 2013–14, Table 10, All households, Selected household characteristics by age of household reference person.

Australian Bureau of Statistics, *Survey of Income and Housing* 2015-16, 13/10/2017

Australian Council of Social Service, *Poverty in Australia 2016*, <www.acoss.org.au/wp-content/uploads/2016/10/Poverty-in-Australia-2016.pdf>.

Australian Institute of Health and Welfare, GEN aged care data, <www.gen-agedcaredata.gov.au/Topics/Services-and-places-in-aged-care>.

Australian Institute of Superannuation Trustees (AIST), *No place like home, the impact of declining home ownership on retirement*, March 2017, <www.aist.asn.au/media/20734/AIST_Housing%20affordability%20and%20retirement%20incomes_FINAL%2021032017.pdf>.

Barnes M, Blom A, Cox K, Lessof C (2006) *The Social Exclusion of Older People: Evidence from the First Wave of the English Longitudinal Study of Ageing* (ELSA) Office of the Deputy Prime Minister, London, UK.

Lane R & Whittaker N, *Sea change, tree change or downsize*, Noel Whittaker Holdings Pty Ltd, Australia 2015.

McCullagh R, *Retirement Villages: a reality check*, NSW Law Society Journal, February 2018.

Morris, A, *The Australian Dream, Housing experiences of older Australians*, CSIRO Publishing, 2016, Victoria.

Productivity Commission, *An Ageing Australia: Preparing for the Future*, 2015, Canberra.

Productivity Commission 2015, *Housing Decisions of Older Australians*, Commission Research Paper, Canberra. <www.pc.gov.au/research/completed/housing-decisions-older-australians/housing-decisions-older-australians.pdf>.

Sorensen G, *Options for the Ageing*, Simon & Schuster, Australia, 1996.

Property Council, *Retirement Living*, <www.propertycouncil.com.au/Web/Advocacy/Retirement/Web/Advocacy/SectorBasedAdvocacy/Retirement_Living.aspx>.

Weston, R., & Qu, L. (2016). *Attitudes towards intergenerational support* (Australian Family Trends No. 11). Melbourne: Australian Institute of Family Studies.

Chapter 6: Supported accommodation

References

[1] ‹www.agedcarequality.gov.au/sites/default/files/media/AACQAConsumerExperienceReportTrends.pdf›.

[2] NSW Parliament, *Aged Care Industry Facts, May 2015*, ‹www.parliament.nsw.gov.au/committees/DBAssets/InquiryOther/Transcript/9768/Aged%20care%20industry%20facts.pdf›.

[3] Australian Institute of Health and Welfare, *GEN aged care data*, ‹www.gen-agedcaredata.gov.au/Topics/Services-and-places-in-aged-care›.

[4] ‹agedcare.health.gov.au/sites/g/files/net1426/f/documents/05_2014/info_booklet_roadshow.pdf›

[5] These figures were taken from *Your Life Choices* tables, September 2017, ‹www.yourlifechoices.com.au/aged-care/cost-of-aged-care›.

Resources

Australian Institute of Health and Welfare, *GEN aged care data*, ‹https://www.gen-agedcaredata.gov.au/Topics/Care-needs-in-aged-carewww.gen-agedcaredata.gov.au/Topics/Services-and-places-in-aged-care›.

Department of Social Services, ‹agedcare.health.gov.au/sites/g/files/net1426/f/documents/05_2014/info_booklet_roadshow.pdf›.

Doyle C & Roberts, G, *Moving into Residential Care*, Jessica Kingsley Publishers, London & Philadelphia, 2018.

Grattan Institute, *Dying Well*, Hal Swerissen and Stephen Duckett, September 2014.

Lane R & Whittaker N, *Aged Care, Who Cares?* Noel Whittaker Holdings Pty Ltd, Australia 2016.

NSW Parliament *Aged Care Industry Facts*, May 2015, ‹www.parliament.nsw.gov.au/committees/DBAssets/InquiryOther/Transcript/9768/Aged%20care%20industry%20facts.pdf›.

Your Life Choices tables, September 2017, ‹www.yourlifechoices.com.au/aged-care/cost-of-aged-care›.

Chapter 7: Relationships in retirement

References

[1] Gawande, A, *Being Mortal*, Profile Books, UK, 2014.

[2] Szoeke,H and Burn, K, *Boomerang families and failure-to-launch: Commentary on adult children living at home*, University of Melbourne, Australia, January 2016.

[3] Ochiltree G, *The changing role of grandparents*, AIFS, AFRC Briefing No 2, 2006, <aifs.gov.au/cfca/publications/changing-role-grandparents>. I have used this article as a basis for my comments rather than referring to specific studies.

[4] Goodfellow, J., & Laverty, J. (2003). *Grandparents supporting working families: Satisfaction and choice in provision of child care*. Family Matters, Issue No 66 Spring/Summer 2003, pp 14-19.

[5] See the Federal Circuit Court website for more detailed information, <www.federalcircuitcourt.gov.au/wps/wcm/connect/fccweb/family-law-matters/divorce-and-separation/how-do-i-apply-for-a-divorce/apply-for-divorce>.

[6] ABS, 2071.0 Census of Population and Housing: *Reflecting Australia - Stories from the Census, 2016,* 28/6/17, <www.abs.gov.au/ausstats/abs@.nsf/Lookup/by%20Subject/2071.0~2016~Main%20Features~Snapshot%20of%20Australia,%202016~2>.

[7] de Vaus, D., & Qu, L. (2015). *Demographics of living alone* (Australian Family Trends No. 6). Melbourne: Australian Institute of Family Studies, <aifs.gov.au/publications/demographics-living-alone>.

[8] There are many studies in this area. A good summary of issues and positive suggestions can be found in this article published by Harvard Women's Health Watch, *The challenges of living alone*, November 2012, <www.health.harvard.edu/mind-and-mood/the-challenges-of-living-alone>.

[9] Reported by Choice magazine, 4 November 2014, <www.choice.com.au/electronics-and- technology/internet/using-online-services/articles/online-dating-sites-review>.

[10] Smith K. R. Zick C. D. Duncan G. J. (1991). *Remarriage patterns among recent widows and widowers*. Demography, p 28, pp. 361–374.

[11] Zheng Wu, Christoph M. Schimmele, Nadia Ouellet, *Repartnering After Widowhood*, The Journals of Gerontology: Series B, Volume 70, Issue 3, 1 May 2015, pp 496 -507, doi.org/10.1093/geronb/gbu060>.

Resources

ABS, 2071.0 – *Census of Population and Housing: Reflecting Australia – Stories from the Census, 2016*, 28/6/17, <www.abs.gov.au/ausstats/abs@.nsf/Lookup/by%20Subject/2071.0~2016~Main%20Features~Snapshot%20of%20Australia,%202016~2>.

ABS 6523.0 – *Household Income and Wealth*, Australia, 2015-16, 13/09/2017

de Vaus, D., & Qu, L. (2015). *Demographics of living alone* (Australian Family Trends No. 6). Melbourne: Australian Institute of Family Studies, <aifs.gov.au/publications/demographics-living-alone>.

Gawande, A, *Being Mortal*, Profile Books, UK, 2014.

Goodfellow, J., & Laverty, J. (2003). *Grandparents supporting working families: Satisfaction and choice in provision of child care. Family Matters*, Issue No 66 Spring/Summer 2003, pp 14-19.

Harvard Women's Health Watch, *The challenges of living alone*, November 2012, <www.health.harvard.edu/mind-and-mood/the-challenges-of-living-alone>.

Ochiltree G, *The changing role of grandparents*, AIFS, AFRC Briefing No 2, 2006, <aifs.gov.au/cfca/publications/changing-role-grandparents>.

Ruddock JS, *The second half of your life*, Penguin Random House, UK, 2015.

Smith K. R. Zick C. D. Duncan G. J. (1991). *Remarriage patterns among recent widows and widowers*. Demography, p 28, pp 361–374.

Szoeke, H and Burn, K, *Boomerang families and failure-to-launch: Commentary on adult children living at home*, University of Melbourne, Australia, January 2016.

Links

Federal Circuit Court of Australia / applying for a divorce:

<www.federalcircuitcourt.gov.au/wps/wcm/connect/fccweb/how-do-i/divorce/apply-for-a-divorce/apply-for-divorce>

Relationships Australia / counselling: phone 1300 364 277

<www.relationshipsnsw.org.au/support-services-category/counselling-services/>

White Ribbon Australia, domestic violence hotlines: 1800 737 732 (24 hr hotline)

Lifeline: 13 11 14

Police/ambulance: 000

Chapter 8: Staying healthy

References

[1] AIHW report, *Australia's Health 2016*, 13 September 2016, <www.aihw. gov.au/reports/australias-health/australias-health-2016/contents/ chapter-3-leading-causes-of-ill-health>.

[2] These figures are based on ABS census reports for 2011-14. Cited in the Australian Institute of Health & Welfare (AIHW) report, *Older Australia at a glance*, April 2017, <www.aihw.gov.au/reports-statistics>.

[3] United Nations, *World Economic Situation and Prospects 2014*, Table E, p148, and Australian Institute of Health and Welfare Bulletin 126, *Healthy Life Expectancy in Australia: Patterns and Trends 1998 to 2012*.

[4] AIHW report, *Australian Burden of Disease Study: impact and causes of illness and death in Aboriginal and Torres Strait Islander people 2011*, September 2016, <www.aihw.gov.au/reports/burden-of-disease/ australian-bod-study-2011-indigenous-australians/contents/summary>.

[5] AIHW report, *National Health Survey: first results, 2014–15—Australia*. ABS cat. no. 4364.0. Canberra: ABS, <www.aihw.gov.au/reports/older-people/older-australia-at-a-glance/contents/health-functioning/health-and-disability-status>.

[6] ABS, *Health of Older People in Australia: A Snapshot, 2004-05*, 28/9/2006.

[7] Australian Institute of Health and Welfare 2012. *Changes in life expectancy and disability in Australia 1998 to 2009*. Bulletin no. 111. Cat. no. AUS 166. Canberra: AIHW. <www.aihw.gov.au/getmedia/17196ce2-161a-47cc-8021-f1368de5947a/13852.pdf.aspx?inline=true>.

[8] Dr L Carstensen quoted in an article, *The aging paradox: The older we get, the happier we are*, by Deborah Netburn, LA Times, 24/08/2016.

[9] L.L. Carstensen et al, *"Emotional Experience Improves with Age: Evidence based over 10 years of experience sampling"*, Psychology and Ageing (2001): p 22, cited at p 94, in Gawande, A, *Being Mortal, Illness, medicine and what matters in the end*, Profile Books Ltd, UK, 2014.

[10] Harvard University (USA) began its longitudinal study of the health and happiness of its sophomores in 1938.

[11] National Bureau of Economic Research, *The Effects of Retirement on Physical and Mental Health Outcomes*, Dhaval Dave, Inas Rashad, Jasmina Spasojevic, NBER Working Paper No. 12123. Revised Jan 2008, <www.nber.org/papers/w12123>.

[12] National Health and Medical Research Council (NHMRC), *Talking about Complimentary Medicine*, NHMRC Ref CAM001, <www.nhmrc.gov.au/guidelines/publications/hpr25-hpr27>.

[13] AIHW 2017. *Cancer in Australia 2017*. Cancer series no. 101. Cat. No. CAN 100. Canberra: AIHW.

[14] ABS, 4833.0.55.001 – *Health of Older People in Australia: A Snapshot, 2004 - 05*, <www.abs.gov.au/ausstats/abs@.nsf/mf/4833.0.55.001/>.

[15] National Ageing Research Institute, *Discussion paper, 4.3 Cardiovascular Disease*, <www.health.gov.au/internet/publications/publishing.nsf/Content/phd-physical-rec-older-disc~chapter-4~chapter-4-3>.

[16] Australian Institute of Health and Welfare 2015. *Australia's welfare 2015*. Australia's welfare series no. 12. Cat. no. AUS 189. Canberra: AIHW, <www.aihw.gov.au/getmedia/c2ff6c58-e05e-49ed-afd7-43bd21eef4e2/AW15-6-4-Mental-health-of-older-Australians.pdf.aspx>.

[17] Australian Orthopaedic Association National Joint Replacement Registry, *Annual Report 2016*, <aoanjrr.sahmri.com/documents/10180/275066/Hip%2C%20Knee%20%26%20Shoulder%20Arthroplasty>.

[18] Australian Bureau of Statistics. (2008). *National Survey of Mental Health and Wellbeing: Summary of Results, 2007*. Cat. no. (4326.0). Canberra: ABS.

[19] Comedian Robin Williams had been diagnosed with a form of Lewy body dementia at the age of 63 and it has been suggested that his despair was so overwhelming that he took his own life.

[20] Whalley, LJ, *Understanding Brain Ageing and Dementia*, p 249, Columbia University Press, New York, 2015 See also pp 259, 288-292.

[21] Grattan Institute, *Dying Well*, Hal Swerissen and Stephen Duckett, September 2014.

[22] World Health Organization. (2003). *WHO definition of palliative care*. Retrieved August 11, 2003, from World Health Organization Web site: <www.who.int/cancer/palliative/definition/en/print.html>.

[23] National Health and Medical Research Council, *Guidelines for a Palliative Approach in Residential Aged Care*, literature review, May 2006, <www.nhmrc.gov.au/_files_nhmrc/publications/attachments/ac14_guidelines_for_a_palliative_approach_to_residential_aged_care_systematic_review_of_literature_1>.

[24] A "good death" is discussed in more detail in the Grattan Institute report, *Dying Well*, Hal Swerissen and Stephen Duckett, September 2014.

Resources

Abel KM, Ramsay R, *Female mind, A user's guide*, RC Psych Publications, 2017.

Australian Bureau of Statistics. (2008). *National Survey of Mental Health and Wellbeing: Summary of Results, 2007*. Cat. no. (4326.0). Canberra: ABS.

Australian Bureau of Statistics, *Health of Older People in Australia: A Snapshot*, 2004-05, 28/9/2006, <www.abs.gov.au/ausstats/abs@.nsf/mf/4833.0.55.001/>.

Australian Institute of Health and Welfare 2015. *Australia's welfare 2015*. Australia's welfare series no. 12. Cat. no. AUS 189. Canberra: AIHW, <www.aihw.gov.au/getmedia/c2ff6c58-e05e-49ed-afd7-43bd21eef4e2/AW15-6-4-Mental-health-of-older-Australians.pdf.aspx>.

Australian Institute of Health & Welfare report, *Australia's Health 2016*, 13 September 2016, <www.aihw.gov.au/reports/australias-health/australias-health-2016/contents/chapter-3-leading-causes-of-ill-health>.

Australian Institute of Health & Welfare (AIHW) report, *Older Australia at a glance*, April 2017, <www.aihw.gov.au/reports-statistics>.

Australian Institute of Health & Welfare report, *Australian Burden of Disease Study: impact and causes of illness and death in Aboriginal and Torres Strait Islander people 2011*, September 2016, <www.aihw.gov.au/reports/burden-of-disease/australian-bod-study-2011-indigenous-australians/contents/summary>.

Australian Institute of Health and Welfare Bulletin 126, *Healthy Life Expectancy in Australia: Patterns and Trends 1998 to 2012*.

Australian Institute of Health and Welfare report, *National Health Survey: first results, 2014–15—Australia*. ABS cat. no. 4364.0. Canberra: ABS, <www.aihw.gov.au/reports/older-people/older-australia-at-a-glance/contents/health-functioning/health-and-disability-status>.

Australian Institute of Health and Welfare 2012. *Changes in life expectancy and disability in Australia 1998 to 2009*. Bulletin no. 111. Cat. no. AUS 166. Canberra: AIHW, <www.aihw.gov.au/getmedia/17196ce2-161a-47cc-8021-f1368de5947a/13852.pdf.aspx?inline=true>.

Australian Institute of Health and Welfare 2017. *Cancer in Australia 2017*. Cancer series no. 101. Cat. No. CAN 100. Canberra: AIHW.

Australian Orthopaedic Association National Joint Replacement Registry, *Annual Report 2016*, <aoanjrr.sahmri.com/documents/10180/275066/Hip%2C%20Knee%20%26%20Shoulder%20Arthroplasty>.

The aging paradox: The older we get, the happier we are, by Deborah Netburn, LA Times, 24/08/2016.

Carstensen L.L et al, "*Emotional Experience Improves with Age: Evidence based over 10 years of experience sampling*", Psychology and Ageing (2001): p 22

Gawande, A, *Being Mortal, Illness, medicine and what matters in the end*, Profile Books Ltd, UK, 2014.

Grattan Institute, *Dying Well*, Hal Swerissen and Stephen Duckett, September 2014.

National Bureau of Economic Research, *The Effects of Retirement on Physical and Mental Health* Outcomes, Dhaval Dave, Inas Rashad, Jasmina Spasojevic, NBER Working Paper No. 12123. Revised Jan 2008, <www.nber.org/papers/w12123>.

National Health and Medical Research Council (NHMRC), *Talking about Complimentary Medicine*, NHMRC Ref CAM001, <www.nhmrc.gov.au/guidelines/publications/hpr25-hpr27>.

National Health and Medical Research Council, Guidelines for a Palliative Approach in Residential Aged Care, May 2006.

National Ageing Research Institute, Discussion paper, 4.3 Cardiovascular Disease, <www.health.gov.au/internet/publications/publishing.nsf/Content/phd-physical-rec-older-disc~chapter-4~chapter-4-3>.

Sharp T, *Live Happier Live Longer*, Allen & Unwin, Sydney, 2014.

Shulman N, MD, Silverman MA, MD, MPH, and Adam G Golden, MD, MBA, *The real truth about Aging, A survival guide for older adults and caregivers*, Prometheus Books, New York, 2009.

United Nations, *Women and Mental Health*, <www.un.org/womenwatch/daw/csw/mental.htm>.

United Nations, World Economic Situation and Prospects 2014, Table E, p148, <www.un.org/development/desa/publications/wesp-mid-2014.html

Whalley, LJ, *Understanding Brain Ageing and Dementia*, p. 249, Columbia University Press, New York, 2015.

World Health Organization. (2003). *WHO definition of palliative care.*

Retrieved August 11, 2003, from World Health Organization Web site: <www.who.int/cancer/palliative/definition/en/print.html>.

Chapter 9: Leisure and learning

References

[1] The term the "Third Age" has been widely used to refer to the post-retirement period of our life. See such books as Weiss RS and Bass SA (ed), *Challenges of the Third Age, Meaning and purpose in later life*, Oxford University Press, 2002, a collection of essays on this topic.

[2] The Older Women's Network NSW, for example, which promotes women's wellbeing, <www.ownnsw.org.au/>.

[3] Merrill Lynch, *Leisure in retirement: Beyond the bucket list*, May 2016, Bank of America, <agewave.com/wp-content/uploads/2016/05/2016-Leisure-in-Retirement_Beyond-the-Bucket-List.pdf>.

[4] *Vacation Deprivation Survey*, Expedia, 2015 cited in Merrill Lynch paper above, Figure 2.

[5] As above p 8

[6] As above p 23

[7] US Bureau of Labor Statistics, *2013 American Time Use Survey*, June 2014.

[8] Deloitte, *Mobile Consumer Survey 2017, The Australian Cut*, <www2.deloitte.com/au/mobile-consumer-survey>.

[9] ACMA, *Digital lives of older Australians*, <www.acma.gov.au/theACMA/engage-blogs/engage-blogs/Research-snapshots/Digital-lives-of-older-Australian>.

[10] ABS, Australian Bureau of Statistics, Data cube, 81460DO002_201415 *Household Use of Information Technology, Australia, 2014-15*, 18 February 2016. <www.abs.gov.au/Ausstats/abs@.nsf/0/2DB0B0DF808896FFCA25825D00792A75?OpenDocument

[11] Many researchers in the USA and Australia have supported this general assertion. Australian baby boomers are estimated to represent 5.5 million people of a population of 24 million. (Australian Bureau of Statistics 2014 *Australian Historical Population Statistics, 2014* (ABS cat. no. 3105.0.65.001))

[12] <www.traveller.com.au/how-baby-boomers-are-shaking-the-travel-industry-gx8sp0#ixzz5Dpv20zBk>.

14 An explanation for this policy was that the company would not be able to guarantee the character of the other person which is not unreasonable.

15 Australian Cruise Association, *Economic Impact Assessment of the Cruise Industry in Australia 2015-16*, August 2016, <www.tourism.australia. com/content/dam/assets/document/1/6/w/s/9/2002041.pdf>.

16 EU, EU policy in the field of adult learning, <ec.europa.eu/education/ policy/adult-learning_en>.

17 Adult Learning Australia is calling on the Australian Government to adopt a formal policy on lifelong learning as an essential feature of a healthy democracy. Providing learning opportunities allows people to overcome barriers and change their lives. <ala.asn.au/2018-is-the-national-year-of-lifelong-learning/>.

18 Dench S & Kegan J, *Learning in Later Life: Motivation and Impact*, Institute for Employment Studies, UK, Feb 2000, Research brief No 183, <webarchive.nationalarchives.gov.uk/20130323040403/https:// www.education.gov.uk/publications/eOrderingDownload/RB183.pdf>.

19 There are studies which support both sides of the argument – that learning style is essentially stable throughout life, or that learning capacity declines as we age which may require change teaching style. An interesting look at this problem from the student's perspective can be found in this research paper, *The learning experiences of older adults as university students*, by Barbara A. Smith, R.N., B.Sc., M.Ed. Doctor of Philosophy, 1999 Department of Theory and Policy Studies in Education University of Toronto.

Resources

ACMA, *Digital lives of older Australians*, <www.acma.gov.au/theACMA/ engage-blogs/engage-blogs/Research-snapshots/Digital-lives-of-older-Australian>.

Adult Learning Australia. <ala.asn.au/2018-is-the-national-year-of-lifelong-learning/>.

Australian Bureau of Statistics, Data cube, 81460DO002_201415 *Household Use of Information Technology, Australia, 2014-15*, 18 February 2016.

Australian Bureau of Statistics 2014, *Australian Historical Population Statistics, 2014* (ABS cat. no. 3105.0.65.001).

Australian Cruise Association, *Economic Impact Assessment of the Cruise Industry in Australia 2015-16*, August 2016, <www.tourism.australia. com/content/dam/assets/document/1/6/w/s/9/2002041.pdf>.

Deloitte, *Mobile Consumer Survey 2017, The Australian Cut*, <www2. deloitte.com/au/mobile-consumer-survey>.

Dench S & Kegan J, *Learning in Later Life: Motivation and Impact, Institute for Employment Studies*, UK, Feb 2000, Research brief No 183, <webarchive.nationalarchives.gov.uk/20130323040403/https://www. education.gov.uk/publications/eOrderingDownload/RB183.pdf>.

European Union, *Adult Learning* policy, <ec.europa.eu/education/policy/ adult-learning_en>.

Merrill Lynch, *Leisure in retirement: Beyond the bucket list,* May 2016, Bank of America, <agewave.com/wp-content/uploads/2016/05/2016-Leisure-in-Retirement_Beyond-the-Bucket-List.pdf>.

Smith, Barbara A., R.N., B.Sc., M.Ed. Doctor of Philosophy, *The Learning Experiences of older adults as university students* 1999 Department of Theory and Policy Studies in Education University of Toronto.

Starts at 60 website, <startsat60.com>.

Weiss RS and Bass SA (ed), *Challenges of the Third Age, Meaning and purpose in later life*, Oxford University Press, 2002.

Chapter 10: Accessing support services

References

[1]Volunteering Australia, *Key facts and statistics about volunteering in Australia*, 16 April 2015, estimated that 31% of the over-65 year population were involved in volunteering.

[2] Australian Institute of Health and Welfare, *GEN Aged Care Data, People Using Aged Care*, <www.gen-agedcaredata.gov.au/Topics/People-using-aged-care>.

[3]Aged Care Financing Authority, *Fifth report on the Funding and Financing of the Aged* Care Sector, July 2017.

[4] Referred to in the ASFA, *Discussion paper: the future interaction of superannuation with aged care and health care*, November 2015, <www. superannuation.asn.au/ArticleDocuments/359/ASFA_Aged-care-health-and-super_Nov2015.pdf.aspx?Embed=Y>, p.11

[5] REST Super report, *The Journey Begins, October 2013*, <www.rest.com.au/restpension/rest-the- journey-begins.pdf>.

[6] Online access can be found at: <www.humanservices.gov.au/individuals/services/centrelink/age-pension#group-125>.

[7] Taken from the Dept of Human Services figures, <www.humanservices.gov.au/customer/enablers/assets>.

[8] Carers NSW assists carers of persons with a disability, their Carer Line is 1800 242 636, <www.carersnsw.org.au/>.

[9] For example, Belardi, L, *Controversial call to regulate admin fees in home care packages*, article in Community Care Review reporting on a call by Alzheimer's Australia to put a cap on administration and exit fees charged by service providers, 16 June 2016.

[10] HealthShare NSW, <www.enable.health.nsw.gov.au/services/aep>.

[11] NSW Nurses and Midwives, *Who Will Keep Me Safe? Elder Abuse in Residential Aged Care*, October 2015, <www.nswnma.asn.au/wp-content/uploads/2016/02/Elder-Abuse-in-Residential-Aged-Care-FINAL.pdf>.

Resources

ASFA, *Discussion paper: the future interaction of superannuation with aged care and health care*, November 2015, <www.superannuation.asn.au/ArticleDocuments/359/ASFA_Aged-care-health-and-super_Nov2015.pdf.aspx?Embed=Y>.

Australian Institute of Family Studies, *Facts and Figures*, <aifs.gov.au/facts-and-figures/ageing-australia>.

Australian Institute of Health and Welfare, GEN Aged Care Data, *People Using Aged Care*, <www.gen-agedcaredata.gov.au/Topics/People-using-aged-care>.

Aged Care Financing Authority, *Fifth report on the Funding and Financing of the Aged Care Sector*, July 2017, <www.gen-agedcaredata.gov.au/Resources/2017_acfa_annual_report>.

Belardi, L, *Controversial call to regulate admin fees in home care* packages, article in Community Care Review, 16 June 2016.

Carers NSW, Carer Line is 1800 242 636,

Centrelink/Department of Human Services: <www.humanservices.gov.au/individuals/centrelink>

Department of Human Services: <www.humanservices.gov.au/individuals/services/centrelink/age-pension#group-125>

Department of Human Services website, <www.humanservices.gov.au/individuals/enablers/countries-have-international-social-security-agreements-australia>

Department of Human Services figures, <www.humanservices.gov.au/customer/enablers/assets>

Department of Health: *Increasing Choice in Home Care – Stage 1*: Discussion Paper Feedback, <agedcare.health.gov.au/programs-services/home-care/home-care-packages-reform/increasing-choice-in-home-care-stage-1-discussion-paper-feedback>.

HealthShare NSW, <www.enable.health.nsw.gov.au/services/aep>

My Aged Care, ph. 1800 200 422,

National Seniors Australia, advocacy organisation,

NSW Nurses and Midwives, *Who Will Keep Me Safe? Elder Abuse in Residential Aged Care*, October 2015, <www.nswnma.asn.au/wp-content/uploads/2016/02/Elder-Abuse-in-Residential-Aged-Care-FINAL.pdf>.

REST Super report, *The Journey Begins*, October 2013, <www.rest.com.au/restpension/rest-the- journey-begins.pdf>.

Volunteering Australia, *Key facts and statistics about volunteering in Australia*, 16 April 2015. <www.volunteeringaustralia.org/>.

Chapter 11: Putting your affairs in order

References

[1] <www.gatheredhere.com.au/guide-to-burial-plots-in-australia/>

[2] <www.gatheredhere.com.au/the-average-cost-of-a-funeral-in-australia/>

[3] NSW Trustee and Guardian: <www.tag.nsw.gov.au/>.

[4] Australian Bureau of Statistics, Cat. 3303.0 - *Causes of Death, Australia, 2016*, 27/9/2017, <www.abs.gov.au/ausstats/abs@.nsf/Lookup/by%20Subject/3303.0~2016~Main%20Features~Australia's%20leading%20causes%20of%20death,%202016~3>.

[5] <www.alrc.gov.au/publications/what-elder-abuse>

Chapter 12: The Retirement Quiz

[1.] Earl, J. K., Leung, C., National Seniors Productive Ageing Centre, National Seniors Australia, & Department of Health and Ageing, Australia (2012). *The retirement quiz: what we need to enjoy a successful retirement.* Braddon, A.C.T: National Seniors Productive Ageing Centre. <nationalseniors.com.au/be-informed/news-articles/retirement-quiz-helps-pre-retirees-plan-future>

Further reading **The Retirement and Resources Inventory** and all the research supporting it have been published in its entirety in the following journal: "Leung, C. S.Y., & Earl, J.K. (2012). *Retirement Resources Inventory: Construction, factor structure and psychometric properties.* Journal of Vocational Behavior, 81 (2), pp 171-182.

ADVANCE CARE DIRECTIVE

Based on the Advance Care Planning template developed by the Hunter New England Health Service 2011

Advanced Care Plan / Directive Template

(Please consider all questions on this template. Cross out section/s you do not wish to answer at this time. Remember to make copies of this plan and give to your GP, your family and trusted friends)

Name: _____

Date of Birth: _____

Address: _____

_____

Completed by proxy: Name: _____

Relationship: _____

If I cannot speak for myself, I would like my doctor to talk about my health care and medical problems with the following person/s:

Name: _____

Contact numbers: _____

I have legally appointed the following: Yes/No

Name and contact number of person appointed: _____

_____

Copies of legal documents held by (name and contact):

_____

Enduring Guardian (for health decisions):

_____ _____

Enduring Power of Attorney (for money/finance decisions):

_____

If I am very sick or badly injured and others need to make medical decisions for me, please consider my following statements when making substitute decisions:

The following things are important to me, and I want them to be considered in Personal Values. Please consider my personal values for the following statements if I am unable to make my own decisions in the future. (Put your initials in the box that is your response to each statement)

I would find life to be acceptable/ OR difficult but bearable /OR unbearable if, for the rest of my life:

- I do not recognise my family and loved ones

- I do not have control over my bladder and bowels

- I cannot feed myself, and cannot wash myself, and cannot do my own personal grooming and dressing

- I cannot move myself around in or out of bed and rely on other people to reposition (shift or move) me

- I can no longer eat or drink and need to have food given to me through a tube in my stomach

- I cannot talk, read or write

- I can never have a conversation with others because I do not understand what people are saying

- I do not get enjoyment from many of the things that I have always enjoyed

Thinking about end of life: Please initial the statement which is closest to your personal belief:

- I am frightened of dying and do not want to think about it happening to me or my loved ones.

- I do not discuss death or dying with others.

- Dying is a fact of life. You just have to deal with it when it happens. I hope that I can talk about it with loved ones and others before my time comes.

- Dying is a natural part of life. I am comfortable discussing death and dying with my loved ones and others. I want to be prepared for when my time comes.

- When my time for natural dying comes, if possible, I would like to be cared for at home or in a home like environment

- In a hospital or hospital like environment I do not know.

- I am happy for my family/person responsible to decide

Name: _____

Signature: _____

Date: _____ or

Proxy Witness name: _____

Signature: _____

Review date/s: _____ _____ _____ _____

Printed in Australia
AUHW012240090320
324816AU00002B/2